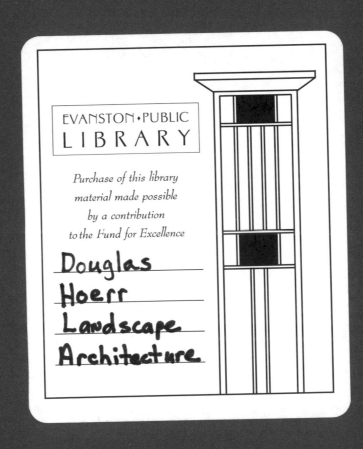

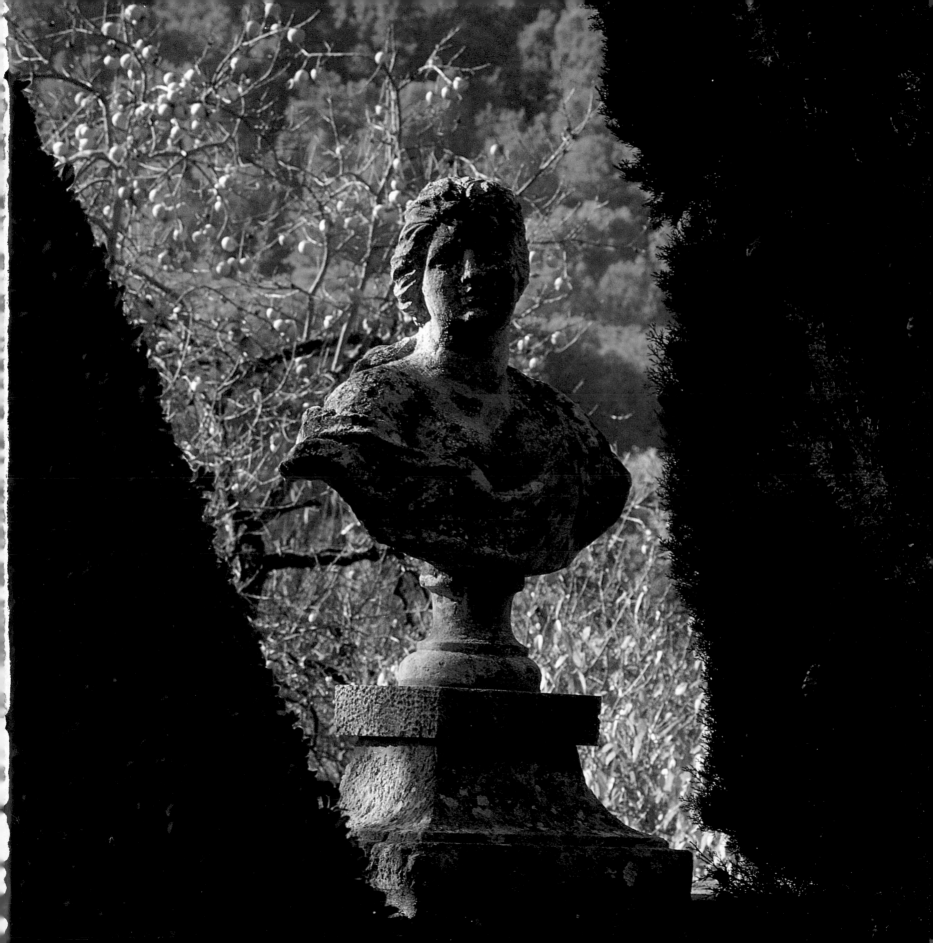

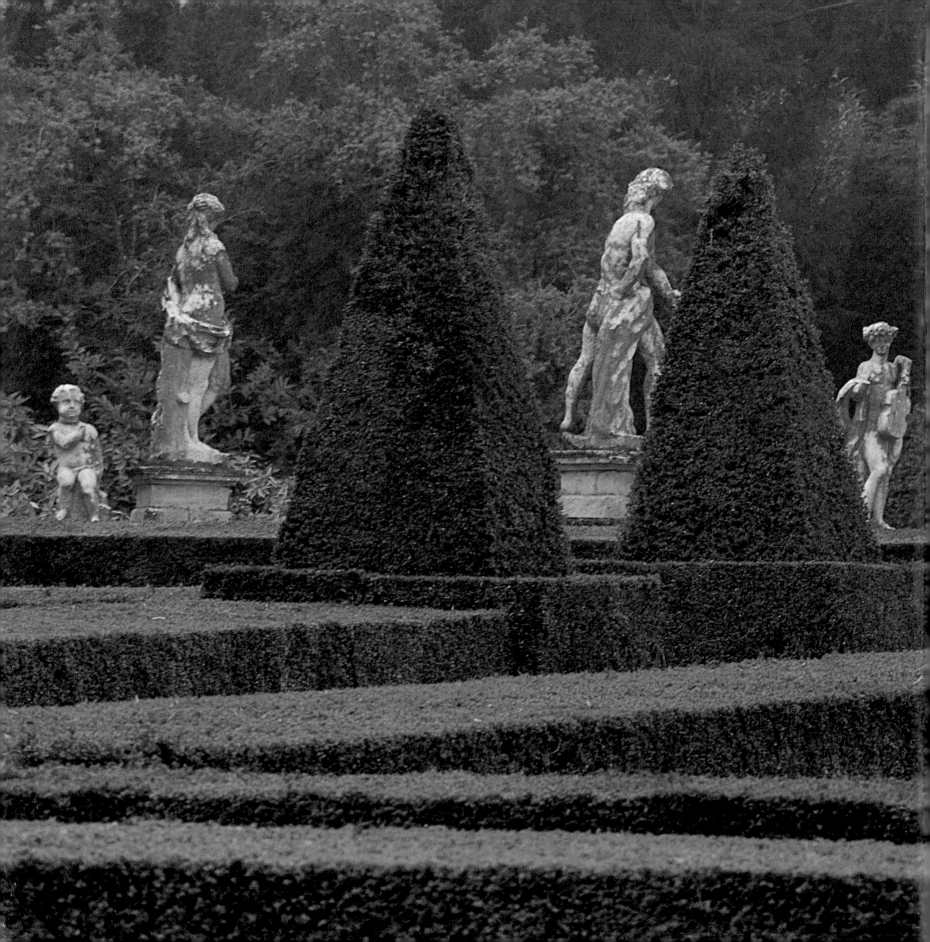

VIVIAN RUSSELL

❧

EDITH WHARTON'S ITALIAN GARDENS

A Bulfinch Press Book
Little, Brown and Company
Boston · New York · Toronto · London

To Molly and Rupert, for your unfailing humor and encouragement, in the hope
that the story of Mrs. Wharton and her gardens may inspire you to adventures of all kinds.
And to the conductor William Christie for his exquisite rekindling of the numinous
spirit of Monteverdi, whose music was written as these gardens were being made
and lingers in them still.

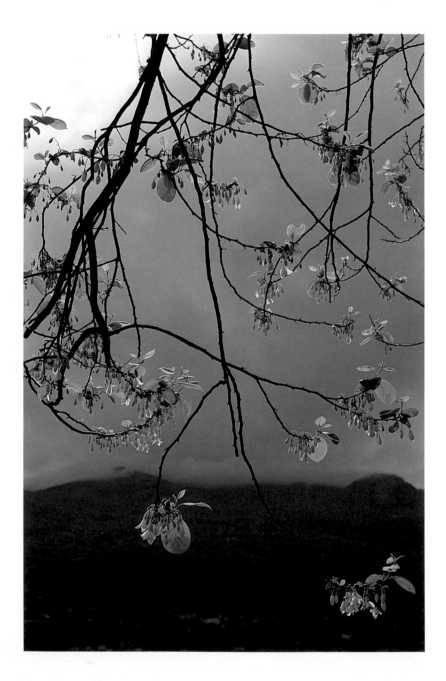

Edith Wharton's Italian Gardens
Compilation copyright © 1997 by Frances Lincoln Limited
Text copyright © 1997 by Vivian Russell
Photographs by Vivian Russell, copyright © 1997 by Vivian Russell
except those listed on page 192

First North American Edition

Edith Wharton's Italian Gardens was produced by
Frances Lincoln Limited, London

ISBN 0-8212-2397-6

Library of Congress Catalog Card Number 97-73771

Bulfinch Press is an imprint and trademark of
Little, Brown and Company (Inc.)
Published simultaneously in Canada by
Little, Brown & Company (Canada) Limited

PRINTED AND BOUND IN ITALY

PAGE ONE *One of the stone figures adorning a balustrade at the*
Villa Cetinale, against a backdrop of persimmons.
PREVIOUS PAGES *The parterre in front of Valsanzibio.*
LEFT *Branches of the snowdrop tree,* Halesia diptera, *at Isola Madre.*
RIGHT *The Fountain of the Organ at the Villa d'Este, Tivoli.*

CONTENTS

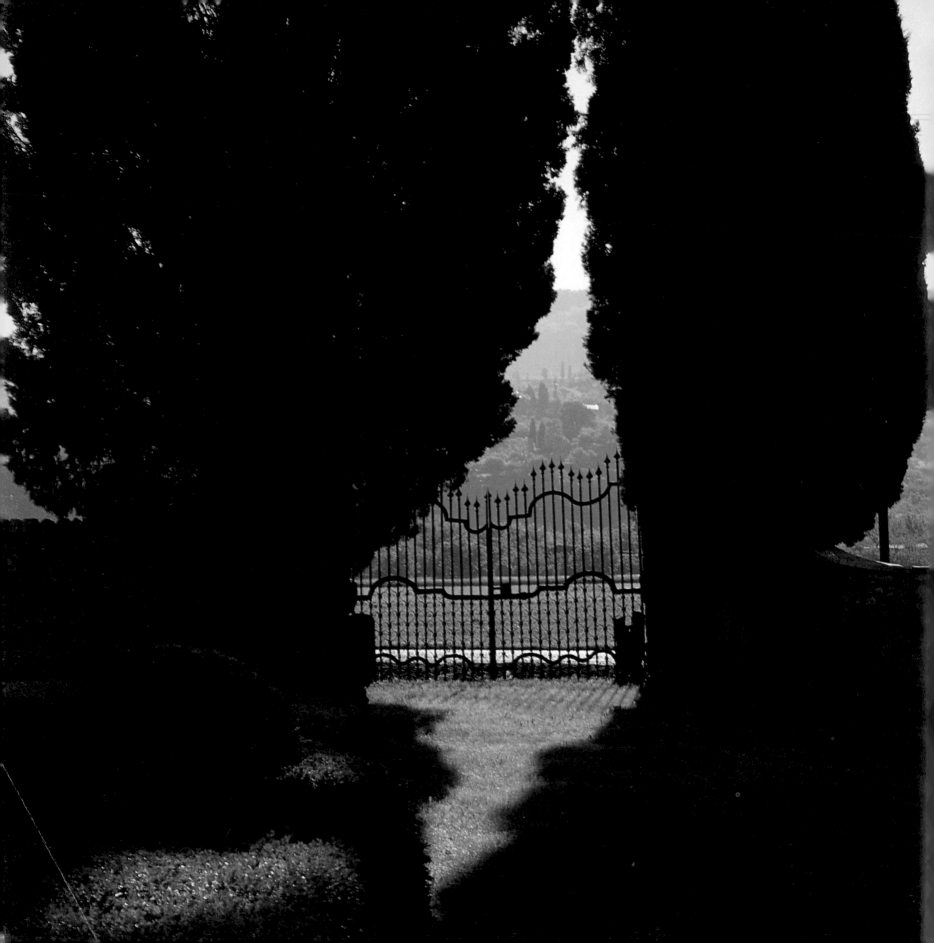

PREFACE

'THE CULTIVATED AMATEUR OF MY YOUTH was encouraged to dash off impressionistic sketches of travels and some of these works opened the eyes and stimulated the imaginations of countless intelligent travellers', wrote Edith Wharton in her late unpublished essay, *Italy Again*. Those 'charming little amateur books', she said, 'after writing one or two of them myself', had earned their right to a place in the sun because they led the 'simple hearted reader' to obscure corners to enjoy unnoticed landscapes and 'feel the secret vibrations of their beauty'.

Thousands of travellers set off in search of the hidden treasures of Italy clutching these literary nuggets, and Edith Wharton's own *Italian Villas and Their Gardens* figured prominently among them. The memoirs of Marchese Iris Origo contain a priceless vignette of such a journey, when she accompanied her mother around Italy in 1911. 'The sight of a cypress avenue leading to a fine villa or the mere mention of its existence in a guidebook, was to my mother irresistible,' the Marchese quipped. A quick word to the chauffeur and a moment later the astonished owners sitting at ease in their loggia or on the lawn would see an English lady, dressed in the height of fashion but swathed in a dust coat, descend from a huge Lancia, followed by a plump, self-conscious schoolgirl carrying a Baedeker, the *Guide Bleu* or Edith Wharton's *Italian Villas and Their Gardens*. ' "I know you won't mind us glancing round for just a moment," my mother would say. Sometimes this technique was entirely successful and we would all end up in a semi-circle on the lawn. But sometimes we encountered only blank stares and stiff manners. "Now do tell me", my mother would confidentially conclude, "what other villas of interest are there in the neighbourhood?" '

Such insouciant *bravura* is as unthinkable today as the equally imperious attitude of other garden visitors of the period, such as Sir George Sitwell. His butler recalled how, in 1909, Sir George sat

Two imposing cypresses mark the old entrance to the garden at Villa Cuzzano, framing a vista of distant promise. 'The lanes and byways led to hidden rarities, lost treasures and forgotten shrines; she knew they were there, it was useless to tell her that they weren't or that she couldn't find them', recalled the writer Percy Lubbock, one of Edith Wharton's friends.

meditating between the giant cypresses at the Villa d'Este in Tivoli just before closing time, when four ancient *custodi* advanced on him. 'Immediately, concluding the old men were brigands (for he always lived a hundred years before his time) he fair biffed 'em with his umbrella. You could hear 'em squawk half a mile away!'

The idea of taking Edith Wharton as our *cicerone,* or guide, and revisiting gardens with her nearly a century after she had described them was a tremendously exciting prospect. I enlisted the help of my friend Elena Pizzi, an American living in Rome, and she contacted all the places Wharton wrote about. By the wayside fell gardens that had vanished altogether and those where permission to photograph was denied, such as Villa Pliniana and the Vatican. I decided to focus on those whose stories could still be told in a visually evocative way, and I put the best of those which were still interesting in their detail in the introductions to each region.

On my travels I found myself, like Henry James, 'up to my neck in that element of the rich and strange for the love of which one revisits Italy'. In the garden of Admiral Andrea Doria, once the pride and joy of Genoa, the terrace below the *palazzo* is inhabited by dozens of vagrant cats patiently grooming themselves on the seats of a deserted open-air cinema; its lower terrace is now traversed by an overground motorway. In between sits what was once an elaborate fountain. The Admiral Andrea Doria, thinly disguised as Neptune, lifts his trident calling for water to fill the dry, cracked and weedy basin below him. The wooden benches placed here and there in the formerly lovely parterre are occupied by shrewder cats who know the film will never begin. In Rome, the white marble statues of worthies on the Monte Pincio, amongst whom Edith Wharton played as a child, have been bedizened with black eyelashes, Hitlerite moustaches and red lipstick. The statues in the niches of the retaining walls of the garden of the Villa Doria-Pamphili are nailed with disclaimers reading 'Made in cement'.

Such is the patina of Italy today. In this book we look with Edith Wharton's eyes through a long telescope, past many centuries, to alight on the gardens as they were first conceived. The old Italian garden, illuminated by the country's magic light, is a garden of ideas, whose paths lead far beyond the garden walls into the realms of philosophy, myth and poetry.

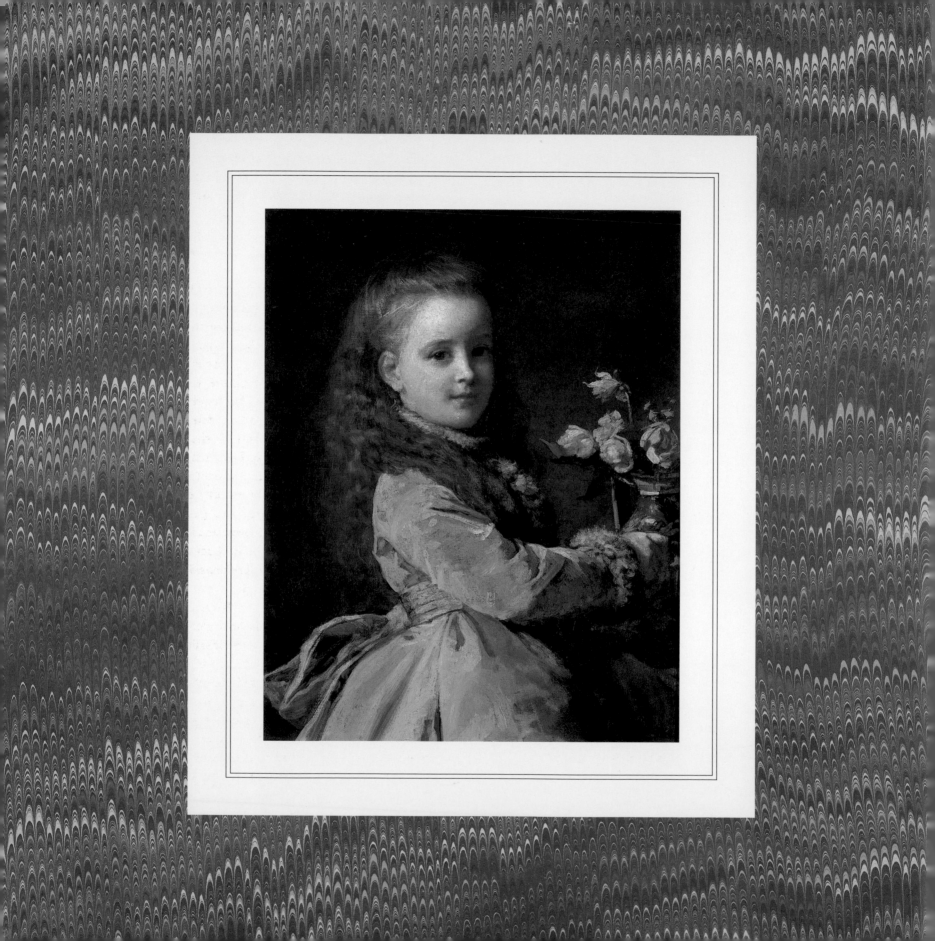

Edith Wharton's life unfolded across the continents of Europe and America, and like all transplanted Americans she could never belong wholly to either. The country she made her own lay somewhere in between, in the vast amorphous ocean she crossed so often that Henry James dubbed her 'the pendulum woman'. It was a kingdom ruled by the cult of the aesthetic, alive with 'secret dreams', 'inner voices' and 'sensations' which she gathered up with the momentum of a great tide washing up on the shores of both sides of the Atlantic, dragging away with her their cultural treasures in the undertow.

Time and again Edith saw herself at sea: 'I was always tossed on the waves of a passionate inner life,' she wrote; 'I never felt anything calmly.' The sea not only fed her imagination but also became the metaphor for her most salient experiences. As a small child she had only to walk the floor making up stories to be 'swept off full sail on the sea of dreams'. Contemplating the master-pieces of Italian art in the Louvre at the age of eighteen, she felt 'as if all the great waves of the sea of beauty were breaking over me at once'. For her knowledge was to 'plunge into a sea of wonders'. Only a year before her death she was lamenting 'what a bore it is to have to take in sail when one has had the freedom of the high seas for so many years.'

The woman who was to become the Pulitzer Prize-winning *grand dame* of American letters was born in 1862, after two older boys, into a bourgeois family of French, Dutch and English colonials who had, over the course of 250 years, become the social aristocracy of New York. They were well ordered, well-to-do, scrupulous in their standards of good manners, education and probity in business. But they were dull. In her youth, Edith deplored their complacent comformity, comparing them to 'empty vessels into which no new wine will ever be poured'. Only as she grew older and witnessed a world changed irrevocably did she begin to appreciate their values, pausing in her autobiography *A Backward Glance* to 'savour the few remaining drops of the old vintage'.

'My mother's rule of behaviour was that one should be polite, my father's that one should be kind,' she wrote in her unpublished memoir *Life and I*. The pursuits of her handsome, much loved father included travel, sport and, perhaps to help him fathom his wife, books on arctic explorations. Edith's 'beautifully dressed, indolent, matter of fact' mother, whom she loved less, kept an exemplary tidy house, but her 'view of life was incredibly prosaic'. Both parents harboured a dread of innovation or originality of character. Into this milieu arrived a child who combined the 'fire of her brain' with a noble and insatiable curiosity and a deep love of beauty, and evolved by her own efforts into one of America's most cultivated and intelligent women.

Edith's journey to enlightenment began at the age of four, when, with her parents and nurse, she crossed the ocean for the first time, bound for the long peninsula of Italy at the start of the family's European odyssey. She would not return to New York for six years. She never forgot the early sunny, violet-scented days of Rome.

EDITH WHARTON AND ITALY

Edith Wharton, painted by Edward May at the tender age of five, around the time that Italy was first revealed to her.
Through the 'trailing clouds of infancy' she remembered her year in Rome as one of 'sunlit wanderings on the springy turf of great Roman villas',
unconsciously absorbing the beauty of the gardens at the Villa Doria-Pamphili, the Villa Borghese, the Palatine and the villas of Frascati.

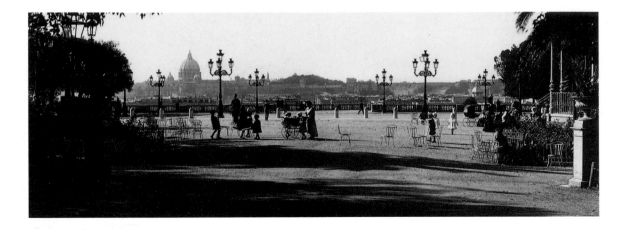

The Monte Pincio gardens in Rome during the period when the young Edith played there with her friends Daisy and Arthur Terry.

Walks 'on the daisy-strewn lawns of the Villa Doria-Pamphili, among the statues and pines of the Villa Borghese, and hunting on the slopes of the Palatine for mysterious bits of blue and green and rosy stone' awakened her sensory antennae. Whilst her mother was assiduously observing the fashionable and adding to her 'inexhaustible memory for details of dress', her small daughter was responding to the first stimuli of her 'inner life'.

The feast of the Roman spectacle – flashing cardinals in scarlet and gold, the golden vision of the Pope floating above them, the stately barouches in which Roman beauties were displayed like peacocks – fed 'my own rich world of dreams' which she already recognized as separate from what she called her 'external life'. Every afternoon little Edith, Daisy Terry and her brother Arthur – children of the American painter Luther Terry, whom the Whartons had met there – gathered with their friends and nurses among the statues and stone benches on the Monte Pincio, named in antiquity as the Hill of Gardens for the grand gardens built there. Edith remembered shaking out her long hair so that it caught the sun, which certainly impressed Daisy, the future Mrs Winthrop Chanler, a lifelong friend who loved Italy as Edith did. Daisy Chanler later remembered Edith's long red-gold hair and her smart sealskin coat. When Edith went back to Rome as a grown-up she met in the '*boschi*' of the Pincio the ghosts of the romping children'.

The impressions the very young Edith absorbed formed the basis of her deep and abiding attachment to Italy, and she used them from the start. She would use her impressions in her first novella *Fast and Loose*, which she wrote at the age of fourteen, setting the marriage proposal in the violet-adorned garden of the Villa Doria-Pamphili. Written more than twenty years later, her first full-length novel, *The Valley of Decision,* was a coloured mosaic as brilliant as the lapidary combinations she collected on the Palatine. Each individual fragment in the tableau of the art, religion, customs and politics of eighteenth-century Italian life that made up the novel shone as evocatively as the precious pieces of porphyry, lapis lazuli and *verde antico* of the Palace of the Caesars.

In primitive travelling conditions, by means of a jolting diligence, the family made an arduous pilgrimage into Spain. The trip instilled in the six-year-old Edith an 'incurable passion for the road'. When she was seven the family moved to Paris, where she learned to read. There her taste for literature developed. Her father had read aloud to her from an early age, from his favourite sermons and Macaulay's *Lays of Ancient Rome*, which she found intoxicating, describing the 'sensual rapture' that both the sound and the sight of words produced as like something 'visible almost tangible'. While they lived in Paris an American friend living there, Mr Henry Bledlow, regularly lunched with the family, and Edith was 'always led in', she recalled, 'with the dessert' and allowed to perch on his knee. ' "Now tell me about mythology please," ' she would request. 'What blessings I have since called down on the teller!' She detested stories for children, which she felt were written with 'indefinable condescension by big people about little ones', but 'the domestic dramas of the Olympians aroused all my creative energy . . . The normal pleasures of my age seemed as insipid as the fruits of the earth to Persephone after she had eaten the pomegranate seed . . . And I can only say that none of the children I knew had the clue to my labyrinth.'

The family left Paris in 1870, when the Franco-Prussian war broke out, and went to Germany, where Edith promptly caught typhoid fever and nearly died. During her convalescence she began to learn German, which would lead 'with raptures into the great ocean of Goethe'. The final stage in the family's peripatetic years took them to Florence, where they spent a winter in a vast rented apartment overlooking the River Arno.

When the family returned to New York, Edith was ten years old. She could speak and almost read three languages besides English, and had begun to form a discerning eye. 'I was born with critical spectacles on my nose,' she once said, but her discriminating faculties also evolved from all she had seen during these early, intensive peregrinations. Inevitably she began to make comparisons. How could New York, built with 'the most hideous stone ever quarried, this cramped horizontal gridiron of a town without towers, porticoes, fountains or perspectives', look anything but 'intolerably ugly' to a child with 'youthful eyes formed by the spectacle of Rome and Paris'? She averted her eyes by burrowing like a true bookworm into the 'kingdom of my father's library', where she began to seek context and meaning for the confusion of impressions she had absorbed. Forbidden to read anything sentimental, outré or modern, Edith landed in the safe and proper arms of classical poetry and literature, her brother's old school books on philosophy and logic, and a haphazardly obtained and inherited array of books on religion, travel, history and art criticism.

Although her parents held 'literature in great esteem, they stood in nervous dread of those who produced it'. Painting and writing were still regarded as 'disquieting', like something between 'a black art and manual labour'. Understandably, Edith kept her literary aspirations to herself. This did not stop her writing in secret though, as her infatuation with the repertoire of the English language consumed her. Poems became sonnets, verse drama became Elizabethan drama, and short stories became novellas and novels. The output was as prodigious as it was varied.

As Edith's childhood melted into adolescence, her life was divided between the world she found in the books of her father's New York library and an outdoor life between the 'wilderness and waves' at Pencraig, their Newport home. For the first time, a garden became part of her autobiographical picture. 'Flowerbeds spicy with "carnation lily rose" and a kitchen garden crimson with strawberries and sweet as honey with Secker pears and quinces' is how she sensually remembered their Pencraig garden.

Governesses improved her languages but gave her no insight or inspiration. The muses who spoke to her from the calfskin-bound volumes, however brilliant in their rhetoric, offered no dialogue. Resonating from the heavens was the voice of the high priest of aesthetics, John Ruskin, 'whose wonderful cloudy pages gave me back the image of the beautiful Europe I had lost, and fed me with visions of Italy for which I had never ceased to pine'.

When her father's failing health necessitated wintering in a milder climate, Edith and her family returned to Europe in 1881 after an eight-year absence, and settled in Cannes, then a haven for the tubercular and the fashionable. Her father bought Ruskin's guidebooks *The Stones of Venice* and *Mornings in Florence* and she and her father went sightseeing together. Ruskin's 'arbitrary itineraries' led them off the Baedeker track and on the occasions when her father could not accompany her on excursions Edith went alone, leaving none of Ruskin's stones uninspected and no path untrodden. It set the exhausting pace and exacting method of her explorations to come.

Ruskin, she said, 'awoke in me the habit of precise visual observation'. But he did much more. He showed her how to respond with informed intelligence to beauty of all kinds. After so many years of trying to reanimate her vague memories of Italy, Edith now stood before St Mark's Basilica in Venice and experienced it through the eyes of the master word-painter: 'while the burghers and barons of the north were building their dark streets and grisly castles of oak and sandstone, the merchants of Venice were covering their palaces with porphyry and gold; and at last, when her mighty painters had created for her a colour more priceless than gold or porphyry, even this, the richest of her treasures, she lavished upon walls whose foundations were beaten by the sea; and the strong tide, as it runs beneath the Rialto, is reddened to this day by the reflection of the frescoes of Giorgione.' This eloquent prose, combined with the image of the Basilica rising before her, would have been electrifying to the highly sensitive eighteen-year-old. The emotion such an aesthetic experience awoke in her she called a 'sensation', a word she used over and over again to describe her most thrilling moments. 'Sensation' provided the impetus for her travels and sustained her in troubled times.

Edith's father died in Cannes the following spring and in 1882 she returned to America with her mother. It seemed as though the door had clanged shut on Italy just as she was on the brink of real discovery. The ground, however, had been prepared. She spent a few weeks in Maine in 1883 in the company of Walter Van Rensselaer Berry, a young Harvard-educated lawyer. In him, a voracious reader like herself with a perceptive, analytical literary instinct, she glimpsed the intellectual communion she so hungered for, but as a romance their friendship came to nothing. In 1885 she married Edward 'Teddy' Wharton – a Bostonian friend of her elder brother – thirteen years her senior, with a sunny and obliging disposition and a wanderlust that matched her own. She could at last submerge herself freely and entirely in delicious Italy. Every February the Whartons packed up their dogs and their housekeeper, Gross, and went to Italy for several months at a stretch, usually via France. They explored a different region on each trip.

Soon after Edith's marriage her eyes were opened to the idiosyncratic beauty of Italian style, which she came to admire as more emotional and full of 'personal invention' and less intellectual than French style. As she was sitting for her portrait in Paris, a chair in the studio caught her eye as 'less skilful in execution' than French furniture, but more appealing for its 'freer, more individual movement'. Inquiry revealed that it was Venetian, and belonged to the much neglected eighteenth century. Always curious about the unusual, Edith made eighteenth-century Italy the focus of her study. During the early trips she was guided by a connoisseur of the eighteenth century, the cultured American, Egerton Winthrop. She read Goethe and the eccentric Charles de Brosses, plays by Carlo Goldoni (the Italian Molière) and Carlo Gozzi, as well as Vernon Lee's 'deliciously desultory' books on the eighteenth century. And so began the 'gradual absorption into my pores of a myriad details' – of landscape, architecture, old furniture and eighteenth-century portraits, and the gossip of contemporary diarists and travellers. She then widened her reading to include Stendhal, whose travel writings make up a volume of 1800 pages, and books on Italy written by fellow enthusiasts such as J. A. Symonds, Charles Eliot Norton and Paul Bourget, their descriptions all vivified by her own repeated spring wanderings.

As she travelled through Italy, Edith's sense of adventure was gratified by the 'rarest and most delicate pleasure' of 'circumventing the omniscience of the guidebook' by reaching overdescribed places by unprescribed routes. She revelled in the 'beauty and tradition and amenity' of the country, glorying in 'the astounding variety of its scenery, all of it enchanting' and delighting in the ordered symmetry with which everything was done. 'La ligne' was everywhere, in the olive groves and avenues of cypresses, and in its architecture. 'The very air is full of architecture. I never weary of driving – looking at doorways, windows, courtyards and walls. What an unerring sentiment for form!'

In 1893 Edith bought Land's End, a house that stood on the edge of Rhode Island's easternmost cliffs, on the bit of land that juts out furthest towards Europe with its 'windows framing the endlessly changing moods of the misty Atlantic . . . and the night long sound of the surges against cliffs'. She also began to integrate what she could of Italy into her American surroundings. With the help of a young Boston architect, Ogden Codman, also sensitized to Europe through his French childhood and travels in Italy, Edith liberated Land's End from the fashionable, fussy style of the 'suffocating upholsterer' and applied the balanced, harmonious architectural simplicity she had observed in Italian villas. She furnished it with choice furniture brought back from Italy and made a formal garden with 'high hedges and trellis work niches' à la française, designed by Ogden Codman, which she embellished with Italianate urns and obelisks procured, somewhat curiously, from a local purveyor of cemetery ornaments.

Blown in on a lucky wind one summer's day was the French author of Sensations d'Italie, the young and already eminent Paul Bourget, and his wife Minnie, despatched by the New York Herald to study the social rockpool of Newport. An intellectual and true connoisseur of Italy, Bourget was astounded to find at Land's End a society hostess who not only furnished her home with Venetian consoles but also shared his passion for Stendhal. Edith found his novels unreadable, as she did those of many in her circle of literary friends, especially Henry James (they became close friends after she met him in the 1880s), but that did nothing to dampen their mutual enthusiasm for exploring Italy together, and over the many stretches of open road and 'sensations' that the two couples shared as they travelled together, a deep friendship developed.

Through Paul Bourget's letter of introduction, Edith met Vernon Lee, who lived at Il Palmerino, in Maiano, on the outskirts of Florence. Only six years older than Edith, Vernon Lee was everything to which she aspired. Vernon Lee was born Violet Paget, to English parents who had moved to the Continent to escape the

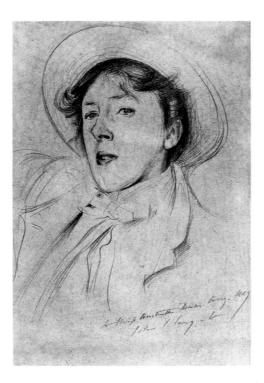

John Singer Sargent's 1889 drawing of Vernon Lee, whom Edith described as 'the first highly cultivated and brilliant woman I had ever known'.

English Sunday, and who hunted and walked their way around the watering holes of Europe. However artless their travelling, at least they mixed with 'picturesque people instead of stodging in New York', as Edith would tartly observe. In Rome, the precocious Violet was taken in hand by the vivacious, artistic and intelligent Mrs Sargent, mother of John Singer Sargent, under whose cultured guidance she discovered literature, art, music, and the history and antiquities of Rome; she also played on the Monte Pincio with John and his sister Emily. But unlike the well-behaved Edith, they amused themselves, so Vernon recalled, by 'bombarding the pigs then kept outside the Porta del Popolo, with acorns and pebbles from the Pincian Terrace; and in burning holes in bay-leaves with a burning-glass, until they were expelled as "*enfants mal élevés*" by the ferocious porter of the Medici gardens'. Such signs of rebellion revealed Violet's *outrée*, iconoclastic personality. Fiercely emancipated, brilliant and original, she was only twenty-four when she published her recondite *Studies of the Eighteenth Century in Italy* under the name Vernon Lee, deliberately sexually ambiguous

for the good reason that 'no one reads a woman's writing on art, history or aesthetics with anything but unmitigated contempt'. To Henry James she was 'a most astounding young female, the cleverest woman I know, a tiger-cat'. Her book *Limbo*, published in 1897, contained a whimsical, evocative and poetic essay on the old Italian garden. For this as much as for the help she was to receive from Vernon Lee, Edith would later dedicate *Italian Villas and Their Gardens* to her.

Edith's natural sensitivity to what her friend the painter Robert Norton described as the 'emotions aroused in her by the physical beauty of colour and form and light', placed in the context of 'atmosphere of association and history', provoked 'an almost wistful longing to communicate' those emotions. But she had to find her writer's voice before she could write confidently about Italy, and this would take up much of the 1890s as, by then in her mid-thirties, she tried to establish herself as a writer. She was ruefully aware that it was not the affable Teddy who would help her find this voice. Whilst full of admiration for her literary talent, he admired the way she kept it separate from the rest of her life even more. The themes of Edith's early fiction, chiefly set in America, are those of scarcely veiled loneliness and entrapment. One story after another was rejected by the publisher, Scribner, and with those early achievers, Paul Bourget and Vernon Lee, however sympathetic, looming erudite and formidable she dared not write on the Italian subject. The watershed years of the 1890s were punctuated by paralysing periods of depression, diagnosed as neurasthenia (the word meant a nervous breakdown). As always when faced with traumatic events, in her writing she returned to her oceanic metaphor, describing the 'seasickness' of her anxiety and nausea that necessitated 'having to pull out of the tide of life and lie in dry dock for repairs'.

But as she struggled to develop as a writer of fiction, she achieved an unexpected success as a writer of fact. Edith and Ogden Codman, having discovered their mutual enthusiasm for the simple Italian style of decorating, decided to collect their ideas into a book. At first poor Edith, her desk stuffed with verses and stories, found she 'could not write out in simple and precise English the ideas which seemed so clear in my mind'. Then once again a lucky wind blew her way, bringing Walter Berry, whom she had seen only briefly in the intervening fourteen years since their summer in Maine, for a long visit. He not only taught her to write with clarity in 'a concise and austere style', with 'high standards of economy of expression and purity of language', but also became her literary counsellor, and gave her the encouragement, guidance and confidence she needed. *The Decoration of Houses,* the book she wrote with Codman, was published to critical and popular acclaim in 1897. The following year, Edith had another nervous breakdown, telling Walter Berry, 'with all my trying I can't *write*' yet. Again, he came to her rescue, and after four months in Washington DC under the care of a renowned neurologist, she produced in rapid succession an entirely new series of short stories that were published by Scribner in 1899 as *The Greater Inclination* and the next year a novella, *The Touchstone.* 'At last', she wrote, 'I had groped my way through to my vocation.'

With her new confidence she could now turn to the place that meant most to her: Italy. In the following years she produced her Italian trilogy, comprising her novel *The Valley of Decision,* her pioneering collection of travel essays *Italian Backgrounds,* written intermittently in the 1890s and published in 1905, and *Italian Villas and Their Gardens,* after which perhaps she felt she had exhausted her subject, for Italy was never the 'hero' of her books again.

During the two years it took her to write *The Valley of Decision,* Edith and Teddy moved from Newport to Lenox, Massachusetts. What had begun with visits to the summer home of Teddy's mother resulted in their buying a 113-acre (44.5-hectare) property there called Laurel Lake Farm, belonging to the Sargent family. The rolling waves of Newport were abandoned for the rolling landscape of the Berkshire hills, for Edith found the winter climate of Newport depressing and felt invigorated in the countryside. She named her new home the Mount after Mount Bonaparte, the country seat of her great-grandfather Major General Ebenezer. The house was built from scratch.

When *The Valley of Decision* was published in 1902, its success earned her the recognition she deserved and needed, especially from Paul Bourget and Vernon Lee, who offered and indeed wrote an introduction to the Italian translation. It greatly pleased and flattered Edith that the book was compared to one of her favourite novels, Stendhal's *The Charterhouse of Parma,* set like hers in north Italy. But the books also differed, for Stendhal begins his story after Waterloo, where Edith's leaves off. She paints a portrait of the social and political fabric of a period when the ideas that led to the French Revolution began to filter over the Alps into Italy, facilitated by Napoleon – ideas that would do away with the old

order of Church and state for ever. Edith's hero, Odo, the future Duke of Pianura, is inflamed with the idea of social reforms, but when he becomes Duke he is opposed and driven out by the very people he is trying to liberate. *The Valley of Decision,* Wharton herself said, 'was not really a novel but a romantic chronicle that unrolled its episodes like the frescoed legends on the palace walls which formed its background'.

In the novel, written as Edith began to consider the prospect of a garden in relation to her new home at Lenox, the theme of the garden is swept into the great mosaic of the age, as bits of looking glass through which larger truths are potently perceived or fleetingly reflected. Based on the Villa Pisani on the Brenta, the garden is saturated with atmosphere; her 'flashing' descriptions of it glitter like gems. It is alive with 'secret vibrations', which to Edith were 'the ultimate and essential message of all works of art': of the 'Marble nymphs and fauns' who 'peeped from thickets of flowering camellias', 'goat faced men' who lurked balefully in the twilight' and Venus, 'the slender dusky goddess detached against the cool marble of her niche'. The affairs of court are compared to the mazes of the ducal garden. A tunnel of clipped limes leads to 'a theatre cut in the turf and set with statues of Apollo and the Muses'. The garden is redolent with the 'drowsy scent of jasmine and wet box borders'. It is deliciously coloured: 'A *cedrario* or orange-walk stretched its sunlit vista to the terrace above the river; and the black cassocks of one or two priests who were strolling in the clear green shade of a pleached alley made pleasant spots of dimness in the scene.' It is used as a metaphor for intellectual freedom: 'Life, cavaliere,' the old dissipated Duke tells Odo, 'is a stock on which we may graft what fruit or flower we choose . . .'

Before his banishment, the Duke is invited 'to the grot beneath the terrace. In this shaded retreat, studded with shells and corals and cooled by an artificial wind forced through the conches of marble Tritons, his lordship at once began to speak of the rumours of public disaffection.' When he leaves, 'the garden alleys were deserted, the pleached walks dark as subterranean passages, with the wet gleam of statues staring spectrally out of the blackness'.

In the novel the garden is a dreamscape: 'Odo stepped out on the terrace, which was now bathed in the whiteness of a soaring moon . . . The hush gew deeper, the murmur of the river more mysterious . . . Seen through the black arch of the arbour the moonlight lay like snow on parterres and terraces.'

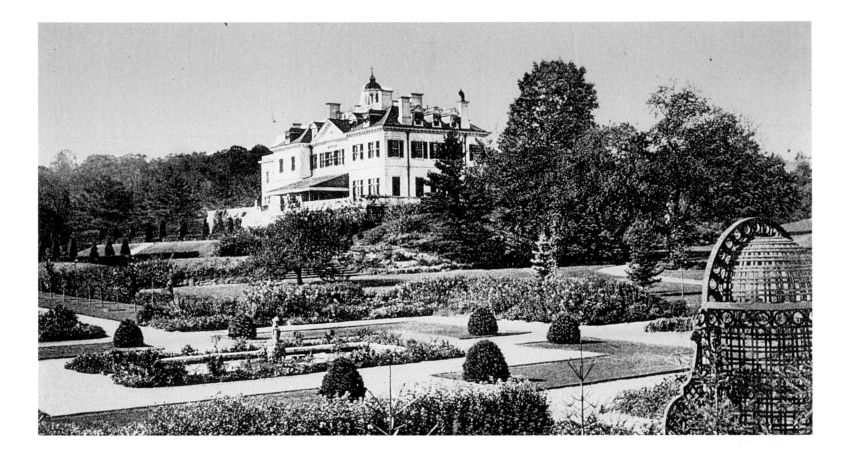

Edith Wharton's home at the Mount in Massachusetts was inspired by Belton House in England, at the time assumed to be by Sir Christopher Wren. From her second-floor apartments, where she spent the mornings writing, Edith could look out over the clipped box, geometrical parterres and statues of the Italianate garden she had created. The garden and surrounding landscape are recognizable in descriptions in her novel The House of Mirth, *published three years after she moved there.*

The editors at *Century Magazine* thought that this poetry-in-prose rendering of an Italian garden would perfectly complement the romantic style of the artist Maxfield Parrish. Shortly after the *Valley of Decision* was published, they asked Edith to write a series of articles to accompany paintings of Italian gardens by him. She was enthusiastic about the idea, as Parrish had already illustrated one of her short stories. The *Century* editors, confident that her prose would be as rhapsodic as Maxfield Parrish's 'moonlight and nightingale' fantasies, underestimated the high-minded approach Edith would take. She may well have written the articles in the atmospheric, painterly vein of her writing in her novel, had she not discovered quite quickly into her researches that no serious work on Italian gardens existed in English. The 1894 peregrinations of Charles Platt, a landscape architect and friend and neighbour of Parrish's in Bar Harbour, Maine, had produced some splendid photographs of less than two dozen of the grandest gardens, but the accompanying text contained not a single date or architect, and Edith instantly recognized the potential of so interesting and unexplored a subject: 'having been given the opportunity to do a book that needed doing, I resolutely took it.' After the critical success of *The Valley of Decision*, 'nothing would appease her creative and critical appetite', noted her biographer, Professor R. W. B. Lewis. She tackled this project with what Paul Bourget dubbed 'energy of culture', which Henry James sometimes found overwhelming, describing the experience of 'travelling under the spur' with the 'rich, rushing, ravening' Whartons.

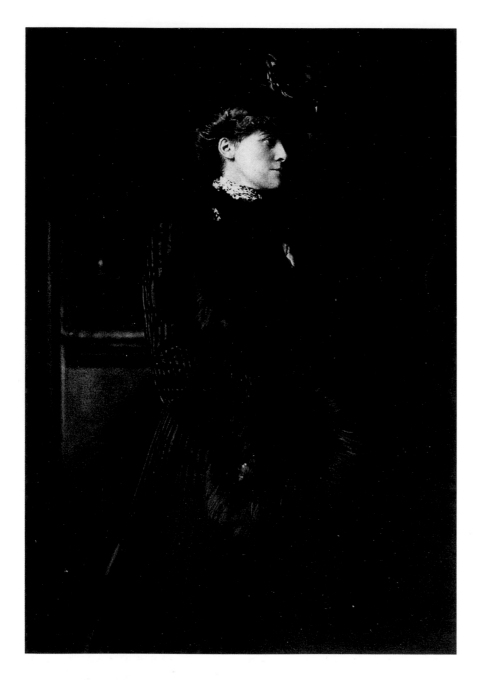

ABOVE *The fashionable and successful Mrs Wharton in Paris in 1907, a period when she was enjoying the fame earned by her novel* The House of Mirth, *which had become a bestseller.*

OPPOSITE *The green and gold jacket to the first edition of* Italian Villas and Their Gardens, *designed by Mark J. Black.*

Edith fully understood that the Italian garden had almost nothing to do with the art of gardening and everything to do with the garden as a work of art. Principles of architecture, the study of painting, sculpture and architectural detail were all disciplines she had long schooled herself in, and which had given her an excellent grasp of the 'plastic arts'. Spanning many years, her reading of Italian literature, poetry and mythology had been comprehensive. In the Renaissance garden, seeped in symbolism, allegory and the visions of poets, she would recognize the enchanted gardens of Tasso, the fables of Ariosto, the philosophy of Petrarch, the spiritual journey of Dante and how these writers were inextricably bonded to the old Italian garden, as indeed was the whole cultural background of Italy.

Edith launched herself into the uncharted waters of her Italian garden voyage on 3 January 1903, when she and Teddy sailed for Genoa. Now fifty-four, Teddy's underlying mental instability was beginning to surface. The doctor had ordered him to spend time in wintery sunshine, and so for three weeks Edith sat under a palm tree in detested San Remo, impatient to be off prospecting for the gold of the Italian garden. From San Remo the Whartons went to Genoa, and from Genoa to Rome, where they arrived at the end of the first week in February for a month's stay.

From Rome Edith wrote to her childhood friend Daisy Chanler, 'You don't need to be told, I am sure, that I have thought of you very often in scenes which are so associated with you. We have been here a month, and we leave, alas, the day after tomorrow, with a sense at once of regret and repleteness. I think sometimes it is almost a pity to enjoy Italy as much as I do, because the acuteness of my sensations makes them rather exhausting.' The highlight of the stay was undoubtedly her first experience of a motor car, driven by the American ambassador, George Meyer, from Rome to Caprarola, a round trip of 100 miles that she was astonished could be accomplished in an afternoon. 'I had a high seat like a coachman's box beside the Ambassador. In a thin spring dress, a sailor hat balanced on my chignon, and a two-inch tulle veil over my nose, I climbed proudly to my perch, and off we tore across the *campagna*, over humps and bumps, through ditches and across gutters, wind-swept, dust enveloped, I clinging to my sailor hat, and George Meyer (luckily) to the wheel.' This 'Witch of Atlas' excursion, she told Daisy, was the most beautiful she ever made in Italy: 'The view on the ridge between Ronciglione and Caprarola, looking down on one side of Lago di Vico, and on the other the wide plain . . . was like one of Turner's Italian visions.'

Edith and Teddy left Rome for Siena, inviting their American friends, the Bucklers, to share their landau. William Buckler's unpublished memoir reveals, according to Lewis, that the trip was meandering, with frequent pauses for Edith to inspect famous if often out-of-the-way gardens. She took photographs, made extensive notes and bought old books in the hope that they might lead her to discover forgotten villas and how the gardens originally looked. Buckler was astonished by the dilapidated state of some of the villas and their inhabitants – there was a great-aunt sleeping in a doorway in one, a grandmother dying on a library couch in another, while at the Villa Lante the cackling of family lunatics rang out from the quarters to which they were confined.

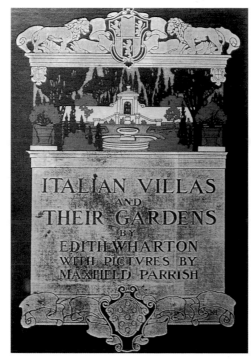

'How I wish you had been with us since we left Rome,' Edith wrote to her friend Sally Norton on 17 March from the Hotel Bristol in Florence. 'At Viterbo, Montefiascone, Orvieto and the delicious villas near Siena! We did not reach here until last night and Miss Paget [Vernon Lee] has such a prodigious list of villas for me to see near here and is taking so much trouble to arrange expeditions for us that I think we shall have to stay here longer than I expected.' Vernon Lee's help was invaluable. Her 'long familiarity with the Italian countryside, and the wide circle of her Italian friendships, made it easy for her to guide me to all the right places, and put me in relation with people who could enable me to visit them . . . thanks to her . . . wherever I went I found open doors.'

On 27 March the Whartons met Paul and Minnie Bourget, who had joined them from Hyères to tour the Brenta and the Veneto together. Edith still found time to squeeze in a cure at the thermal baths of Salsomaggiore near Parma, explore the lakes and reach Paris by 15 April. 'Our time', she wrote in a masterful understatement, 'is painfully short.'

Ten days later Edith returned to America, 'where the atmosphere is thin enough to permit my over-crowded sensations to settle'. Her first article, which appeared in the November 1903 issue of *Century Magazine*, illustrated with one of Parrish's 'brilliant idealizations' of the Italian scene, prompted a 'distracted letter' from one of the editors, Richard Watson Gilder, who found the text 'too dry and technical. Could I not, Mr Gilder pleaded, introduce into the next number a few anecdotes, and a touch of human interest? My answer was curt.' Edith, her literary conscience bristling, was adamant in wanting to do justice to a subject 'which hitherto had been treated in English only in the most amateurish fashion'.

It is a great shame that *Century Magazine* did not honour Edith's pioneering work by including in the articles the plans she went to considerable lengths to obtain, because by omitting them the editors obliged her to use her allocated space for describing what the plans would have explained. Otherwise she might have chosen to include more of those 'flashing gems' a reviewer of *The Valley of Decision* described as 'iridescent bubbles blown from the lips of fancy'. Even so, the writing, as Lewis says, is 'infused with a somber charm of style and a stateliness of movement' and the articles, published all together as a book, *Italian Villas and Their Gardens,* in 1904, paved the way for architectural students, landscape gardeners and enthusiasts such as Inigo Triggs, Sir Geoffrey Jellicoe, Jock Shepherd and Sir George Sitwell, who all followed in her footsteps and paid tribute. One of her earliest readers was Egerton Winthrop's nephew Lawrence Johnston, and her book influenced his groundbreaking English garden, Hidcote.

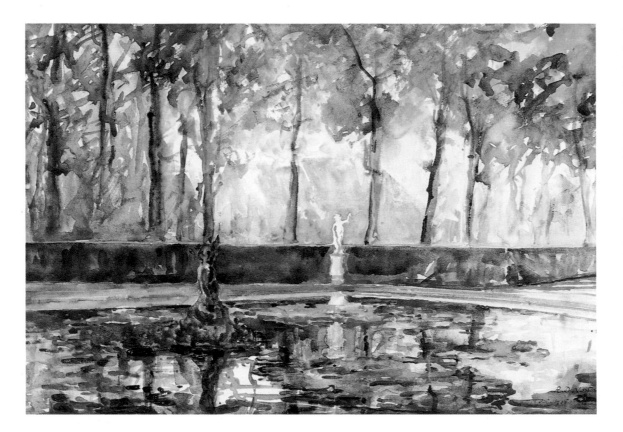

Edith Wharton cared for her gardens with passionate devotion. She ministered to her plants as if they were young charges; perhaps they replaced the children she never had. 'Edith was very learned about gardens,' reported Berkeley Updike, the stylish printer of her books, on a visit to the Mount, and she and a neighbour, Miss Charlotte Barnes, used to hold 'interminable and to me rather boring conversations about the relative merits of various English seedsmen and the precise shades of blue or red or yellow flowers that they could guarantee their customers. I have never thought it very interesting to hear about other people's gardens and have laughed at the prosey discourses of their owners until I had one of my own, when I found myself victimizing guests in precisely the same way.'

Although she commissioned her niece Beatrix Farrand to design the kitchen garden at the Mount, Edith wanted to do the rest of the landscaping there herself. Teddy was also involved, 'opening up vistas through trees' with mixed results. In her later years, Edith admitted how her Italian book influenced the Italianate rendering of a garden that elicited the comment from the Austrian ambasssador, as he looked out from the terrace over a formal garden, rock garden, trees, rolling hills and lake: 'Ah, Mrs Wharton, when I look about me I don't know if I am in England or Italy.'

She never made a garden in Italy, seeming to have exhausted her subject, and henceforth treated it, she said, as 'dessert' whilst France became her 'daily bread'. She made two gardens in France, her two saints she called them: Saint-Brice outside Paris, and Sainte-Claire, built on an Hyères hillside overlooking the Mediterranean. She spent her winters there in the company of two of the greatest gardeners of this century, Lawrence 'Johnnie' Johnston and her neighbour Charles de Noailles.

The art critic Bernard Berenson had by this time replaced Walter Berry and Henry James as her intellectual confidant. Bernard and his wife Mary Berenson's villa, I Tatti, near Florence, became her spiritual home and she visited them every year, usually *en route* to or from Hyères. Sainte-Claire, she wrote to Berenson, 'was no mere parterre of heaven; it is the very "cielo della quieta" that Dante found above the seventh heaven . . . I've found the Great Good Place'. The Italian poets remained alive for her and were constantly referred to. Berenson said she knew more about Dante than any other amateur. In 1933, deeply chagrined by what she sensed as the rumblings of yet another war, she wrote to Berenson suggesting a sojourn in his summer villa: 'Let us act as Boccaccio's set and forget about it.'

At the age of seventy-three she stood before the masterpieces of the Italian Exhibition in Paris, as she had in the Louvre in her youth, and experienced them this time not as 'waves' but as 'a great tidal wave of beauty'. But right behind it was the inexorable 'tidal wave of fatigue' of her failing health. 'Yes: the garden is the only life preserver left,' she wrote to her young friend and gardening chum, Louis Bromfield.

The ink was barely dry on her memoirs, in which the Rome of her childhood was distilled into 'the scent of box hedges . . . and the texture of weather-worn, sun-gilt stone', when she had her first stroke. Her last weeks before she died in August 1937 were spent quietly being wheeled about the garden at Saint-Brice, seeing friends for the last time, reminiscing and dozing on the sofa. 'What weary lonely days when I dreamed of Italy,' she wrote.

Italy had shone like a beacon into the unenlightened world of her childhood. It had been her first love and she had loved it then innocently and instinctively; and as she grew up and looked upon it with informed and lucid eyes, she loved it even more. It had beckoned her like a siren – the same siren who had called on her to make the long pilgrimage of a writer her life's work. And perhaps, during those final weeks in summer, as her life was ebbing away, she may have remembered a much earlier summer, thirty-eight years before, when she was on holiday with Teddy and the Bourgets, high up in Switzerland in an immaculate landscape of 'precise gardens and subjugated vines' dotted with chalets. It resembled an 'old maid's paradise that would be thrown into hopeless disarray by the introduction of anything so irregular as a work of art'. From the cool, comfortable but uninspired heights of the Splügen Pass, she watched the diligences arriving from Italy, all hot, dusty and dishevelled. 'Was it better', she wrote of those moments, 'to be cool and look at a waterfall, or to be hot and look at Saint Mark's? Was it better to walk on gentians or on mosaic; to smell fir needles or incense? Was it, in short, ever well to be elsewhere when one might be in Italy? . . . Gradually we began to

picture our sensations should we take seats in the diligence on its return journey . . . We did not say much to each other, but one morning at sunrise we found a travelling carriage at the door. No-one seemed to know who had ordered it, but we noticed that our luggage was being strapped on behind.' She saw the other diligence waiting in the silent square: 'There they stand, side by side in dusty slumber, till the morning cow bells wake them to departure. One goes back to Thusis; to the region of good hotels, pure air and scenic platitudes. It may go empty for all we care. But the other . . . wakes from its Alpine sleep to climb the cold pass at sunrise and descend by hot windings into the land where the church steeples turn into *campanili*, where the vine, breaking from perpendicular bondage, flings a liberated embrace about the mulberries, and far off, beyond the plain, the mirage of domes and spires, of painted walls and sculptured altars, beckons across the dustiest tracts of memory. In that diligence our seats are taken.'

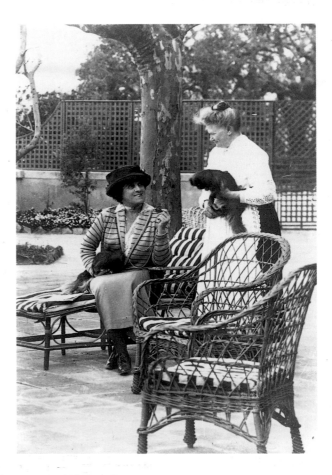

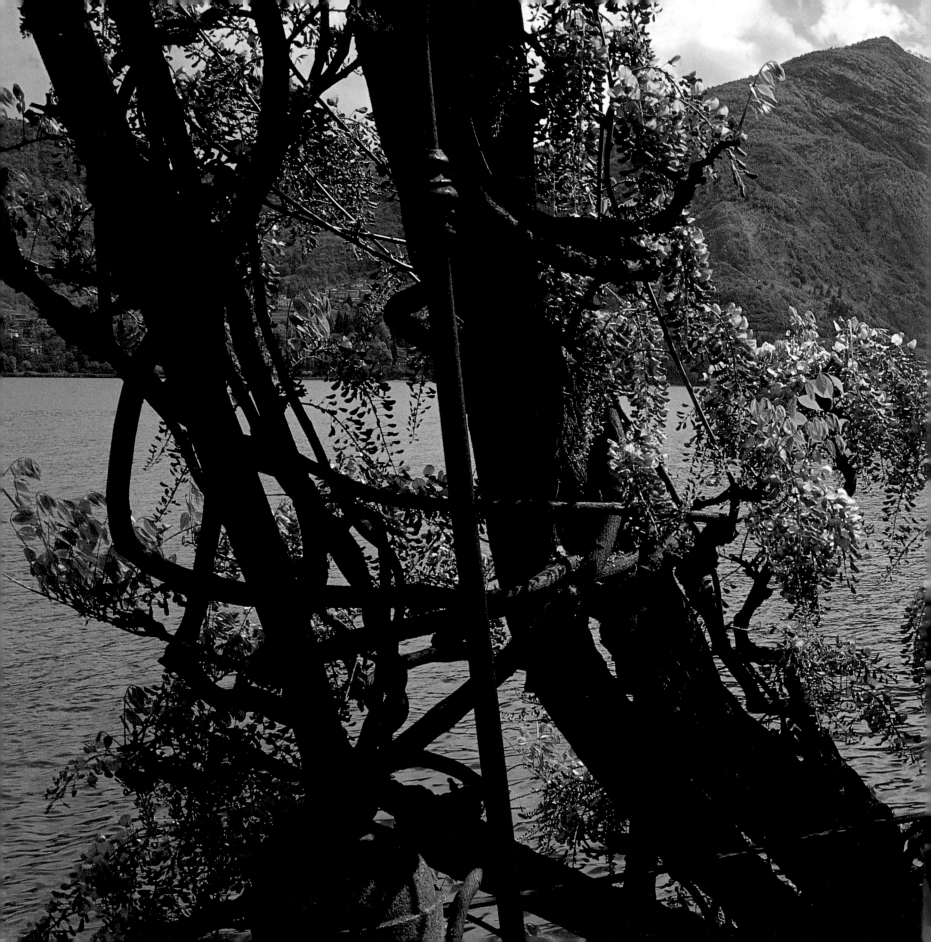

GARDENS OF LOMBARDY

NINETEENTH-CENTURY TRAVELLERS crossed the high Alps and entered Italy through the Brenner Pass, the Splügen Pass and over Mount Cenis – but no crossing was so grand, so high and treacherous as the Simplon Pass. 'The Simplon', wrote Lord Byron after he had made the crossing in 1816, 'is the most superb of all possible routes. It is magnificent in its nature and in its art both God and man have done wonders – to say nothing of the devil, who must certainly have had a hand (or a hoof) in some of the rock and ravines through and over which the works are carried.'

The Simplon was barely passable in 1800, when Napoleon made it his route between France and Italy. It had remained virtually unchanged since 1644, when John Evelyn had made an epic crossing on a mule and by a miracle survived. He and his party had crept along a narrow and treacherous track in mist so thick they could neither see nor hear one another, proceeding almost blindly across 'ravines of stupendous depths' over unprotected bridges of unfelled fir trees, surrounded on all sides by the 'terrible roaring of cataracts'. It took Napoleon's 30,000 men six years and five million kilos of gunpowder to blast through the massive mountain walls, and to build the 653 bridges over ravines and chasms that were needed to make the road continuous.

Considered the wonder of its day, the new route over the Simplon offered a bracing and dramatic rite of passage into the Promised Land of the Grand Tour, and became the time-honoured way of entering Italy. Among the clutch of early travellers was, in 1814, Caroline of Brunswick, later Queen Caroline, wife of George IV, followed soon after by Byron, Stendhal and Shelley. Turner painted and sketched his way along the route, as did Ruskin in 1844, the same year that Dickens made the crossing with his wife, five children, servants and the family dog. The young Henry James walked part of the way in 1869, and the French writer Théophile

Gautier also crossed the Simplon, leaving a description in *Italia,* published in 1852, that is as harrowing as Evelyn's.

Travelling from the cold air of the high Alps into the warmth of Italy, carriages lurched and lumbered along vertiginous routes carrying travellers clutching their Baedeker, Bradshaw or Murray guidebooks, which hastened to reassure them that the world ahead was free of the 'perils of precipices and robbers' presently surrounding them. English carriages, reported Byron, were regularly 'stopped and handsomely pilfered of various chattels'. But however alarming, the Pass afforded a breathtakingly beautiful descent into the dreamland of Lombardy. 'Down, down on, on into Italy we went', wrote Henry James to his sister Alice: ' . . . a rapturous progress thro' a wild luxuriance of corn & vines & olives & figs & mulberries & chestnuts & frescoed villages . . . One can't describe the beauty of the Italian lakes, nor would one try if one could; the floweriest rhetoric can recall it only as a picture on a fireboard [firescreen] recalls a Claude. But it lay spread before me . . . in the long gleam of the Major [Lake Maggiore] . . .'

Beyond lay a vast green plain, as if, remarked Evelyn fancifully, 'Nature had here swept up the rubbish of the earth into the Alps to form and clear the Plains of Lombardy.' From the vast horizon, frequently blanketed in fog, rose the spires of Milan, the city of bankers. Its long moneyed arm had reached into the 'smiling landscape' of the Italian lakes and built villas and gardens there for the vanity and pleasure of the rich.

One by one travellers alighted from their carriages and fell under the spell cast by the purity of the transalpine light playing upon the splendour of the scenery. It was a landscape that stretched from the highest highs of its perpetually snowy white peaks to the bottomless depths of its brooding, deep blue lakes. Wharton found it had 'an air of perennial loveliness'. The mountains were covered in forests of rich chestnut and sombre fir. Through this dark canopy

PREVIOUS PAGES *The heady beauty of the Lombardy landscape never failed to impress, startle and inspire early travellers. The weather was as temperamental as the people, prone to sudden storms and violent squalls even in settled spells of sparkling sunshine. Its fabled mists hung oppressively in the air and clung to the hills until blown away by the fierce north wind, the tramontana, after which every detail of the scenery was revealed with startling clarity. This wisteria, in one of the few 'undisturbed corners', as Wharton described them, of 'old garden magic', overlooks Lake Maggiore, next to the Villa Carlotta. The mist is just clearing.*

OPPOSITE *The Simplon Pass was treacherous even after the road was made, as this vignette after Turner shows. Imagine poor John Evelyn carrying his medicinal herbs back from the Botanic Garden at Padua on mules in the seventeenth century, when there was no path.*

RIGHT *Looking across Lake Maggiore to Bellagio. The mist has now lifted, revealing the clarity of light that gave the region its 'air of perennial loveliness'.*

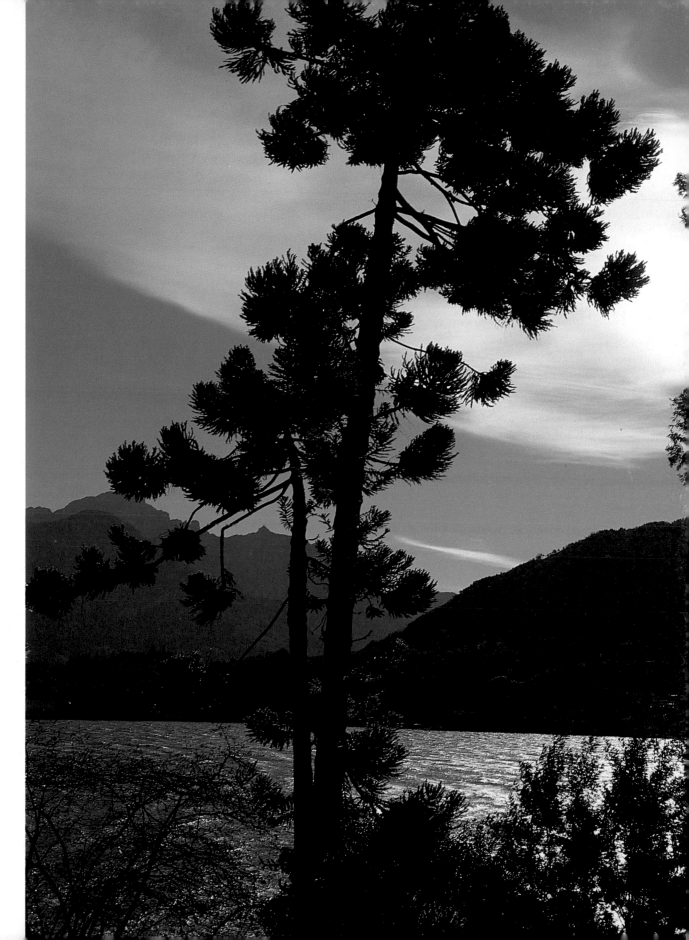

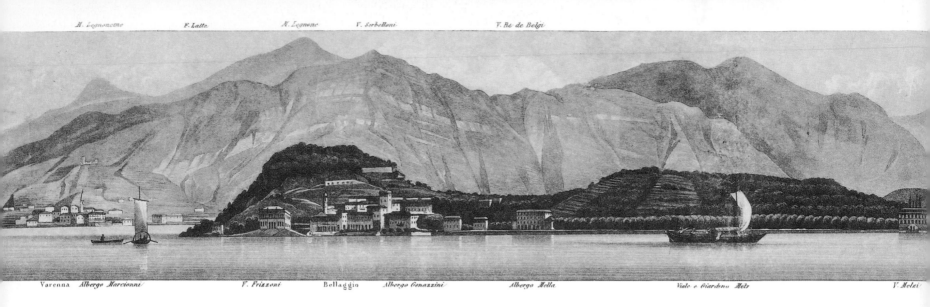

rose the white church towers of white-walled villages built near torrents and streams, and in Shelley's 'glens filled with the flashing light of the waterfalls'.

The Murray guidebook to the north of Italy, first published in 1842, whose overriding aim, noted Henry James, was 'to alleviate the grinding chore of travel', proposed various itineraries in the Lombardy region. Playing the part of an experienced and cautioning nursemaid, it offered minutiae on every point of interest. You were all but taken by the hand, placed in a boat and floated off to the garden paradises of the Borromean Islands. On your way there you could see for yourself if Isola Bella really did resemble 'a huge Perigord Pie stuck round with the heads of woodcocks and partridges'. In Arona, you were led step by step up into the head of the colossal 106-foot (32.5-metre) bronze statue of San Carlo Borromeo, where you were instructed to 'squeeze yourself through the folds of the upper and lower drapery of his skirt', and so clamber up the coppery insides of the saint by means of crampons to the top, where 'you could rest by sitting down in the recess of the nose which serves as an arm chair' – with the proviso that 'this should not be attempted by the nervous, or those of corpulent dimensions'. You were guided through the villas of the Milanese gentry inhabited during the season of *villeggiatura* – the Villa Carlotta, the Villa d'Este and the Villa Pliniana – and told of the terraces, gardens and excellent views from the Villa Serbelloni hotel, but warned of 'complaints of insolence of the landlord to English ladies'. Murray didn't tell the tourist (but Stendhal, in *Voyages in Italy*, did) that the Villa Serbelloni had been built on the site of an old castle, the Villa Sfrondata, which belonged to the

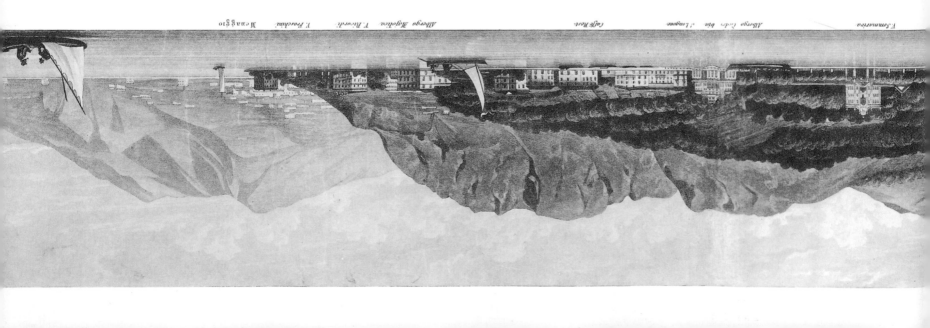

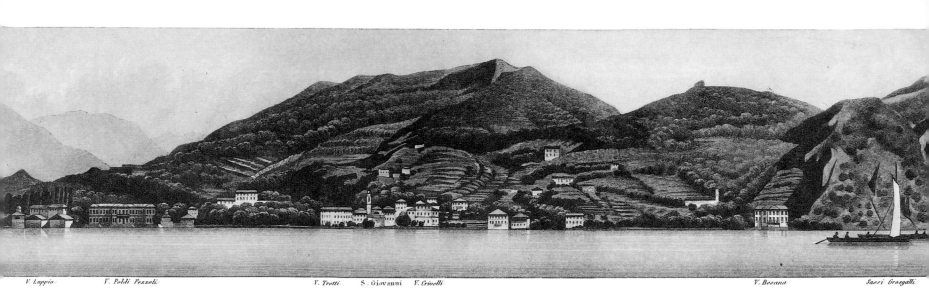

niece of Pope Gregory XIV. Visitors to the villa were shown where she flung her lovers over the precipice and into the lake when she tired of them. 'We saw the spot but we did not see the lovers', noted Stendhal.

Like a genie released from its bottle, the *genius loci* liberated the imagination, and the scenery that beguiled the tourists also stirred poetic, literary and musical Muses. 'The Lake of Como has figured largely in novels of "immoral" tendency', pronounced Henry James, referring to the hero of Stendhal's *Charterhouse of Parma*, Fabrizio del Dongo, based on Cardinal Alessandro I Farnese (later Pope Paul III), who began the great Caprarola villa and whose story Stendhal, as the French consul in Rome, moved to Lombardy for diplomatic reasons. The whole atmosphere was decidedly operatic – even Henry James found himself 'fairly wallowing in a

libretto'. By the shores of Lake Como, that ever-flowing fountain of inspiration, Bellini composed *Norma* and *La Sonnambula*, Rossini *Tancredi*, and Verdi Act II of *La Traviata*. To try out their arias the composers could avail themselves of the services of Madame Giuditta Pasta, the Maria Callas of her day, and her husband the tenor Giuseppe Pasta, who had a villa on Como. Another diva, 'La Grissina', sang at Isola Bella for Napoleon, who had a tempestuous affair with her. Liszt, forced into exile by an amorous liaison, wrote

A panorama of Como, showing the villas along the shore. The almost mythical landscape of the lakes was as filled with muses as Mount Parnassus, inspiring the composers and writers who visited and stayed. The surrounding hills, planted with chestnut trees by the Milanese dukes to provide for people when food was scarce, supplied a verdant backdrop.

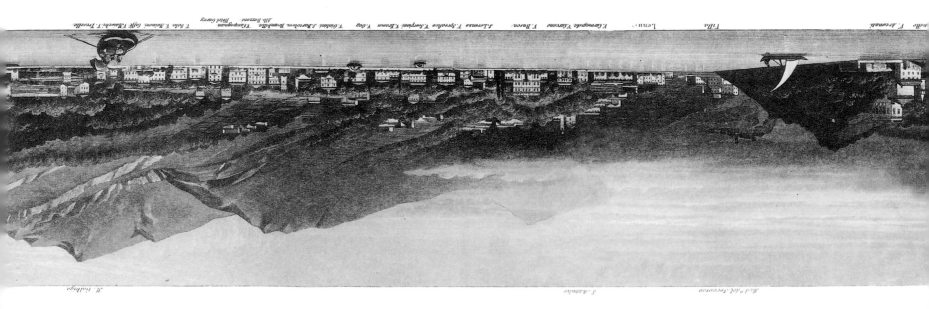

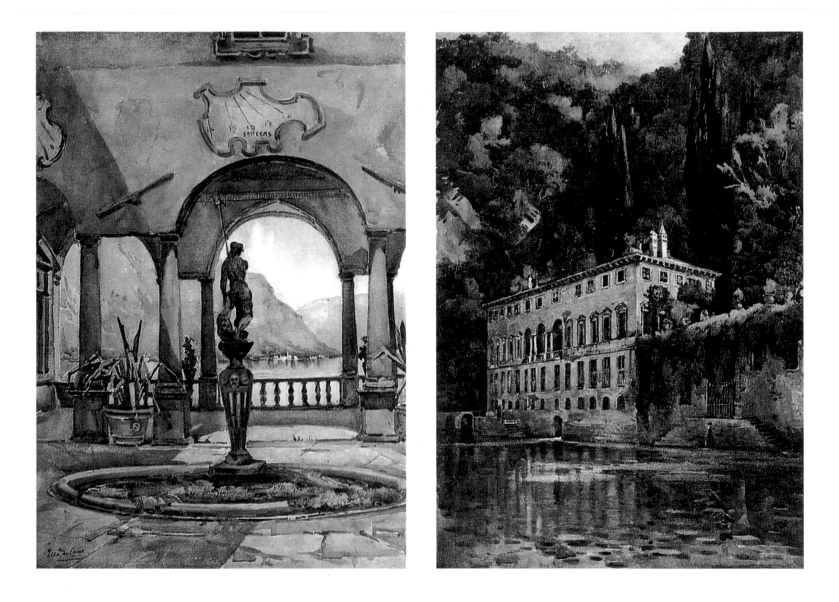

Watercolours of the loggia and spring (left) and the Renaissance Villa Pliniana (right) on the shores of Lake Como, painted at around the time of Edith Wharton's visit by Ella du Cane. Wharton enthused: 'The contrast of this dusky dripping loggia, on its perpetually shaded bay, with the blazing blue waters of the lake and their sun-steeped western shores, is one of the most wonderful effects in sensation that the Italian villa-art has ever devised.' The spring was discovered by Pliny the Elder in the first century AD. So famous did it become that Leonardo da Vinci, living in Milan under the patronage of the Sforzas, came to study and draw it. Pliny the Younger's letters, in which he discussed the layout of his villas near Rome and in Tuscany, became the foundation for Renaissance garden design. Evoking the bubbling spring as the sacred spring of Parnassus and his idea of otium – a life of elegant and intellectual leisure – his writings formed the idea of a garden as a place of spiritual, intellectual and physical nourishment.

his 'Dante Sonata' on the shores of Como, where, on Christmas Day 1837, his daughter Cosima was born, the future wife of Richard Wagner, to whom Isola Bella may have suggested Kundry's enchanted garden in his opera *Parsifal*.

Sitting on a kind of geographical cusp, Lombardy was, by nature, a land of contrasts. The duality of its character, cunningly exploited by garden architects, was everywhere: in the rises and falls of its topography, the highs and lows of its temperature, and the light and dark of its sun and shade. Pliny the Younger, who became Lombardy's most famous early citizen, understood and later represented this inherent dichotomy in the first century AD. He left his native Como at the age of fourteen, but remained wistfully attached to the lake, which had, he said, 'both use and beauty'. When he inherited land from his uncle, Pliny the Elder, he built two villas on either side of Lake Como, one situated high up, the other low down. The higher one, in Bellagio, sat on a ridge straddling two bays, with a view of the Alps more superb than that of any other villa on the lake. He named it 'Tragedia', after the knee-high buskin or cothurnus boot worn by actors in classical Greek tragedies. The lower one, in Lenno, near the Tremezzina bay, hugged the shore; this he called 'Comedia', after the low shoes worn by comic actors. 'Each', he said, 'seems the more attractive to the occupant by contrast with the other.' The Villa Tragedia was aptly named, for it was replaced by the Villa Sfrondata, a shrine to rejected lovers.

Both Plinys became preoccupied with a little bubbling spring at the other end of Como. From the younger Pliny's description of 'the spring which rises in the mountain, and running among rocks is received into a little banqueting room', it seems that it had already been integrated into a house in the first century. It ebbed and flowed by regular amounts three times a day, but Pliny the Younger, who camped and dined beside it, drinking from its water, could not work out the nature of this phenomenon, and offered seven possible explanations for 'this wonderful appearance'. In this story, we find the germ of the essential and most inspired elements of the Italian garden: a passion for the understanding and manipulation of water, and the metaphor of a small spring as the source of all creativity.

A Renaissance palace, the Villa Pliniana, was built over the spring in 1570. When Shelley came to Lake Como in April 1818 he was taken to it, felt the poetic muses stirring there and wished to rent it for the summer. Although neglected, the bubbling spring was still ebbing and flowing as it had in Pliny's time and now featured as a fountain in the courtyard. The villa, according to Shelley, was 'built upon terraces *raised from* the bottom of the lake'. And above, 'from among the clouds as it were, descends a waterfall of immense size, broken by the woody rocks into a thousand channels to the lake'. When Wharton visited Villa Pliniana in April 1903, she marvelled at the way the architect had captured the torrent on its descent from the waterfall and carried it 'through the central apartment of the villa. The effect produced is unlike anything else, even in the wonderland of Italian gardens.'

Villa Pliniana was a purist's paradise: in it Wharton found the essence of Lombardy, uncompromised and unadulterated by the passion for the 'new English garden' that had by then mutilated many other gardens. To her, the Renaissance garden was consecrated ground, and demolishing it to make way for a fashionable English-style park designed to show off sub-tropical and exotic trees and shrubs was an act of desecration: 'The fury of modern horticulture', she fumed, had 'swept over Lombardy like a tidal wave', tearing across the hallowed ground of the old Italian garden, obliterating terraces and groves, pleached alleys and boxed parterres, and leaving a trail of devastation that included winding paths, spotty flowerbeds and rolling lawns. 'Here and there, some undisturbed corner remains . . . but these old bits are so scattered and submerged under the new order of gardening that it requires an effort of the imagination to reconstruct from them an image of what the old lake-gardens must have been before . . .'

Lombardy's equable climate and abundant water supply, she acknowledged, had always allowed the garden architects of the Italian lakes to use flowers in profusion, 'mingling bright colours with architectural masses'; and, loving flowers herself, she understood this 'passion for horticulture' but believed it should remain within the architectural framework of the garden. She accepted that old Italian garden architecture could be 'artificial' and 'avowedly conventional': it could even be 'a complete negation of nature'. She admitted that the fantastic landscape of the lakes 'justified in the garden architect almost any excesses of the fancy'. But what the gardens were not permitted to be was English. The Lombardy gardener who heeded her impassioned plea for conservation could, as the custodian of a museum piece, look forward to a life of raking terraces, clipping box and picking lemons, basking in the warm glow of Edith Wharton's blessing.

THE BORROMEAN ISLANDS

NEARLY FIVE HUNDRED YEARS AGO, Count Lancellotti Borromeo bought two rocky fishermen's islands on a bend at the north-western end of Lake Maggiore, surrounded by a panorama of snow-capped Alpine peaks. One became a botanical paradise, the other a Baroque masterpiece. Isola Bella and Isola Madre, still owned by the Borromeos, are Italy's most glittering islands.

The Borromeos were a wealthy, cultivated and philanthropic Milanese family, comprising the great and the good of their day. Their name derives from *buon Romeo*, meaning 'devoted pilgrim to Rome'. Theirs was a *casa santa* if ever there was one, for on the family tree hangs a galaxy of cardinals, archbishops, a pope and a saint – San Carlo Borromeo.

During the fifteenth and sixteenth centuries, a series of Visconti and Sforza dukes ruled Milan and presided over Lombardy. They were a paradoxical combination of artistic enlightenment and gross corruption. While they irrigated the sunny Lombard plain to encourage the cultivation of mulberry trees and rice, patronized Leonardo da Vinci and laid the cornerstone of Milan Cathedral, they disposed of one another with astonishing insouciance and imagination. The practices in the Church were scarcely less corrupt. Into this climate Carlo Borromeo was born in 1538, destined to become the great reformer of his day. Although the guidebooks tell you that from an early age Carlo Borromeo became a priest and lived the simple life of a hermit on Isola Madre, preaching from a tiny church, in reality he was a *bon viveur* in his youth, leading a life of exhausting social pursuits. That was all changed by the election of his uncle as Pope Pius IV, who made him a cardinal at the age of twenty-two and despatched him to Rome, installing him in the Villa Pia on the Vatican hill to reflect on more serious matters. So serious did Borromeo become that he devoted his life to saving souls and championing the poor.

Borromeo earned the undying love of the people with his humanity and courage when he risked his life during the great plague of 1576–7 to distribute the sacrament in person. But his uncompromising efforts, in the spirit of the Counter-Reformation, to cleanse the Church of its scandalous abuses earned him enemies. The Umiliati order of priests attempted to assassinate him as he prayed in his private chapel, but the bullet they fired bounced off his back. This was read as divine intervention: a miracle.

When Borromeo died at the age of forty-six, he was displayed in Milan Cathedral. 'To form an idea of the *étalage*, you must imagine that a jeweller, for reasons of his own, has struck an unnatural partnership with an undertaker . . . The black mummified corpse of the saint', wrote Henry James, 'is stretched out in a glass coffin, clad in his mourning canonicals, mitred, crosiered and gloved, glittering with votive jewels.' This grisly peepshow became one of the most popular attractions of the Grand Tour. Charles de Brosses went after he had visited the copper-skirted colossus erected to the saint at his birthplace, Arona, and was not able to resist remarking on the length of the saint's nose, which, he said, never seemed to end. As he was kneeling in front of his patron saint a rat scurried in and began gnawing away at the tip 'with no respect for beatitude'.

San Carlo lay preserved in the aspic of moral rectitude, but the world moved on. In 1797, Napoleon visited the Islands and he carved the word *battaglia* (meaning 'battle') on the trunk of a bay laurel on Isola Bella. He was taken to Isola Madre to admire the rearing of pheasants and asked for one to take with him. When he returned two years later after the Battle of Morengo had made him Emperor of France and King of Italy, he was warmly welcomed by Prince Borromeo, in spite of having destroyed the Rocca d'Arona, their family home. His victory was celebrated on the Islands with receptions and a gala concert with La Grissina. At the same time, in Milan, Stendhal reported overhearing the conversation of the workmen hanging up banners in the Cathedral for San Carlo's feast day. The two names on their lips were San Carlo and Napoleon – both single-minded, and adored.

Count Borromeo's early death in 1513 put a stop to plans to develop Isola Bella, which would probably have looked very similar to Isola Madre had it been landscaped at the same time. By the time the Borromeos turned their attention to taming that island of 'bare, splintering rock', a new century had begun, heady with the novelty of the Baroque. The classical laws of finite proportion made way for the free use of infinite space and the imagination was opened to splendid and dramatic effects, one of which was the idea of turning the entire island into a floating garden.

GARDENS OF LOMBARDY

An eighteenth-century view of the Borromean Islands by an unknown artist. 'The Borromei converted their rocky islands into the hanging gardens which to travellers became one of the most important sights of the "grand tour",' wrote Wharton. Amongst the most eloquent was Dickens: 'The beautiful day was just declining', he wrote, 'when we came upon Lago Maggiore, with its lovely islands. For however fanciful and fantastic Isola Bella may be, and is, it is still beautiful. Anything springing out of that blue water, with the scenery around it, must be.' Wharton, too, added her poetry: 'Are they real? No; but neither is the landscape about them. Are they like any other gardens on earth? No; but neither are the mountains and shores about them like earthly shores and mountains. They are Armida's gardens anchored in a lake of dreams, and they should be compared, not with this or that actual piece of planted ground, but with a page of Ariosto or Boiardo.'

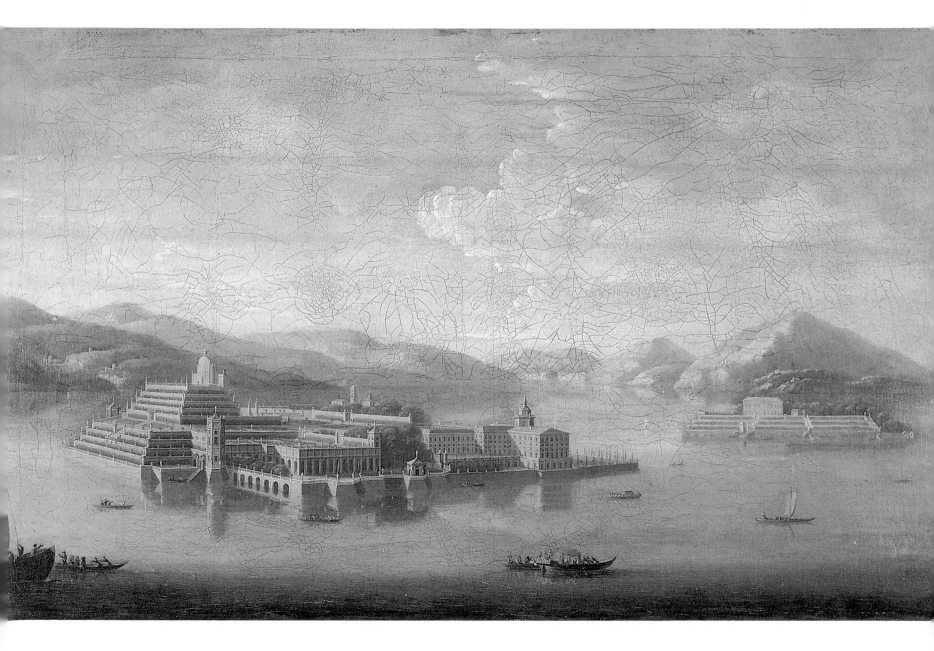

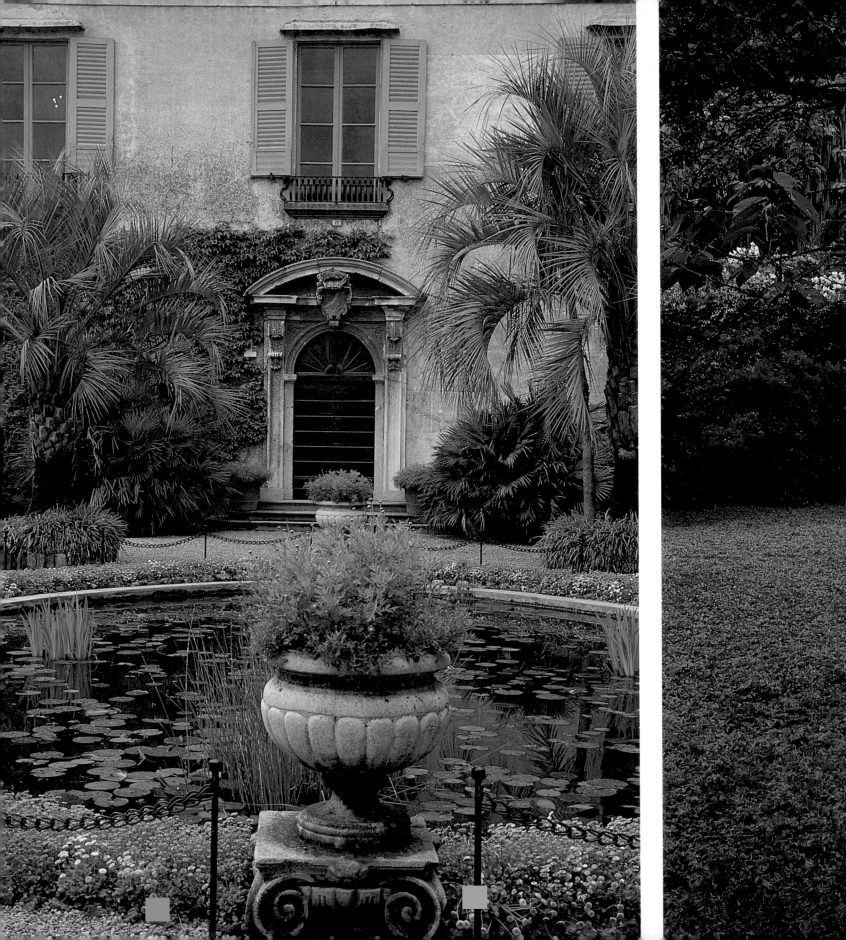

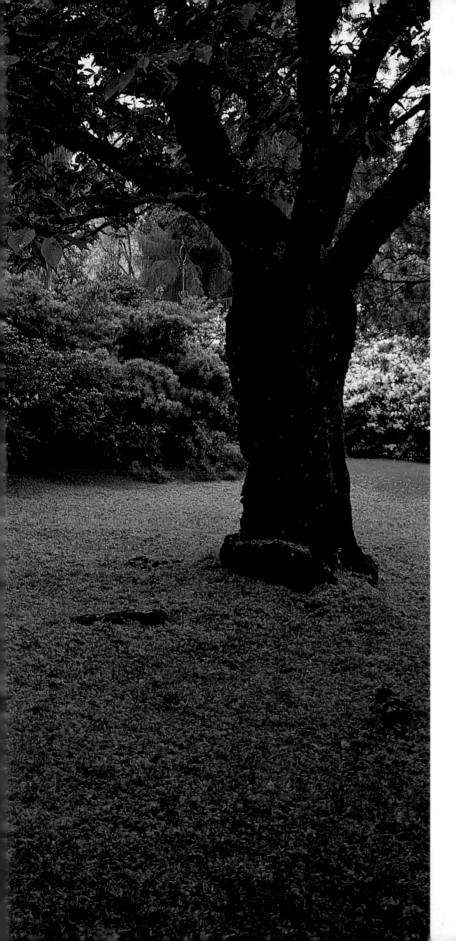

ISOLA MADRE

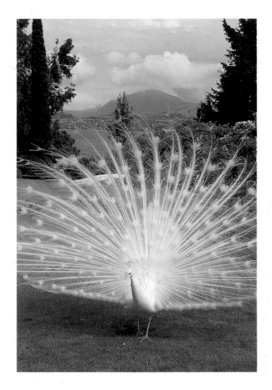

EDITH WHARTON damned Isola Madre with faint praise, as a garden of 'no special interest save to the horticulturist'. But John Ruskin loved it. A letter written to his father on 23 August 1845 begins, 'I am certainly becoming a very commonplace sort of person. Here is a fine day at last and I got up early to have a morning walk in Isola Madre, and I enjoyed it quite as "the public" do. I like the aloes and the laurels and the stone pines and the regular gravel walks and the "vedutas" cut through foliage, and everything . . .' The next day he wrote to his mother, 'I am going actually to draw some *garden* for you out of Isola Madre, and study some of its bee haunted aloes tomorrow morning if it be fine – it is sweet to see

'The Isola Madre,' wrote Edith Wharton, 'the largest of the Borromean group, was the first to be built on and planted.' The palazzo she described as 'the plain Renaissance palace'; the garden is an island fantasy of flowers and peacocks.

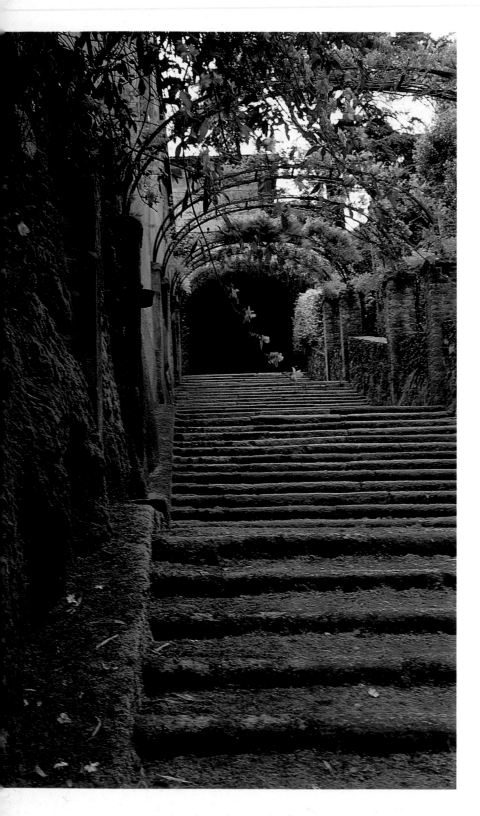

the aloe with two or three hives of bees about it making its yellow blossoms yellower.'

Isola Madre was a paradise garden from the start, blessed by the aura of San Carlo, which must have hung in the air like incense, for Ruskin always called it 'San Carlo's isle'. Because of its amenably flat terrain, Isola Madre was the first of the two Borromean Islands to be tamed and work began on its garden and palace soon after its purchase in 1501. The Renaissance *palazzo* took two years to build on the ruins of a Roman fortress; the loggia was built in the eighteenth century. To the ancient olive trees on the island, lemons, mulberries, fruit orchards, orange trees and vineyards were added. A woodland of laurels, firs, cypresses and other evergreen trees encircled by vineyards was created for the pheasants and Numidia hens that Napoleon was later to admire.

The equable climate of mild sunny winters and humid summers encouraged the cultivation of more sophisticated plants. In the nineteenth century the high retaining walls fortifying the island were torn down, the fields of vines and mulberries were dug up and a picturesque English-style park was introduced, in which many ornamental trees were planted. The terraces were exoticized with palms, papyrus, lotus blossom and bananas, and now there are collections of magnolias, cornus, myrtles and tree ferns.

High hedges of camellias and bay laurels and stands of holm oak *(Quercus ilex)* protect the island from the winds. There is no protection, however, from the Brazilian parrots that feed on the fresh new shoots in spring. A bright and decorative green, they lend a tropical look to this island heaven, already made famous by the white peacocks introduced 150 years ago. The birds nest high up in the cedar of Lebanon, and are a favourite of the present Principessa Borromeo, who stays at Isola Bella for a month every year, and brings her friends across to visit Isola Madre.

No one lives in the *palazzo* any longer, which now houses a museum. Yet the island was once a place of pilgrimage as well as a

LEFT *A pergola draped in wisteria and primrose jasmine (*Jasminum mesnyi*).*

OPPOSITE, CLOCKWISE FROM TOP LEFT *Banks of azaleas make a sparkling backdrop to the white peacocks, which are a welcome change in the Italian garden from stone statuary;* Davidia involucrata; *camellia;* Magnolia 'Yellow Bird'; *laburnum; a snowdrop tree,* Halesia diptera *– one of only three in Europe.*

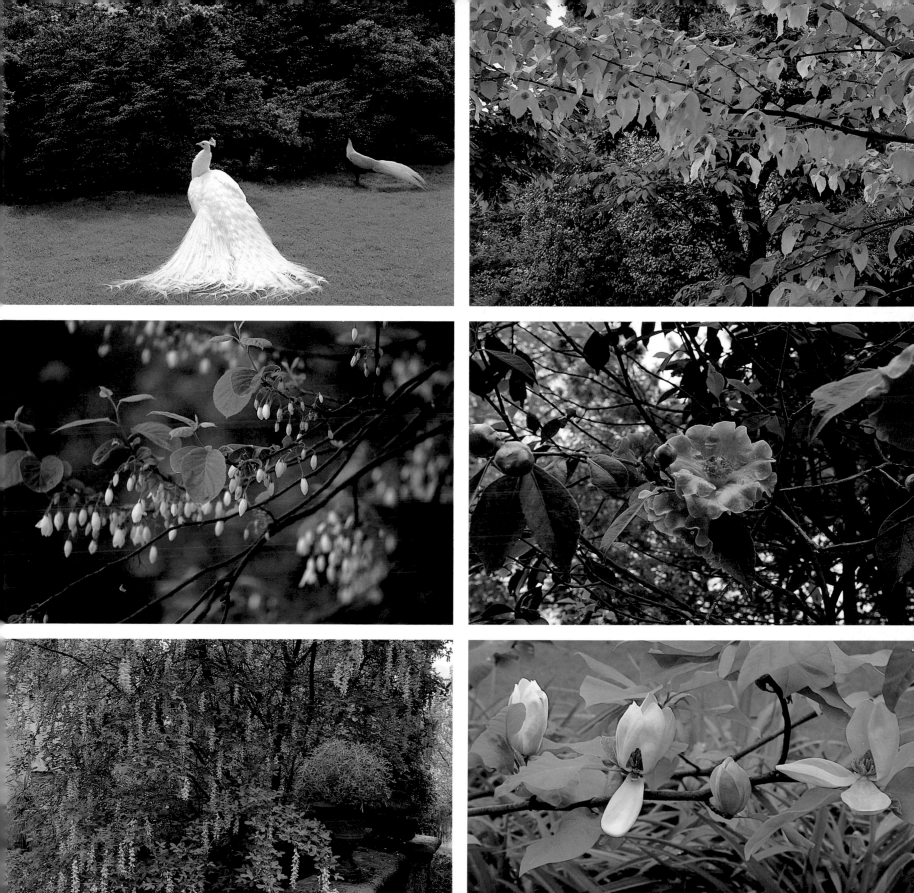

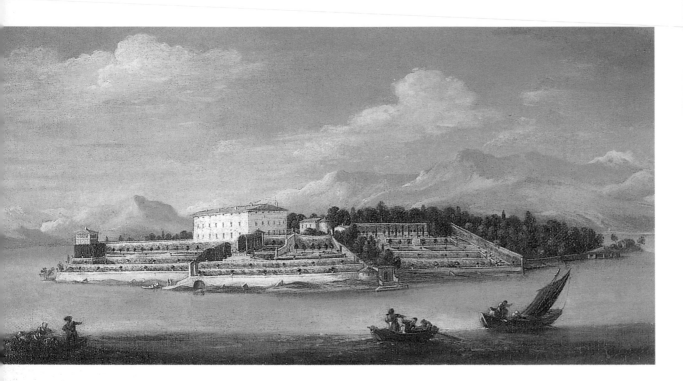

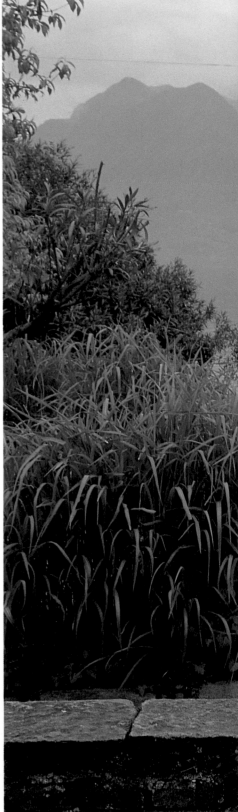

favourite haunt of prime ministers, presidents, European and English royalty, including Queen Caroline and Queen Victoria. Its isolated position also made it ideal for quarantine during times of plague, and a place of confinement for members of the Borromeo family deemed to be afflicted with 'queerness'.

The ubiquitous diarist John Evelyn sailed past the Isola Madre in 1646. He was the first of many travellers to remark on the garden's 'walks all set about with Oranges and Citron trees, the reflection from the Water rendring the place very warme . . .' and its prospect of the snow-capped Alps, covered with pine trees and ferns. The hypersensitive Henry James, who submerged himself in the experience of the Italian lakes, imagining himself 'as a hero of romance whose chief end was to float forever in an ornamental boat from one stately stretch of lake laved villa steps to another', left this memory of an August excursion from his hotel in 1869: '. . . as the afternoon began to wane, took a little boat at the terrace-stairs, lay out at my length beneath the striped awning and had myself pulled out to these delicious old Borromean Islands – the Isola Madre and the Isola Bella . . . They're a quaint mixture of tawdry flummery and genuine beauty – a sort of tropical half-splendid, half slovenly Little Trianon & Hampton Court.'

ABOVE *The terraces and palazzo of Isola Madre as they appeared in the middle of the eighteenth century, when Antonio Jolli painted this view.*

RIGHT *The lowest terraces afford views across the blue waters of Lake Como. Wharton described the lake scenery as appearing 'to have been designed by a lingering and fastidious hand, bent on eliminating every crudeness and harshness and on blending all natural forms, from the bare mountain peak to the melting curve of the shore, in one harmony of ever varying and ever beautiful lines'.*

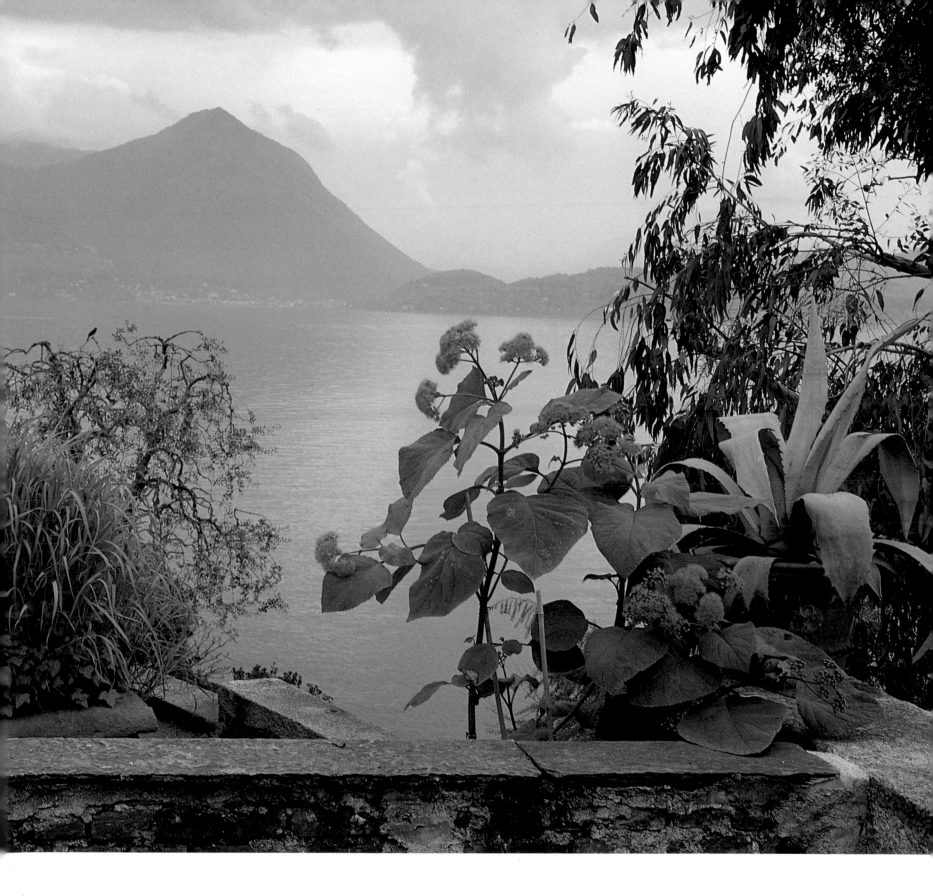

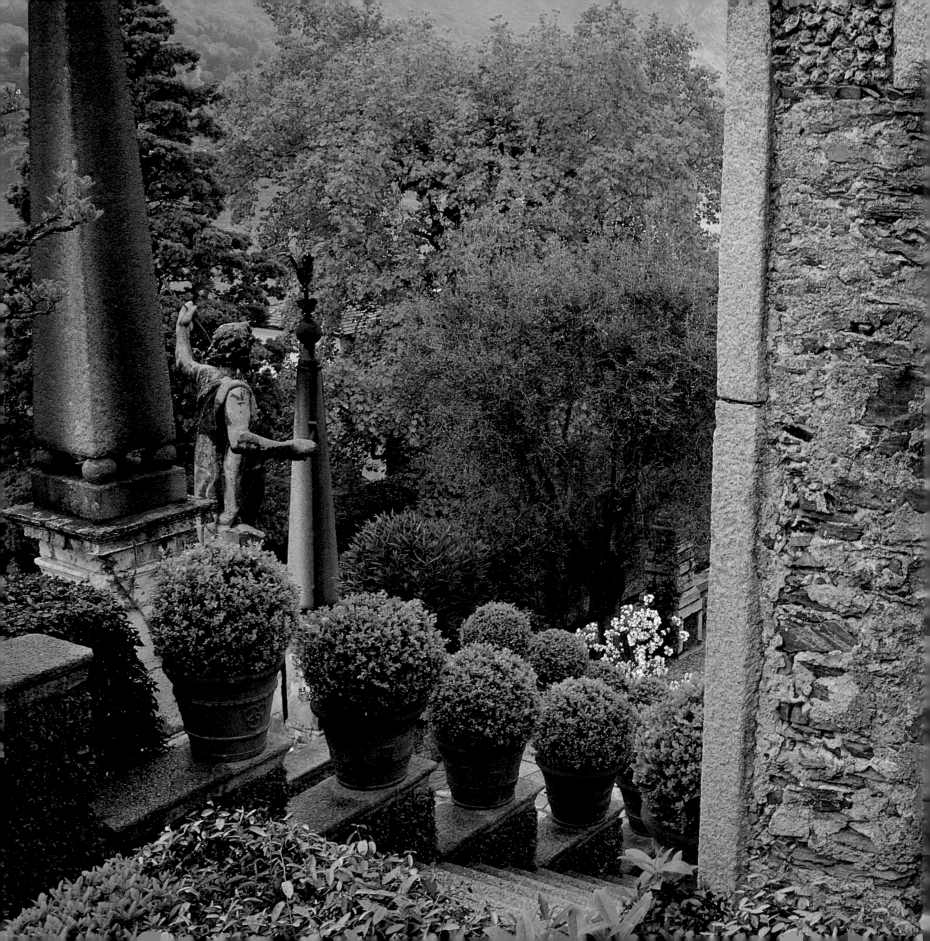

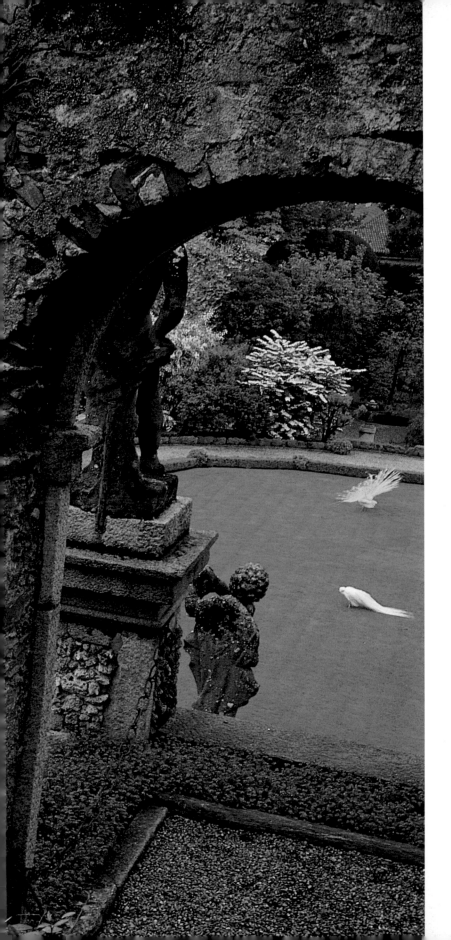

ISOLA BELLA

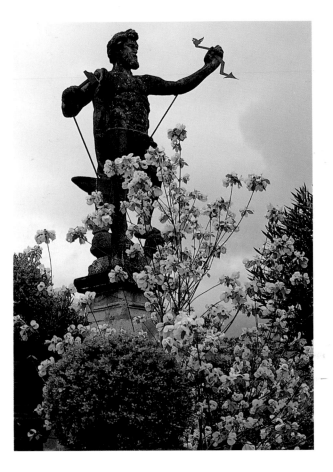

The architect Angelo Crivelli's unique concept for the Isola Bella was an island designed as one of the great galleons of the sixteenth century that sailed the seas trading or hoping to find gold in the New World. From the top of the water theatre, which represents the 'poop', there are views down on to the main 'deck' (left). Green box, white cornus and pale blue myosotis make an elegant scheme to complement the stone and cement; the expanse of green lawn was used as an outdoor theatre. Standing between two obelisks is a statue of Jupiter (detail above), god of the sky and weather, holding a bolt of lightning with which he destroyed his enemies.

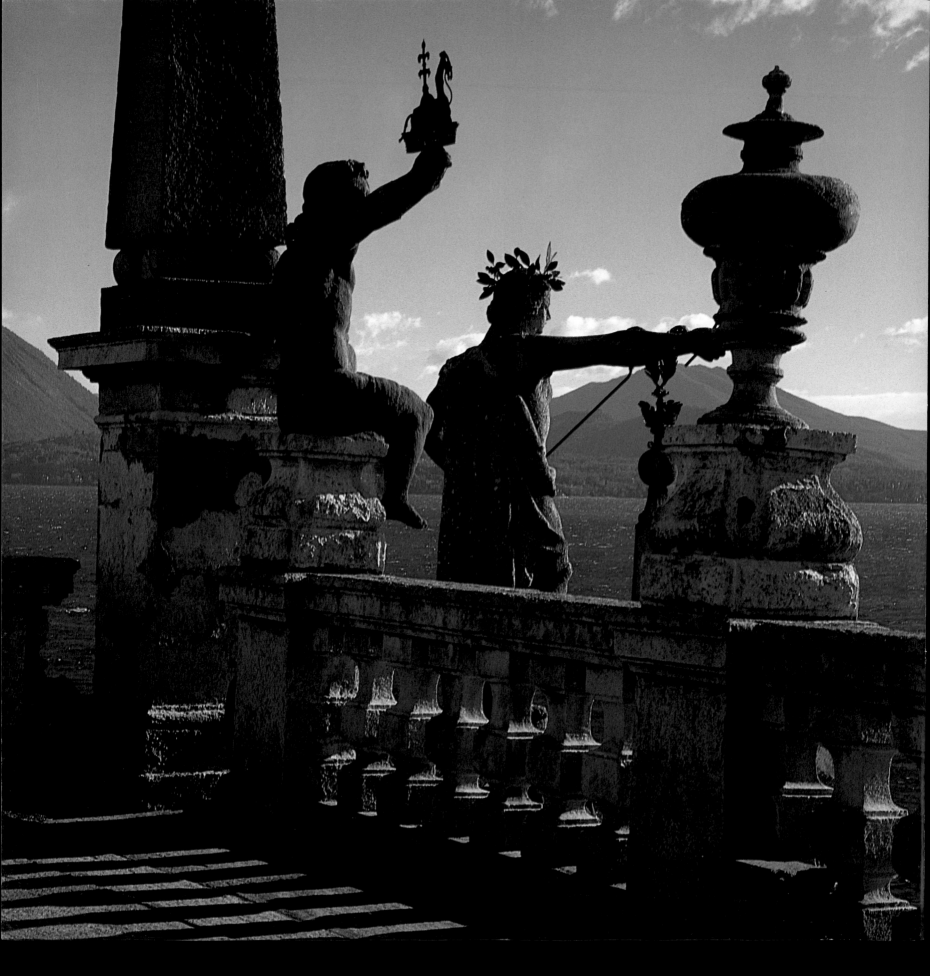

ISOLA BELLA

'FROM THE GARDEN STUDENT'S POINT OF VIEW, there is nothing in Lombardy as important as Isola Bella', stated Edith Wharton emphatically at the end of her lengthy description of the island. Unlike the gardens in Lombardy that had fallen victim to the eighteenth-century craze for English parkland, Isola Bella remained firmly anchored to its seventeenth-century mooring. Devised as an architectural entity, it would have been awkward to change: to have structurally altered even one part of it would have been to sacrifice the whole. Isola Bella is not so much a garden as a monument within which a garden has grown. 'I've seen the garden built in 1670,' wrote Stendhal. 'Built is the word.'

When the Borromeos came to consider what to do with Isola Bella, sensuality had returned to replace restraint, and the imagination had opened to splendid and dramatic effects in art and architecture. A flamboyant Baroque showpiece, Isola Bella would make real the dreamscapes of the fashionable poets Ariosto and Tasso. The idea of transforming the whole island into a garden may have been inspired by the enormously popular allegorical romance, *Hypnerotomachia Poliphili*, written by Francesco Colonna in 1499, in which the whole Island of Cythera is laid out as a garden. Count Carlo Borromeo III, nephew of San Carlo Borromeo, commissioned the architect Angelo Crivelli to draw up the plans and work commenced in 1632. The prow of the ship, represented by the *palazzo* standing at the narrow end of the island, faced north to the Alps. At the south end lay the stern, with a 'poop' of ten terraces rising like a truncated pyramid to the 'bridge' or top terrace. Enclosed by balustrades, the terraces were planted with grass alternating with swirling *broderies,* which were never allowed to grow high enough to fudge the design, so they preserved the smooth, polished look of 'decks'. The flat area between the stern and the prow – the 'waist' of the ship – contained a long parterre, also decorated with low *broderies*. The nautical theme was further

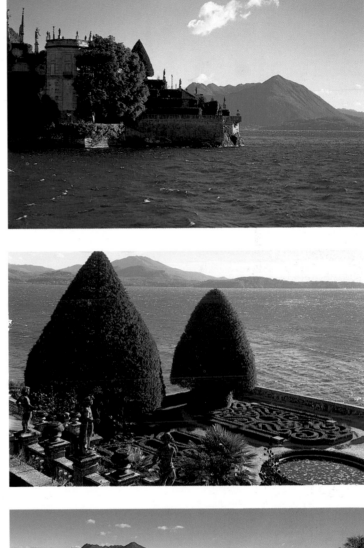

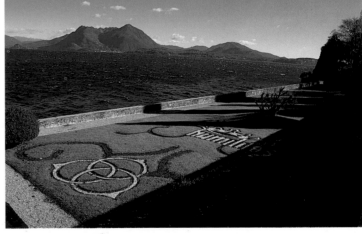

The statues on the balustrade enclosing the top deck of the vessel are like crew or passengers hailing passing ships (left). The way the decks rise as terraces to suggest a 'stern' is easy to see from the lake (right top). Water for the water theatre was drawn up from the lake through the turret. The poop deck was the jardin d'amour, *dedicated to the seasons and Flora (right centre). This deck (right below), planted with grass and low* broderies, *shows how flat all the decks were in their original design before the later planting. Its motto, 'humilitas', always raises a sceptical eyebrow.*

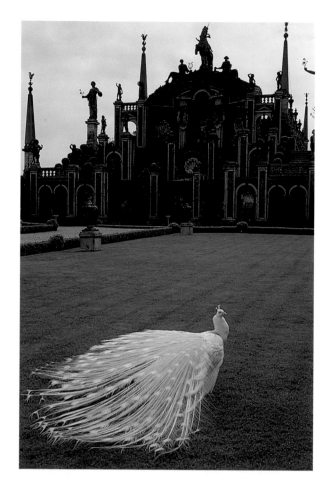

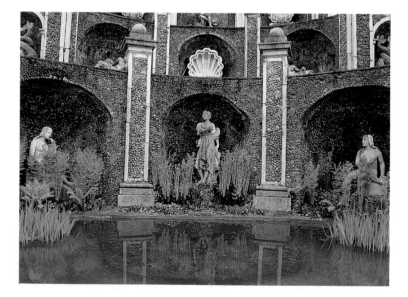

embellished by the great shell-shaped Baroque water theatre constructed in three levels against the 'poop', with large shells and statues set into its niches.

It was originally intended that the ship should have a 'forecastle' consisting of a dome on top of the *palazzo* crowned by a mast, but this was never built. The fact that the full concept was not realized may explain why Wharton thought that the palace and garden had not been designed 'with regard for each other'. Yet from the topmost terrace 120 feet (36.5 metres) above the lake, far above its towering trees, one has the illusion of captaining a sailing vessel. Only the Borromeo unicorn and a few obelisks that could pass for masts clutter the scene; the statues might be the crew or its passengers. From here you can see how cleverly Crivelli adapted his plan to disguise the fact that the shape of the island did not allow for a straight axis between the prow and the stern, or palace and garden. Where the axis veers off at an angle, he built a courtyard with a statue of Diana, surrounding it with a small *bosco*. The unsuspecting visitor loses his bearing upon entering this deception, and exits still thinking he is walking in a straight line.

In 1670, a year before the garden was completely finished, a lavish inauguration took place with mock naval battles and choruses hidden behind shrubberies, and singers who sang from boats in the water. Fifteen years later, Gilbert Burnet, later Bishop of Salisbury, visited the garden and wrote the first full-length account of it. His idiosyncratic style and prodigious use of commas so amused Wharton that she quoted him at length, dubbing him the 'breathless bishop'. He marvelled at the 'noble walks', 'noble stairs' and 'fragrant smell, the beautiful Prospect', and finished with a resounding 'perhaps the whole World has nothing like it'. As a result, it quickly became one of the star attractions of the Grand Tour, and all the literary luminaries reported on it, but no one ever surpassed the breathless rhapsodies of Bishop Burnet.

Not all visitors reacted with the same childlike wonder. In 1739, a grumpy Charles de Brosses, blown in by a gamut of winds as contrary as his character, delivered his Gallic assessment, meting out praise and criticism in equal measure. The fountains, he sniffed, were dry. The two hexagonal garden pavilions that Wharton was later to find so beautiful spoiled the whole prospect, he said. But there were enchanting corners in the garden – groves of pomegranates and orange trees, corridors of grottos, and above all vast bowers of lemon and citrus trees laden with fruit. Even so,

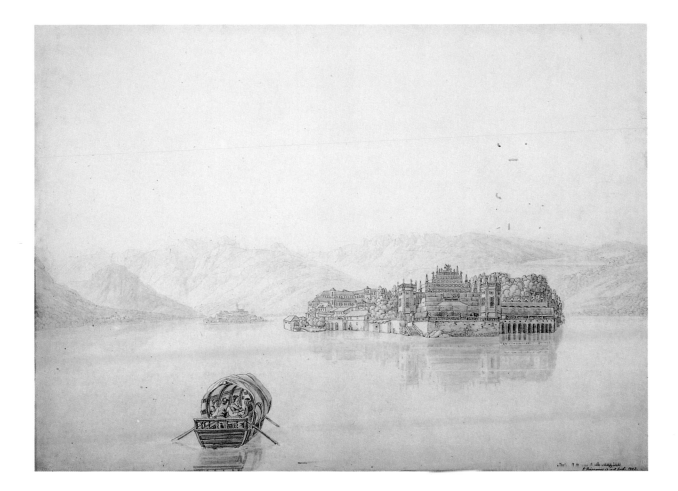

ABOVE *Peter Birmann's* Isola Bella on Lake Maggiore, 1805, *shows a view of the island facing north. The creation of Isola Bella was such a huge undertaking that neither Count Borromeo who commissioned it nor Crivelli who designed it lived to see it finished, and the palazzo was never completed. Lying on a bed of clay, the island had to be stabilized and vaults and supports were driven through the bed of the lake to provide foundation. Tons of earth, Baveno granite, tufa and ashlar stone were brought from the mainland in boats to construct the garden. On the island's eventual completion, the admiration it excited soon combined with euphony to contract Isola Isabella, as it was named (after the Count's mother), to Isola Bella.*

OPPOSITE *A pebbled effect of light and dark stones highlights the architectural lines of the water theatre and provides a marvellous foil to the statues. These convey an allegory of the family's triumph and culminate in the Borromeo unicorn silhouetted against the sky. Peacocks float about the lawns where theatricals were performed, like spirits of the Baroque era.*

de Brosses continued ungallantly, 'the gardens are badly maintained in many places (and in this respect the Italians are far inferior to the French)'.

In 1844 Ruskin wrote a heartfelt lament about the state of the garden: 'Isola Bella is fast going to decay; it made me melancholy to look at it. All green, damp, shattered, covered with weeds and dead leaves, and yet the flowers and foliage of surpassing beauty, and more impressive to me than ever.'

Some writers criticized the garden for being too contrived. Byron found it 'Fine but too artificial'. Rousseau, tempted to set his *Nouvelle Héloise* there, also found it too 'artificial' for such a natural heroine as his Juliet. Even Baedeker found it 'in questionable taste'. But Sir George Sitwell understood that Isola Bella should be taken on its own terms as 'a thing by itself'. Wharton, a purist in many ways, defended its style, pointing out that the garden was as 'unreal'

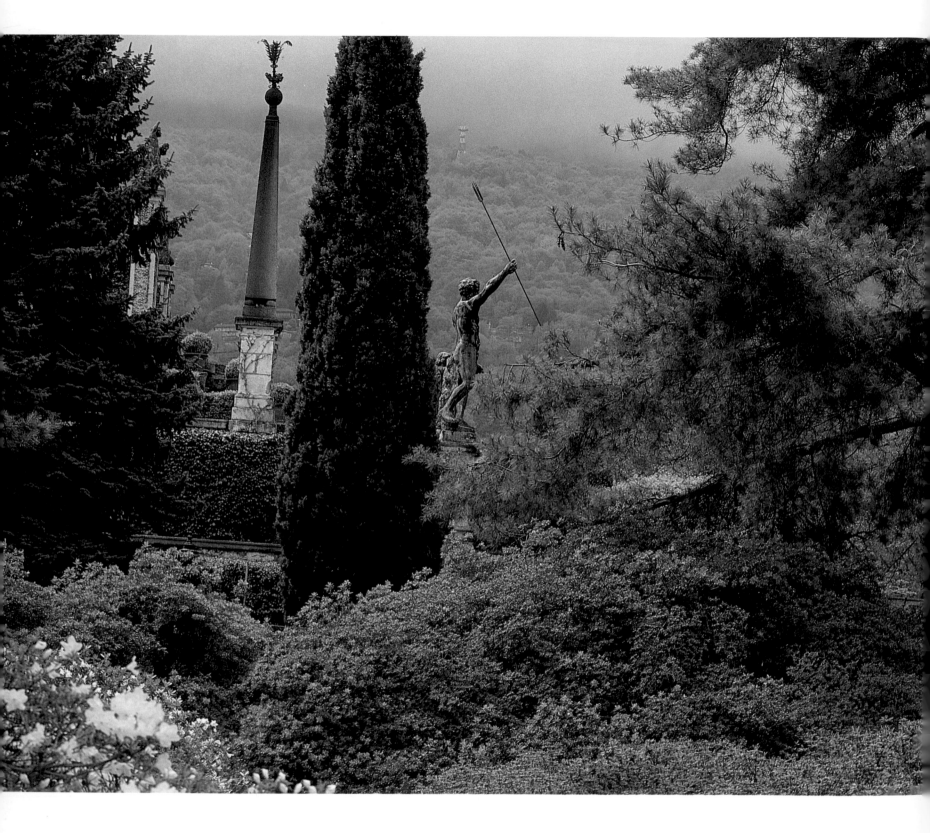

as the scenery, and that all garden-making – whether stylized in the 'laboured naturalism of Repton or Capability Brown' or the 'frank artifice of the Italian garden-architecture' – is, by definition, artificial. 'Both these manners are manners,' she argued; the garden should therefore be judged on its own aesthetic merits.

It is perhaps of greater concern that the planting of the garden is now so at variance with the original design. Originally, the only trees on the island were those used to camouflage the trick change in axis. Yet by 1882 there was a floral mantle: the Baedeker guidebook published in that year reported 'cedars, magnolias, cypresses, orange trees, laurels, magnificent oleanders and other luxuriant products of the south', which Wharton confirmed, adding a few of her own – 'roses, camellias, jasmine, myrtle and pomegranate'. Today, the great parterres planted with cannas and bananas are more appropriate to a Rousseau-type jungle of sub-tropical exotics than a Baroque water theatre. One hopes for a return to the integrated beauty of its original planting, to have the terraces as 'polished decks' again, brushed by the elegant white peacocks dragging their long white tails over them.

Meanwhile the island sits placidly on the lake, bearing the brunt of the fierce tramontana, the north wind that races down from the Alps, together with the vicissitudes of informed opinion that blow hot and cold over it. Sir Geoffrey Jellicoe gave it both the greatest criticism and the greatest praise. When he and Jock Shepherd conducted their seminal study of Italian gardens, published in 1925, they deemed Isola Bella too 'decadent' to include, accusing the architect of 'turning what was probably once a beautiful island into one of the most vulgar places in existence'. After a lifetime's experience working in a world that has become truly vulgar, Sir Geoffrey's perspective so changed that he wrote of it as 'possibly the most romantic folly in the classical world'.

LEFT *The vegetation, growing with almost tropical luxuriance, has obscured the original design. 'In the equable lake climate', observed Wharton, '. . . the passion for horticulture seems to have developed early, and the landscape-architect was accustomed to mingle bright colours with his architectural masses, instead of relying on a setting of uniform verdure.'*

RIGHT *Wisteria covers the bows of the 'stern'. 'The southern extremity of the island terminates in a beautiful garden-pavilion, hexagonal in shape, with rusticated coigns and a crowning balustrade beset with statues,' wrote Wharton.*

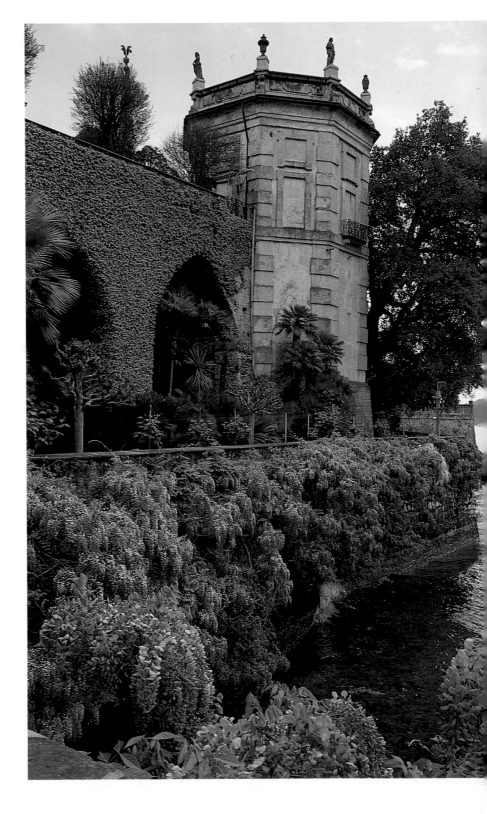

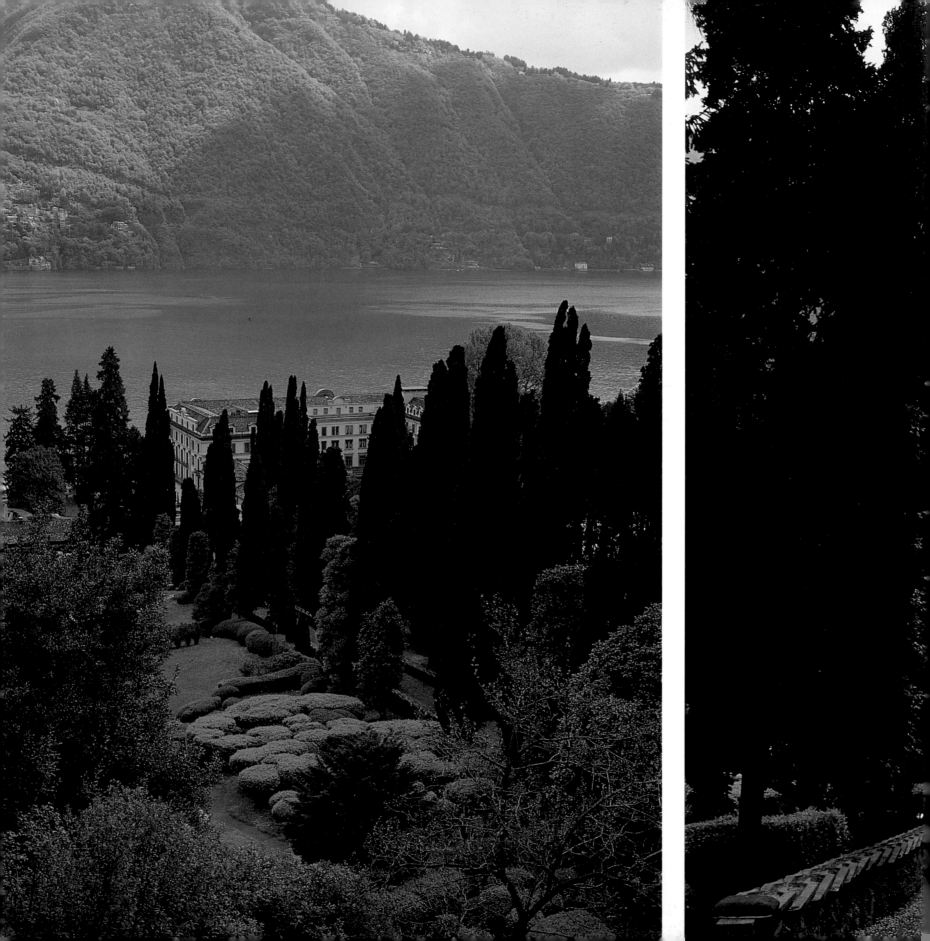

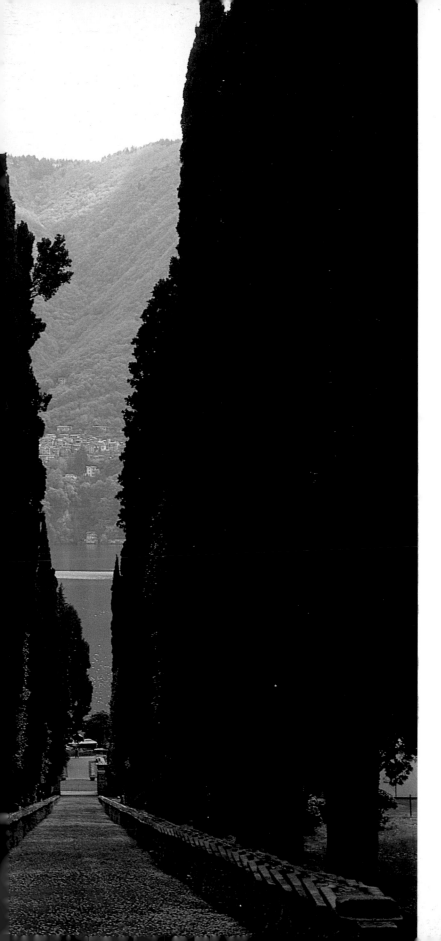

VILLA D'ESTE

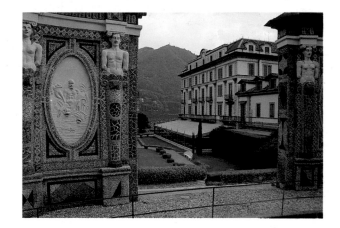

AS IF TO MATCH THE SPLENDOUR of the steep mountains that form a towering crown around Lake Como, the Villa d'Este at Cernobbio at the southern end of the lake is palatial, and has been from the moment it was conceived until its present incarnation as a sumptuous hotel.

Nuns and Jesuits, princes of the Church and princesses of the realm have prayed and played here. Fortunes have been lost in the extravagant gamble of owning the villa – with the players themselves making up the hand of a royal flush. An English queen, a Russian empress, a count and a marquis, and their lovers, guests and households have all indulged their fantasies and stamped their conceits on the house and gardens of the Villa d'Este. Today, the guests are of the paying variety, but the Villa d'Este still caters to the fashionable vanities of the day. A jogging route has been laid out through the Renaissance garden; an indoor swimming pool and gym complex now occupy the old *limonaia*; while the *giardino segreto* has been swallowed up into the bowels of the kitchen.

'In the gardens of the Villa d'Este there is much of the Roman spirit – the breadth of design, the unforced inclusion of natural features, and that sensitiveness to the quality of the surrounding landscape which characterizes the great gardens of the Campagna,' wrote Edith Wharton. This harmony is apparent in the long view of the villa and grounds from the bosco (far left) and in the sensational 'corridor' of magnolia and cypresses (left). The front of the villa can be seen from the mosaico (above).

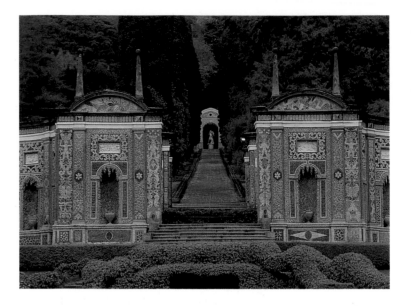

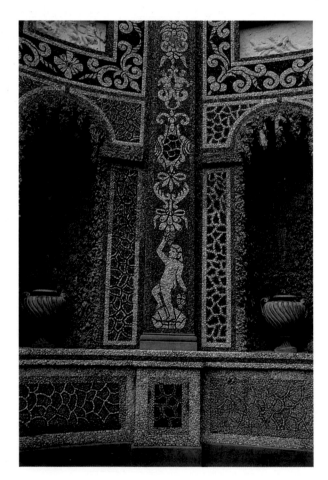

Situated on the sunny side of the lake, opposite the shady Villa Pliniana, the Villa d'Este had already been a hotel for thirty years at the time of Edith Wharton's visit and for a long time was one of the highlights of the lake tour. 'Along the shores of Como, where the ground rises so abruptly from the lake,' she explained, 'landscape effects were difficult to produce . . . Behind the Villa d'Este, the mountains are sufficiently withdrawn to leave a gentle acclivity.' This 'gentle acclivity', which she may not have found so gentle had she climbed to the top, accommodates the central axis of the garden which, exceptionally, was placed alongside the villa so that the view to and from the lake remains open and clear. Set back from the lakeshore, the garden consists of a large parterre divided into four squares. Steps from the parterre lead up to an oval fishpond flanked by pebble- and stucco-walled pavilions, which mark the first stage in the ascent up the hillside. From the fishpond, a *tapis vert* bordered on either side by a cascade sweeps steeply up to a statue of Hercules set inside a rotunda 300 feet (91.5 metres) above the lake.

The cascade is the only surviving fragment of the original garden. The Villa d'Este was built on the site of an old convent in 1568 by Tolomeo Gallio, the new Cardinal of Como and son of a wealthy silk merchant. Como had become a centre for the manufacture of fine silk following the introduction of mulberry trees to the Lombardy plain by the Dukes of Milan, and the profits from this industry funded many of the villas. To design his garden, Gallio chose Pellegrino Tibaldi, a painter, sculptor and architect and a follower of Michelangelo. He was Milan's most prominent and prolific architect, and Carlo Borromeo, the Archbishop of Milan, also employed him to work on Milan Cathedral.

The architects working in Rome at this time demonstrated their infatuation with Imperial Rome in the gardens they were designing. With Pliny's birthplace practically on his doorstep, Tibaldi also made the most of this association. A cascade was made up of shapes like Roman couches, a group of the plane trees so admired by Pliny was planted by the water's edge, and his favourite ivy was used decoratively to swathe the stonework and as garlands.

The next phase in the garden's construction came when the wealthy Milanese Marquis Calderara inherited the property in 1794. He married a much younger woman, a ballerina from La Scala called 'La Pelusina', and left Milan to settle in Como. They planted the avenue of cypresses and built the *mosaico*, a grotto,

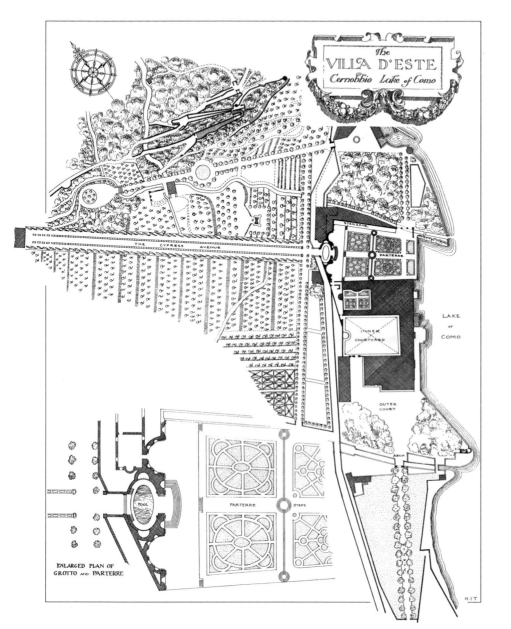

The VILLA D'ESTE
Cernobbio Lake of Como

temple to Minerva and the Neoclassical temple to house a statue of Hercules.

After her husband's death La Pelusina married the Napoleonic general Count Pino, and to welcome him back from his Spanish campaigns had mock battlements resembling those that she may have danced around on the stage of La Scala built along the top of the hillside. Made of cement, the battlements must have been entirely covered in ivy when Wharton saw them, to have provoked no comment. Perhaps it was this camouflage of ivy that turned them into the 'summerhouses' she mentions which, together with the 'romantic ivy-clad bridge' produced the 'sylvan' effect she found so appealing.

Since the early nineteenth century the Villa d'Este has been associated with the restless Queen Caroline. During her self-imposed exile, estranged from her husband George IV, she visited the Marquesa Calderara Pino at the Villa Garrovo, as it was then called. Even though Queen Caroline was already facing financial ruin, she decided that she must have the villa. The Marquesa Calderara Pino and her husband were 'persuaded' to sell in order not to offend a royal personage and, once installed, Caroline declared, 'My palace is most *superbe.*' She renamed it the 'New Villa d'Este' after Guelfo d'Este, an ancestor whom she had recently discovered she shared with her husband. The said Guelfo had founded both the House of Brunswick – Caroline's family – and the House of Hanover – George IV's – before leaving Germany in 1504. He subsequently joined the court of Cardinal Ippolito I d'Este of Ferrara, to which the fabled Ariosto also belonged. In honour of her Ariosto connection, Queen Caroline immediately replaced the statue of Hercules at the head of the cascade with that of Ariosto. Queen Caroline's tenure from 1815 to 1820, though brief and by no means continuous, was of great benefit to Lake Como, for she built a road through the property, linking Cernobbio and Moltrasio – the first to run along the lakeside. For the work, she employed some of the men who had built the Simplon Pass. She named the street 'La Strada Carolina'; it has now been renamed 'Via Regina'.

The Villa d'Este seems to have been alive with dramatic muses. When Napoleon was vanquished in 1814, Count Pino continued to train his soldiers among the fake battlements and conducted mock naval battles on the lake. Queen Caroline built a theatre, where she put on Italian operas and threw lavish *fêtes champêtres* in which she would dress up and act. But these were nothing compared to the high drama of the intrigues instigated by George IV through his agents in Italy. Their task was to catch Queen Caroline *in flagrante* with her lover Bartolomeo Pergami, or to bribe someone to say they had, so that the King could divorce her. Spies hid behind bushes and crawled about the garden, duels were fought and the atmosphere became so tense that Caroline sought refuge on Isola Madre. She finally returned to England in 1820, where she was put on trial for adultery, and her builders, gardeners and oarsmen were all brought over to London to testify against her. She was acquitted, but died shortly after, quite possibly from the strain of it all.

One of the villa's last tenants, the Russian Empress Maria, wife of Alexander II, rented it in 1868 and spent two years there. She opened the gardens to the public and on those days had herself rowed out on to Lake Como swathed in sable and cashmere while the visitors were treated to a puppet show. For his plots and characters the puppeteer need have looked no further than the various scenarios that made up the villa's eccentric history.

RIGHT *The Hercules Temple at the end of the corridor was built at the beginning of the eighteenth century. The façade has recently been restored, but the stalactites across the top of the arch are original. Queen Caroline replaced the statue of Hercules with one of Ariosto to celebrate her connection with the Estes of Ferrara, after whom she renamed the villa. During the period of Italy's reunification the villa was the headquarters for anti-Austrian activity, and to play down their patriotism in the face of the enemy the owners removed Ariosto, replacing it with one of Hercules flinging the dying Lichas into the sea, presumably echoing the torrent and cascade below.*

FAR RIGHT *One of Edith Wharton's 'sylvan temples', dedicated to Minerva (top). The torrent that pours down the mountain with such force (centre) once isolated the villa from the land, and it was only accessible from the water until Queen Caroline built her Strada Carolina along the lake shore. Standard wisterias border the cypress and magnolia corridor (below).*

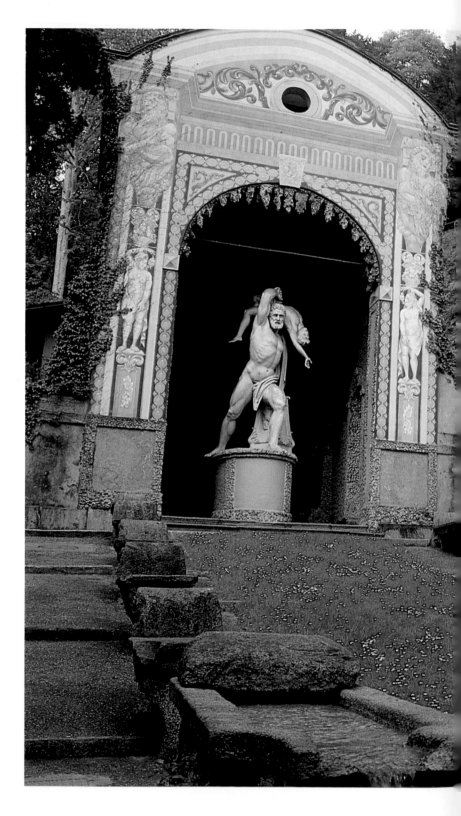

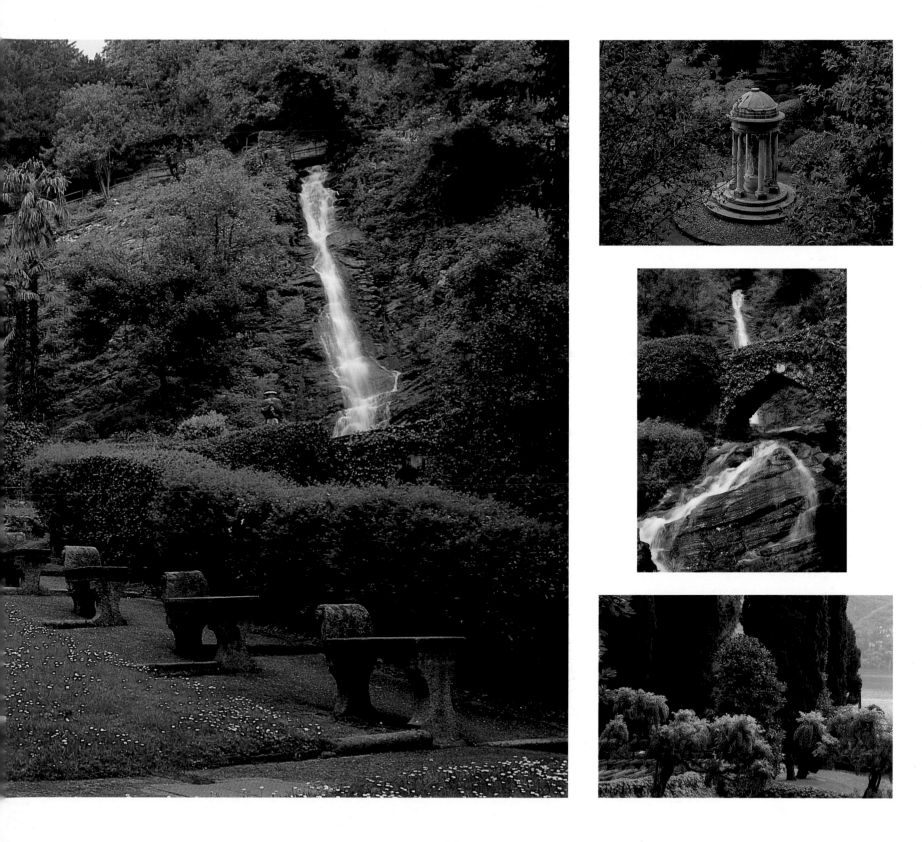

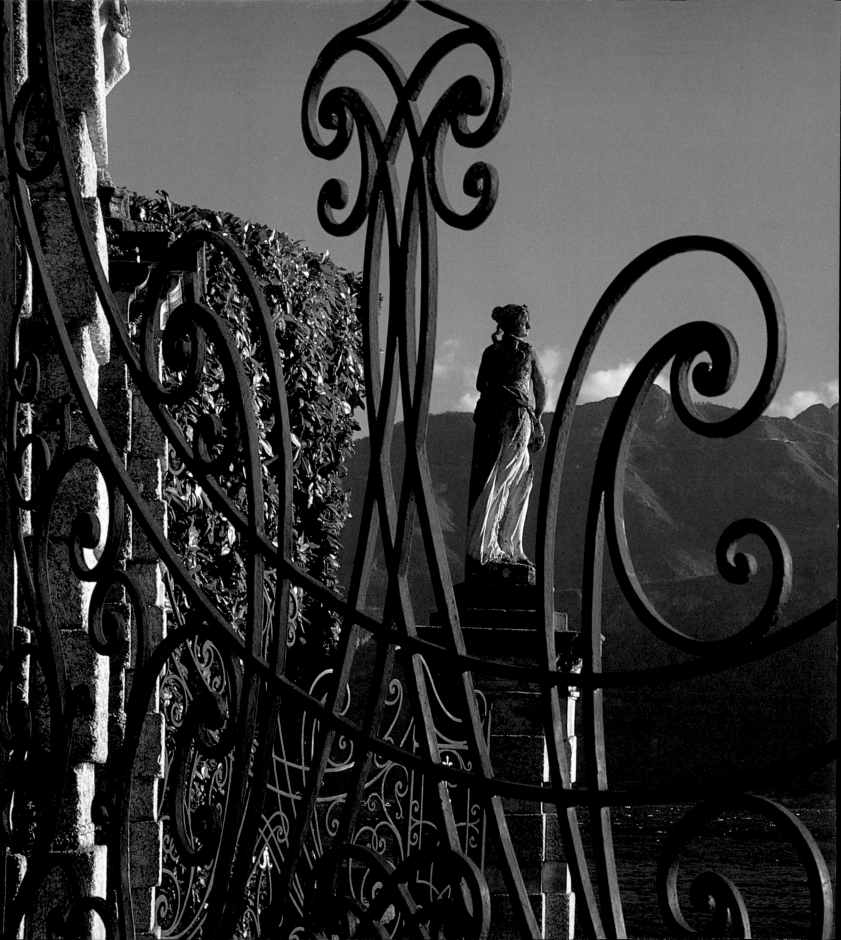

VILLA CARLOTTA

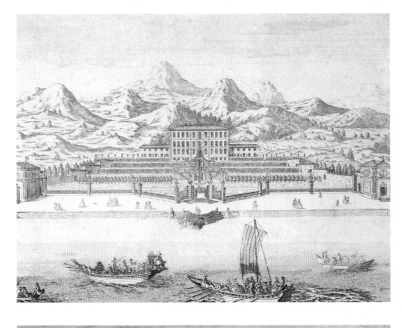

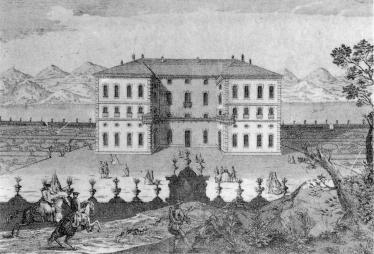

ABOVE *Views of the villa from the front and back, by Marcantonio Dal Re,
from* Le Ville de Delizia *(1763).*

LEFT *The wrought iron gates were much admired by Wharton. Their swirling
'C's stand for Clerici, the name of the first owner of the villa. Beyond the gates
is one of the statues of the four seasons; others are by the water's edge.*

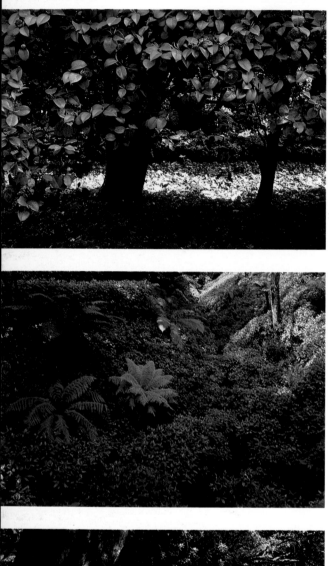

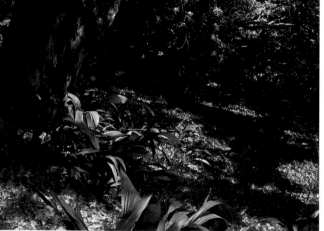

FARTHER ALONG LAKE COMO from the moneyed exclusiveness of the Villa d'Este sits that honeypot of the modern coach tour, the Villa Carlotta, between Tremezzo and Cadenabbia. For the crowds that decamp there daily, it provides unabashed thrills by way of brilliance in scenery, colour and botanical variety, with enough statues and terraces to reassure the dazzled tourist that he really *is* in Italy.

The Villa Carlotta lies near the site of Pliny's Villa Comedia on the deliciously warm bay of the Tremezzina. This is where, Stendhal informs us, all the shivering Milanese flock in cold weather since 'winter is unknown' – a claim he supports by citing an orange tree that had survived unprotected there for sixteen years.

Edith Wharton glanced over this garden, all but dismissing it in two curt sentences as she beat her familiar funerary drum for the old gardens of Como sacrificed to the 'fury of modern horticulture'. But while it is true that only the 'fine gateways and the architectural treatment of the terraces bear witness to the former beauty of its grounds', it is also true that there were other beauties she could have described. One wonders if she ventured beyond the garden's terraces, for how else could she fail to mention them? She might have found the cool green glade of tree ferns that cuts deep into the mountain more 'sylvan' than the cliffs of Villa d'Este. Had she slipped through a large inviting opening along the azalea path, she would have found herself in the secluded, twilight *bosco* of *Rhododendron arboreum*, where sunbeams filter over the gnarled roots, grey bark and mossy nooks of a forest floor carpeted in pink petals. The weird interplay of light and shadow that characterizes the Italian *bosco* is usually conducted beneath a canopy of the sturdy, but comparatively dull grey ilex; here in late spring the atmosphere has been suffused with a rosy glow.

The garden's secluded pathways are washed with dappled shade in late spring. On the second terrace is a camellia walk (left top). Tree ferns are grown in pots in a cool glade (left centre). As soon as the autumn rains start the ferns are removed and stored in the greenhouse for the winter to protect them against the torrent of water that pours down the hillside. Just off the main azalea path is an enchanting giardino segreto *carpeted in fallen petals from the tree-like* Rhododendron arboreum *(left below and right).*

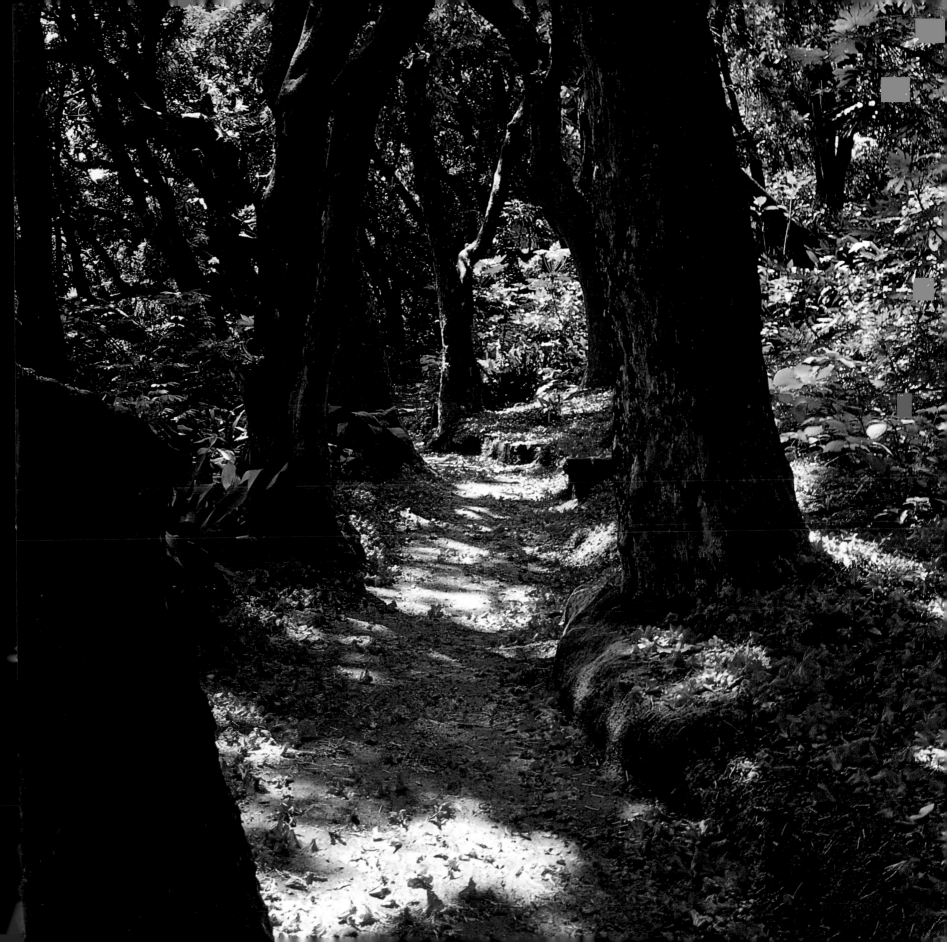

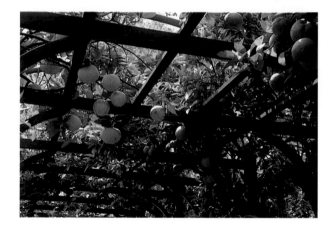

Villa Carlotta is as much a garden to look out of as one to look into, and is sited, of course, to capitalize on the views. Had Wharton climbed up to the villa, she would have stood on the top terrace with a panorama of unspoiled grandeur before her, a hedge of box at her feet and the scent of a lemon-covered pergola rising up to meet her from a terrace below. This would have potently and outstandingly recalled that old garden magic as only she could feel it. Yet of this Wharton makes no mention. The Villa Carlotta was one of the very last gardens of her exhausting four-month tour. Her husband was ill and she had a boat to catch – perhaps she only had time to survey it from the road, or perhaps all the azaleas put her off.

Today the view is exactly the same – only the box hedge has gone. How rare it is to find a landscape unchanged from when the garden was first conceived. For how many other gardens can this claim be made? The faithful pilgrims who worship at the shrine of Villa Lante near Viterbo, for instance, never mention the television antennae, the modern housing, the laundry lines or the electricity pylons that make up the view, or the overhanging woodland that so darkens and chokes the garden. The *Catch 22* of a borrowed landscape is that sooner or later you have to give it back. In the gardens themselves, the irritating pampas grass, inelegant squares cut out of lawns to house the execrable palms, bananas and cinerarias that Wharton so deplored are at least only cosmetic blemishes. Garden art – as expressed in *broderie* parterres, pleached alleys and marble terraces – can be reinstated, but a whole landscape cannot be reclaimed. For this reason perhaps, the Villa Carlotta still holds an ace up her sleeve.

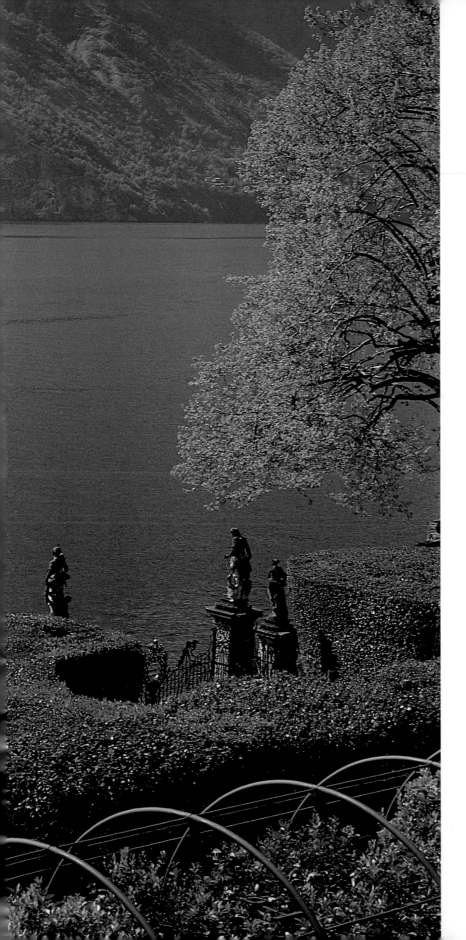

VILLA CARLOTTA

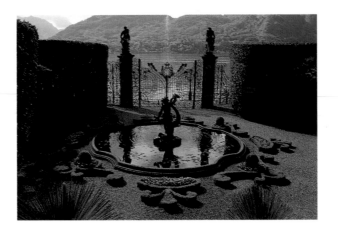

The Villa Carlotta is thought to have been built around 1745 by an unknown architect for the eccentric Marshal Giorgio Clerici, the 'C's of whose surname appear intertwined in the villa's iron gates. The top terrace, on which the villa stands, and the lowest terrace next to the road would most impress both houseguests and *le grand public*, so they were made the widest and were laid out with elaborate curving 'C' patterns of low box *broderie*. On the parterres adjoining the villa, the airy elegance of the *broderie* was later replaced by Florentine cypresses, which then gave way to densely planted trees and shrubs that were already mature when Wharton came. Looking at this congested terrace today, it is hard to imagine just how flat and spacious it originally was. Meanwhile, most of the *broderie* on the lowest terrace was replaced with hedges of myrtle, reported by Murray's guidebook of 1874 to be already 20 feet (6 metres) high. In the ensuing years the myrtle was replaced by thickets of laurel – better suited to absorb the noise and fumes from the traffic that roars up and down the length of the lake.

FAR LEFT *The lemon-covered pergola on a middle terrace.*

LEFT *Looking towards the shores of Lake Como from the garden. Geoffrey Jellicoe wrote 'Sympathy [is] required not with surroundings of the country but with the flat surface of water, itself a very formal setting. Gardens set out to catch this spirit of water, simplicity and horizontality, and to reflect it in their lines. There is more of the lake than the land in the unbroken series of terraces that build up from the water's edge to the house of Villa Carlotta.'*

ABOVE *On the bottom terrace is the Fountain of Cupid with a dolphin.*

On Clerici's death, the villa passed to his daughter Claudia, who married Giovanni Battista Sommariva di Lodi in 1795. This ambitious man had risen from modest beginnings to a prominent career in law, finance and politics. Across the lake, between 1801 and 1810, Sommariva's rival, Francesco Melzi, was building the sumptuous Villa Melzi, at a cost of three million francs.

Scarcely less competitive than the great cardinals of Rome, Sommariva embellished his villa's façade with stucco and bought woodland and vineyards to increase the size of the property. On the roof he erected a balustrade and added a clock in the 'empire' style. He carried his ostentation to its peak by building a 'Temple of Friendship' at the highest point of his garden, covering it with a metal roof so that blinding light bounced off, spoiling Melzi's view.

In a genuine play of one-upmanship, whatever one had the other had to have too. They both planted *Rhododendron indicum* and towering sequoias; commissioned statues by Canova; and turned their houses into museums which all Milan came to see. While Melzi commissioned the statue of Dante and Beatrice that would inspire Liszt's 'Dante Sonata', Sommariva acquired Thorwaldsen's frieze of the 'Triumphal Entry of Alexander into Babylon', commissioned by Napoleon to decorate the Simplon arch leading into Milan and left unfinished when he was vanquished in 1814. He had the frieze completed by having himself and the artist added on the end.

Stendhal visited both villas often, sometimes accompanied by friends. At the Villa Melzi he wrote passages of his 1800-page

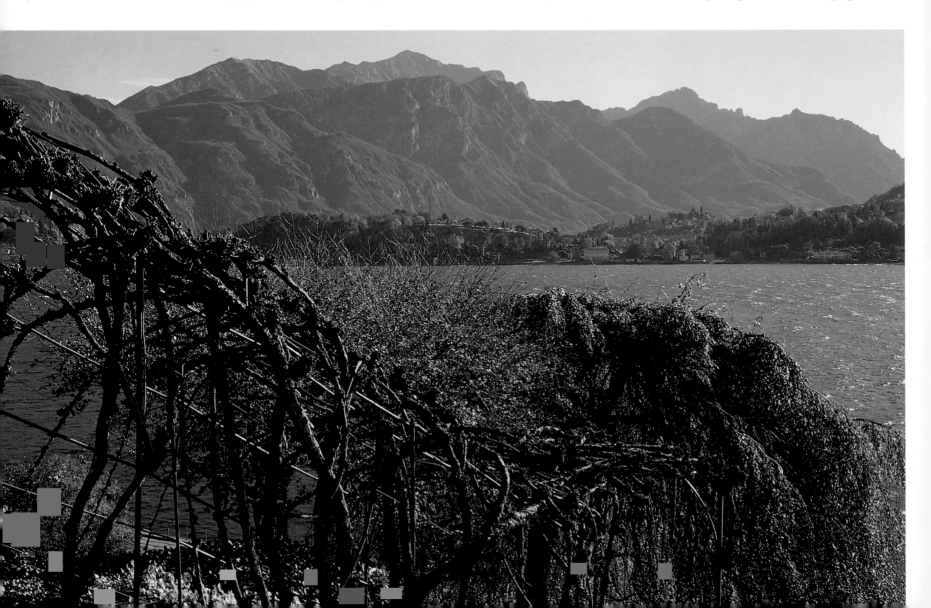

VILLA CARLOTTA

Voyages in Italy, and in 1818 was a house guest at the Casa Sommariva, as the Villa Carlotta was then called. It was in this part of Como that he set the opening scenes of *The Charterhouse of Parma*, published in 1839, but it was the Villa Melzi which earned his praise as 'one of the enchanting spots in the neighbourhood', an opinion revealed long after Sommariva and Melzi both lay safely buried in the mausoleums they had built in their gardens.

In 1840 Casa Sommariva was bought by Princess Marianna, wife of Albrecht of Prussia. Today the Temple of Friendship, with its blinding metal roof has gone, and now it is the hot pink and red azaleas planted by the Princess's daughter, Princess Carlotta – after whom the villa is named and who was given it on the occasion of her marriage in 1857 – that dazzle visitors to the Villa Melzi.

BELOW LEFT *The garden in winter. Villa Melzi is just visible on the other side of the lake, near the town of Bellagio. The vine-covered tunnel leading from the top terrace to the lemon pergola terrace provides shade in summer.*

BELOW RIGHT *The garden is at its most brilliant in May. This was the season when Princess Charlotte, who planted the azaleas, gave her great house parties. Her guests were taken out in distinctive green-and-white striped ducal barges to the middle of the lake to admire the sight from the water.*

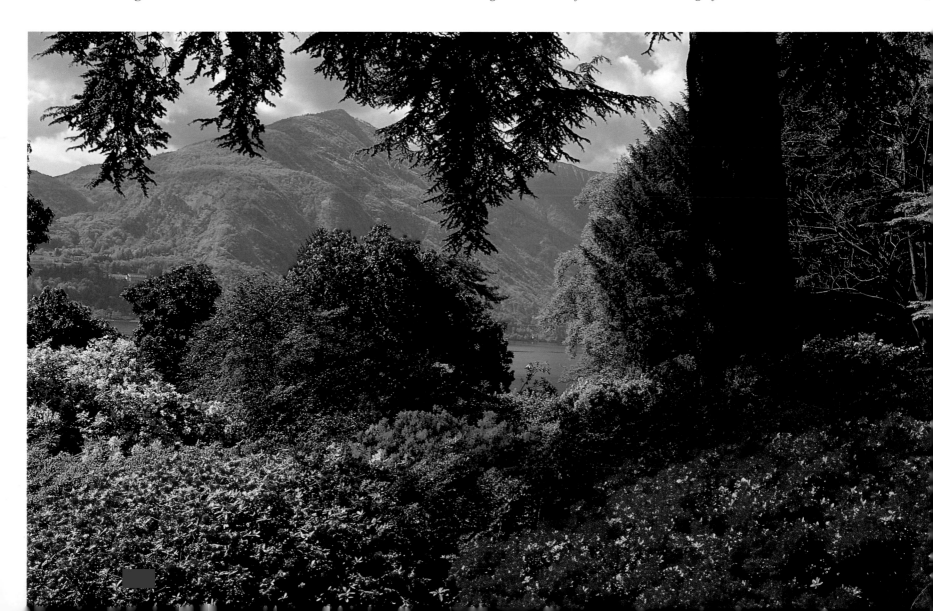

VILLA CICOGNA

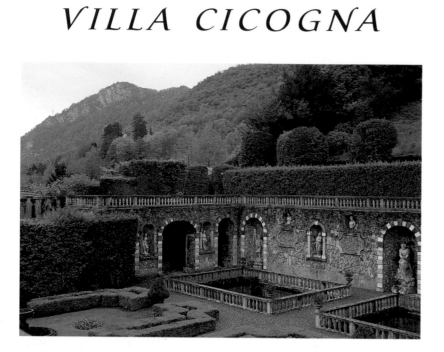

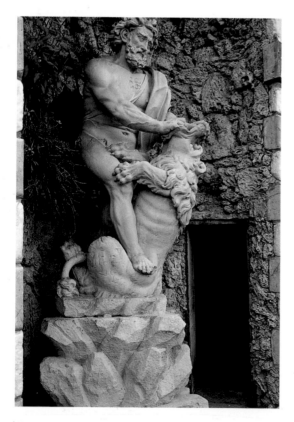

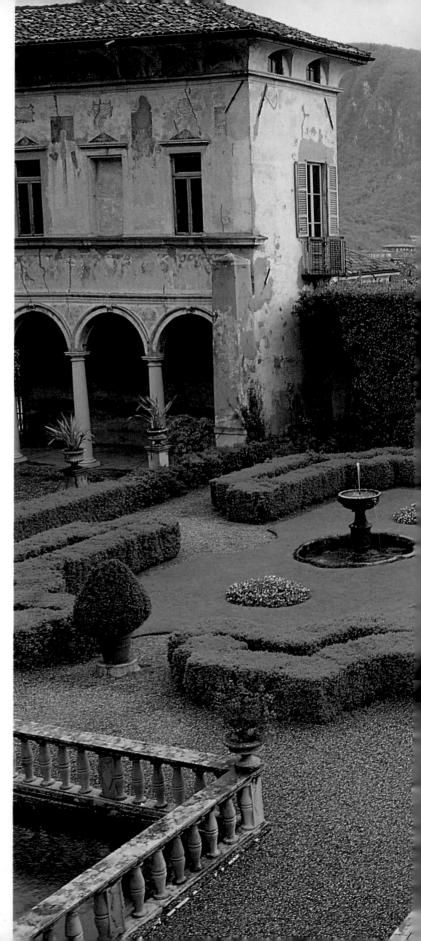

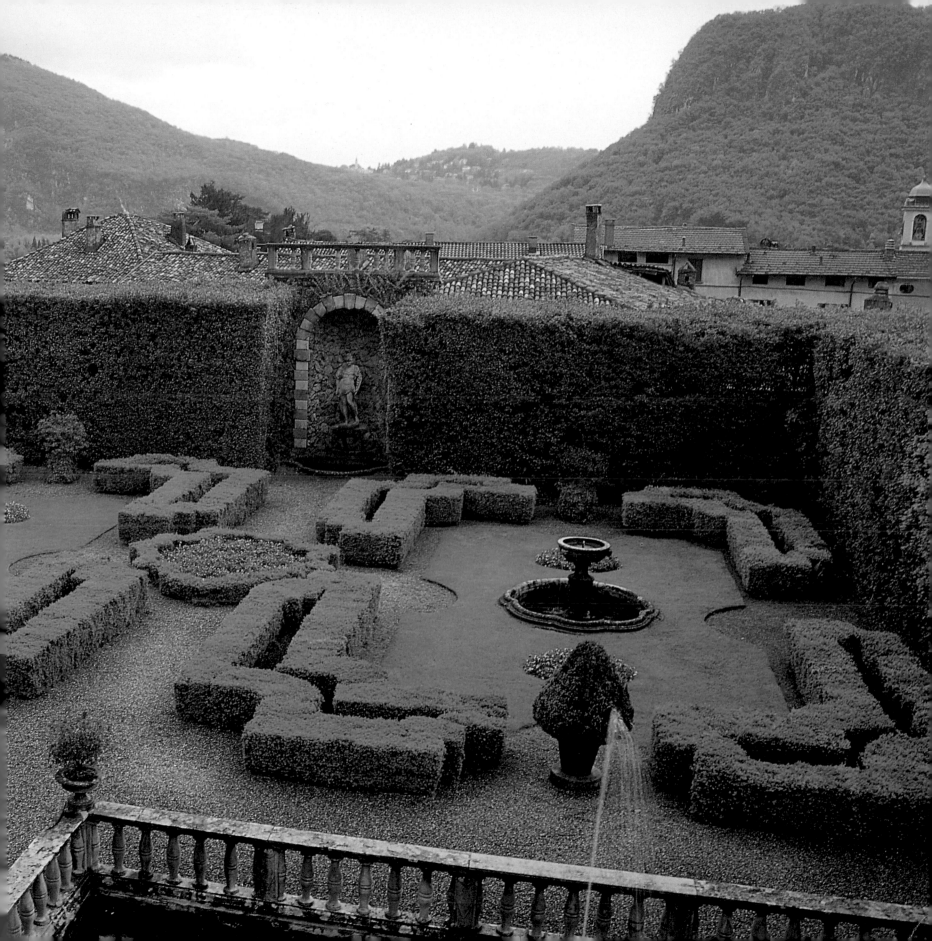

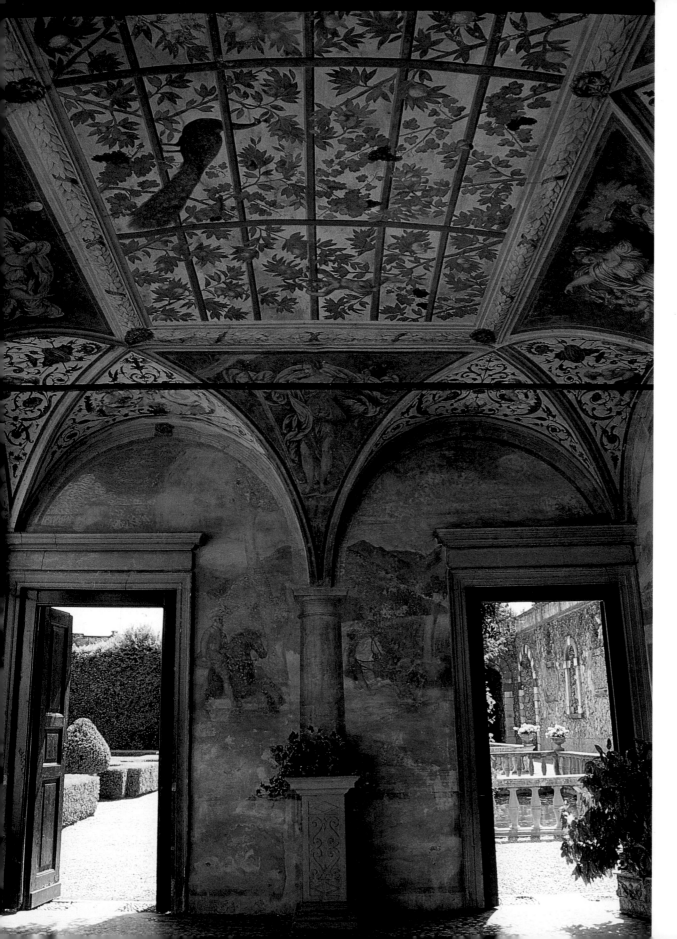

PREVIOUS PAGES *From a bedroom window, views across the sunken garden with its peschiere lead to the bosco beyond, where the Cicognas hunted with the Viscontis half a century ago (left above). A statue of Hercules forcing apart the jaws of the Nemean lion stands in a central niche in the sunken garden (left below). The view from the bosco across the sunken garden towards the Viggiu Alps near Varese (right). Part of the fresco that used to decorate the entire villa is still visible just under the eaves, where it has been protected from the sun. The pipework for the scherzi d'acqua still lies under the paths, awaiting restoration.*

LEFT *Renaissance architects made much use of the arcaded loggia described by Pliny to effect a transition between the inside of the villa and the garden. Here the garden is brought into the architectural fabric of the house through frescoes of flowers and trellises that resemble those painted by Giovanni da Udine at the Villa Farnesina in Rome. The frescoes were done by the Campi brothers of Cremona. They were preserved beneath a layer of thick whitewash that was applied during the plague that swept through Lombardy in the seventeenth century, and which was only removed in 1800.*

OPPOSITE *An 1813 plan of the garden shows that the overall layout has not changed, but the shapes of the parterres have been altered.*

THE VILLA EDITH WHARTON described as a 'charming old place' once stood alone against a wooded hillside on the outskirts of Bisuschio, its exterior walls decorated with vividly coloured frescoes. Set against a backcloth of leafy green, it must have been a painter's dream, even in an age when it was not unusual for frescoes to decorate the exterior walls of entire villages. These have all faded, and the sprawl of Bisuschio now clusters around its feet, but the Villa Cicogna, impregnable as an oyster, still harbours its pearls.

The villa started life early in the fifteenth century as a hunting lodge in what Wharton described as 'the lovely but little-known hill country between the Lake of Varese and the southern end of Lugano', whose forest was the province of happy hunters and black bears. In 1476, the dissolute, tyrannical Duke of Milan, Galeazzo Maria Sforza, who moved from hunt to hunt accompanied by his retinue of courtiers, courtesans, clowns, monkeys, parrots and leopards, was a guest of Agostino Mozzoni, head of a family of landowners. While they were out hunting boar together, the Duke was attacked by a bear. Agostino Mozzoni's dog threw itself at the animal, and by momentarily distracting it gave Mozzoni the opportunity to kill the bear. The dog lost its life, and later that year so did the Duke, who was attacked in church on Christmas Eve. Before his death, however, he had arranged favours and exemptions for the Mozzonis and their ensuing wealth enabled them, over the years, to transform their hunting box into a Renaissance villa of great allure.

In the first half of the sixteenth century, the brothers Francesco and Maino Mozzoni built the present villa, which was further enhanced by Francesco Mozzoni's son, Ascanio, so that by 1560 it had been transformed, wrote an admiring Wharton, into 'an early Renaissance building of great beauty with a touch of Tuscan austerity in its design. The plain front, with deep projecting eaves and widely spaced windows, might stand on some village square above the Arno; and the interior court, with its two-storied arcade, recalls, in purity and lightness of design, the interiors of Brunelleschi's tradition . . . The walls of the court are frescoed in charming cinque-cento designs, and the vaulted ceiling of the loggia is painted in delicate trellis-work, somewhat in the manner of the semi circular arcade at the Villa di Papa Giulia.'

If Wharton was reminded of gardens she had just been to see herself, it is because Ascanio Mozzoni had gone to the newly built

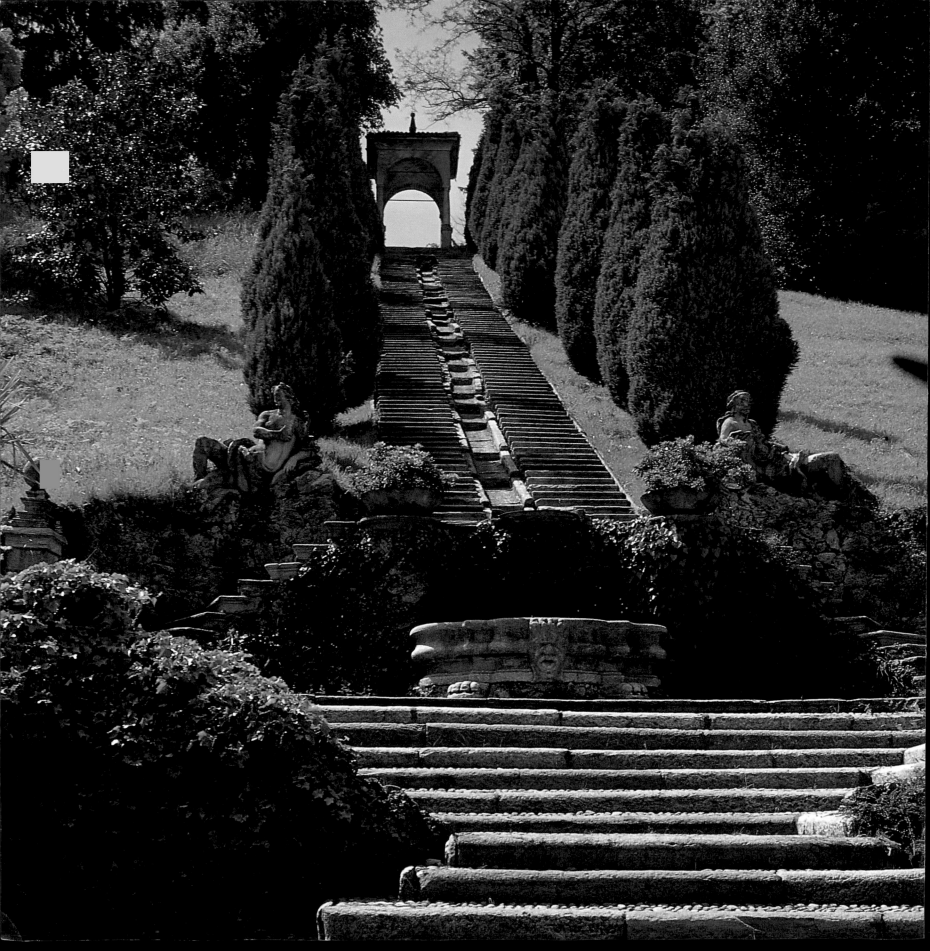

gardens of the Medici in Florence, and the papal gardens of Rome, for ideas and inspiration in laying out his own. He selected what pleased him and scaled it down to create this gem of a garden. Everything here has been preserved; only the 'enchanting views across the southern bay of Lake Lugano' have disappeared, hidden by tall trees.

The Villa Cicogna was well off the tourist trail of the tours proffered by Murray and Baedeker guidebooks, and never made an appearance in any of the journals of well-known travellers. This unmarked, unsung, and by and large unmentioned villa was first discovered, it seems, by Wharton in 1903. Soon after Wharton's discovery, the Villa Cicogna was visited by Sir George Sitwell, who included a mention of it in his long essay *On the Making of Gardens* (1909), but only amongst a clutch of other gardens.

'The Villa Cicogna', Wharton noted, 'still gives a vivid idea of what an old Italian country house must have been in its original state.' Even today, the interior frescoes, Renaissance furniture and stucco ornament are so perfectly preserved that it feels as though the Mozzoni of the sixteenth century have only just stepped out of the rooms. The villa has benefited from five centuries of continuous ownership by the same family, and although every part of the villa is now open to the public and the family has moved into the guest house next door, they still treat it as their home, recently celebrating a family wedding there.

The 'real beauty of any garden', argued Sitwell, 'lay in its relation to the individual, that it should be a "background for life", not a glittering museum piece.' Visitors to this garden feel the day-to-day life that a garden should be part of, and this makes it one of the best loved stops on the garden circuit.

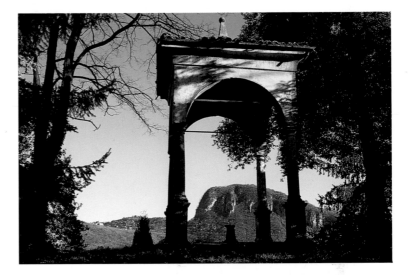

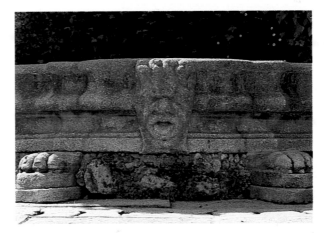

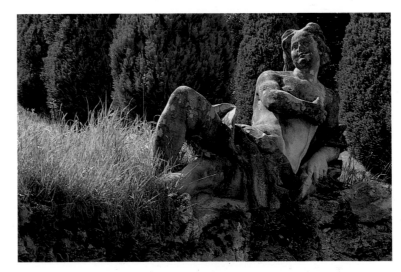

There is a fine view straight up the scaletta d'acqua *from the* piano nobile *of the villa (left). The cascade was originally fed by a reservoir, which visitors can easily find in the woods above along with the Heath-Robinson-like network of watercourses and aqueducts that lead to it; the waterfall is now powered by an electric pump. The gloriette at the top (right) is reached by climbing 156 steps (right top), while the lion basin sits at its base (right centre). Reclining statues mark the first stage in the ascent (right below).*

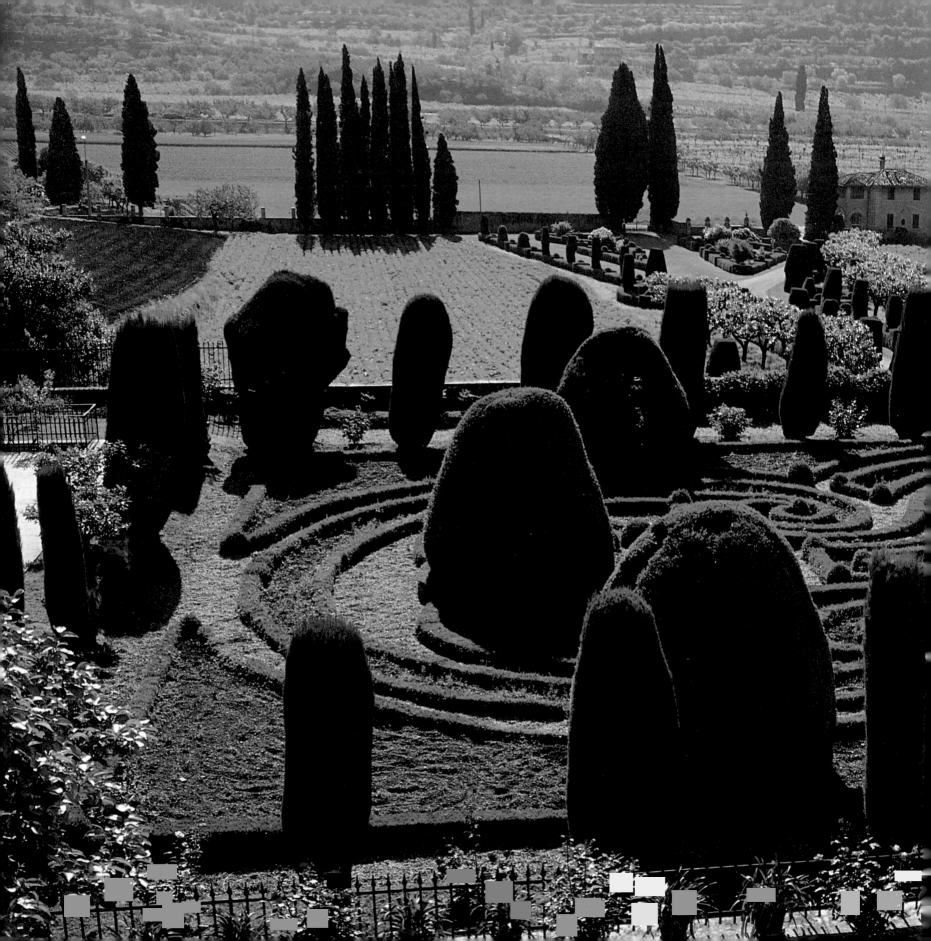

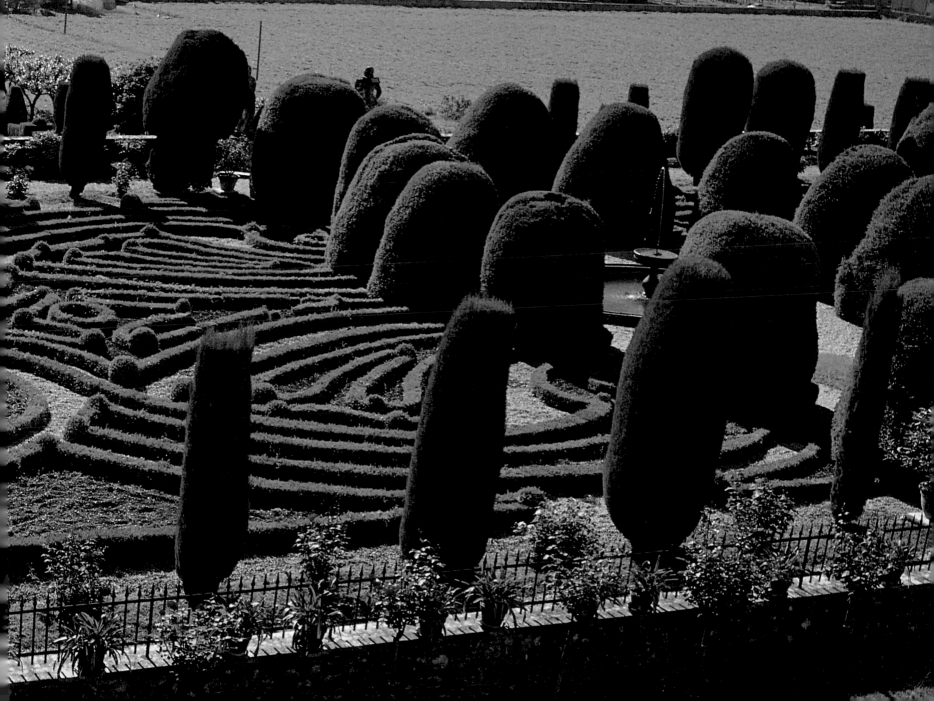

WHEN IN THE THIRTEENTH CENTURY spring thawed the snow on the Alpine peaks and water poured into the north-east region of Italy, there were no cavernous lakes to absorb it, and it rushed instead into dozens of rivers and streams, regularly bursting their banks. The consequent damming, diverting and banking up of its rivers and the draining of swampland into canals has been a preoccupation of the Veneto for centuries. The two largest rivers, the Adige, flowing through Verona, and the Po, which creates fertile plains, were often represented as river gods in the region's gardens.

Padua had to cope with a dangerous Brenta: 'Paduans dyke up Brenta's tide', Dante recounted in his *Inferno*, 'to guard their towns and castles.' The Brenta connected Venice to Padua and the engineering works caused so many disputes between the cities they finally had a war over it.

The powerful republic of Venice, whose enormous wealth was generated by the monopoly its merchant ships had over trade routes, became the centre from which culture and influence radiated, and all the gardens of the Veneto benefited from its cosmopolitan character. Marco Polo, Dante and Petrarch were all born within fifty years of each other and each lived for a time in Venice. Marco Polo set off from Venice for the Orient and his drawing of a Tartary Castle in the territory of Genghis Khan may have influenced the crenellated Castle of Cataio 200 years later. Valsanzibio was built by the procurator of St Mark's and was inspired by the writings of Dante; the Villa Pisani was built by a doge; the botanic garden of the University of Padua was endowed by Venetian patricians and the Prato della Valle erected to these benefactors; and the main grotto of the Giusti Gardens was decorated with shells brought back from Cyprus.

In the city of Venice itself, it was a Frenchman – Napoleon – who laid out the public garden, which contained a large collection of animals but rarely any people. George Sand explained that 'the Venetian ladies dread the heat and would not think of going out during the day; but they also dread the cold and do not venture out at night . . . Civilised males prefer to frequent places where there is a chance of meeting the fair sex . . .' For all its wealth, the island-bound city had little space for private gardens. 'At any season', wrote the famous American chronicler of Venice, W. D. Howells, of the garden at the back of the Palazzo Giusti, 'the lofty palace walls rose over it, and shut it in a pensive seclusion which was loved by the old mother of the painter and by his elderly maiden sister. These often walked on its moss-grown paths, silent as the roses and oleanders to which one could have fancied the blossom of their youth had flown; and sometimes there came to them there, grave, black gowned priests . . .' Secrecy and isolation made these gardens potent; the scents of the fruits and jasmine of the garden of the Palazzo Capello – where Henry James set his *Aspen Papers* and Gabriele d'Annunzio his *La Fuoco* – were highlighted because the garden, 'enclosed like an exiled thing by its girdle of water, becomes all the more intense from its banishment, like the soul of the exile'.

Venetian souls, marooned in a lagoon, were released from their humid prison and claustrophobic solitude when the great families began to build their villas of the *villeggiatura* in the sixteenth, seventeenth and eighteenth centuries. Accustomed to life on the water, they built them along the Brenta River, which had been

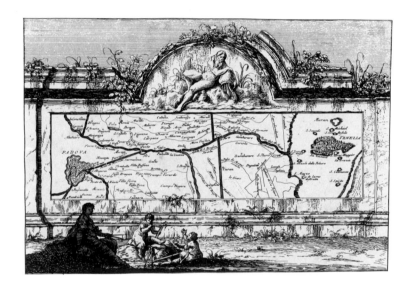

PREVIOUS PAGES *The parterre at the Villa Cuzzano and the view over the Veneto landscape.*
ABOVE *This map, presided over by a river god, shows the Veneto landscape criss-crossed with rivers, including the Brenta, connecting Padua to Venice.* RIGHT *A river god in the gardens of Villa Barbarigo at Valsanzibio.*

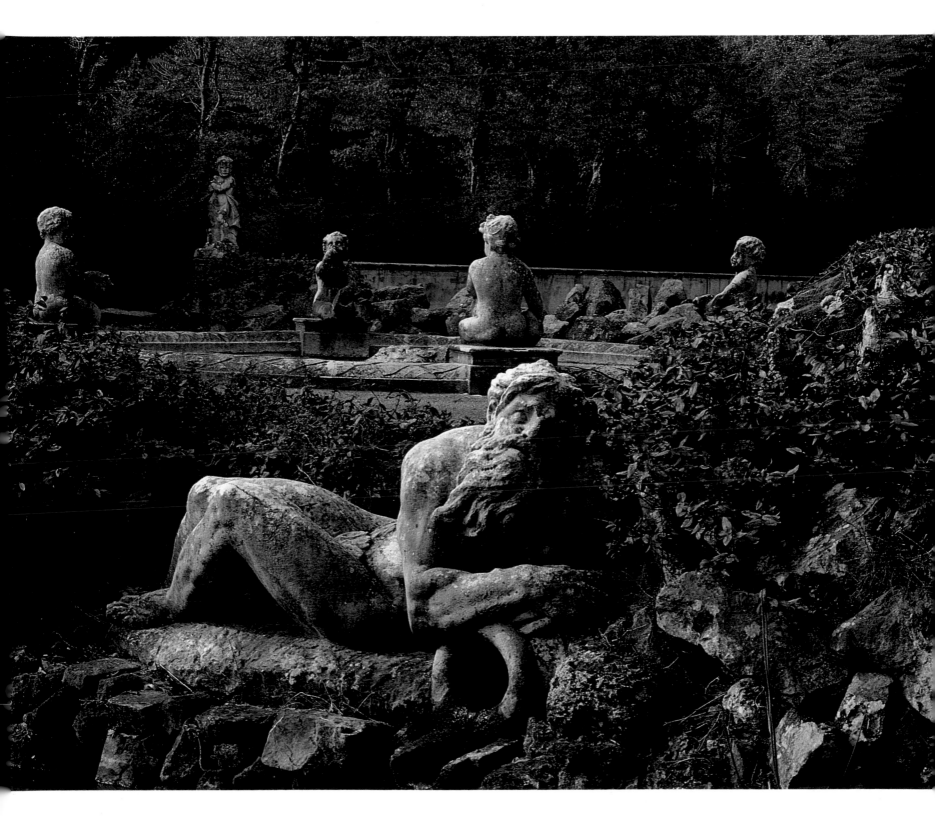

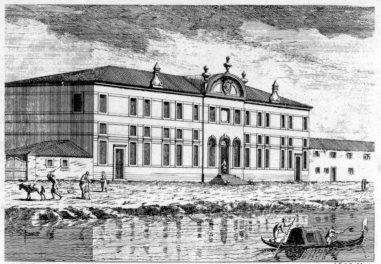

Veduta del Palazzo de' NN.HH. Mocenighi.

J.F. Costa del et inc.

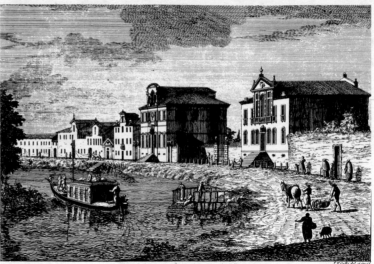

Veduta della Volta fuori delle Porte della Mira.

J.F. Costa del et inc.

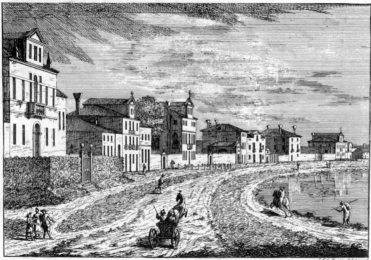

Veduta verso il Taglio.

J.F. Costa inv. del et incid.

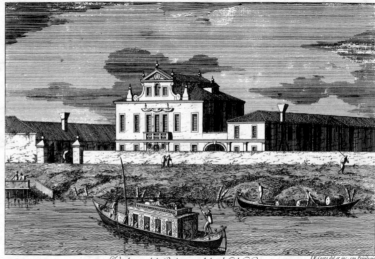

Veduta del Palazzo del N.H. Corner

J.F. Costa del et inc. con Privilegio

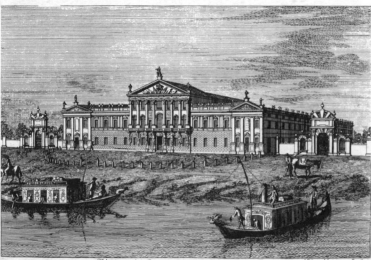

Veduta del Palazzo delli NN.HH. Pisani

J.F. Costa del et inc. con Privilegio

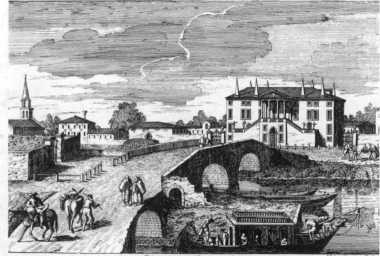

Veduta delle Porte di Strà

J.F. Costa del et inc. con Privilegio

dammed and diverted so many times it was as tame and lifeless as a mill pond, with small front gardens and all the main gardens laid out behind. 'Along the Brenta,' wrote Edith Wharton, 'the villas sit side by side, in "a prevailing note of amenity" suggesting a lief of neighbourliness and sociability.' These villas were modelled on or designed by 'local' architects such as Palladio and Scamozzi, their interiors might be frescoed by another local artist, Tiepolo. In 1645, John Evelyn sat in a boat drawn by horses along its twenty-mile length admiring 'both sides deliciously planted with country villas and gentleman's retirements. Gardens planted with Oranges, Figs and other fruit, belonging to the Venetians.' Of 'the celebrities that might be cited', Wharton tells us 'there dwelt the Signor Procurante, whom Candide visited on his travels, the famous Procurante Pisani, and Lord Byron, who in 1819 carried off the Guiccioli to his villa at La Mira on the Brenta.' This was the large and gloomy Villa Foscarina, Byron tells us, with 'more space than splendour – and not much of that, and like all Venetian ex-marine habitations too near the road – they seem to think they can never have dust enough to compensate for their long immersion.'

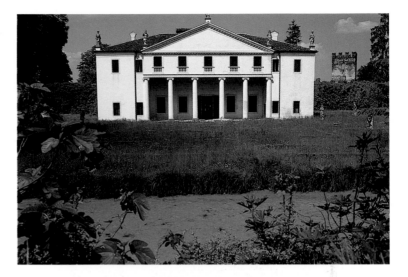

When Wharton and Walter Berry made their 1911 tour of northern Italy, they sent Henry James a series of jocular postcards in verse. The one from here reads: 'In such a place, in ties unholy, how could he live with La Guiccioli?' seeming less dubious about Byron's scandalous 'last attachment' with Terese Guiccioli, whom he seduced the same year she left the convent and married Count Guiccioli, three times her age, than about the gloomy villa.

After Venice lost her monopoly of the trade routes and began her economic decline, 'the Brenta continued to be a favourite *villeggiatura* of the Venetian nobility until the middle of the nineteenth century'. But as Wharton tells us, by the time she visited them 'no traces of their own gardens remain except for the statues which bordered their walls'. Today, the villas crumble in ramshackle gardens, or are over-restored pastiches with indifferently planted parterres. Sometimes a solitary statue and a pair of gates are all that is left of a once glorious villa.

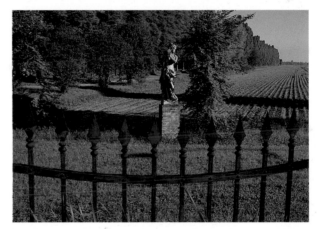

When she visited the villas on the Brenta, Edith Wharton found that 'the houses still remain almost line for line as they were drawn in Gianfrancesco Costa's admirable etchings, "Le Delizie del Fiume Brenta", published in 1750 (left); but unfortunately almost all the old gardens have disappeared.' Some of the Brenta villas today (right).

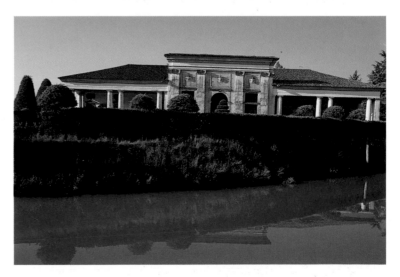

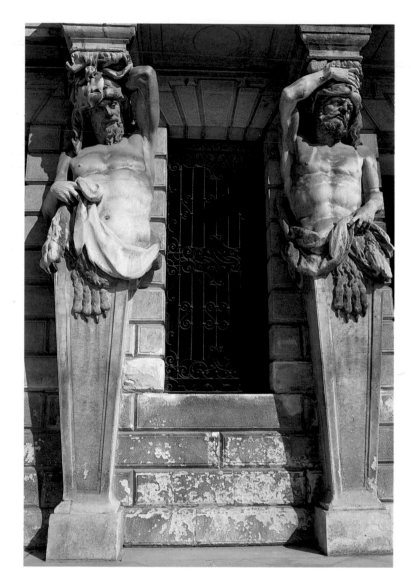

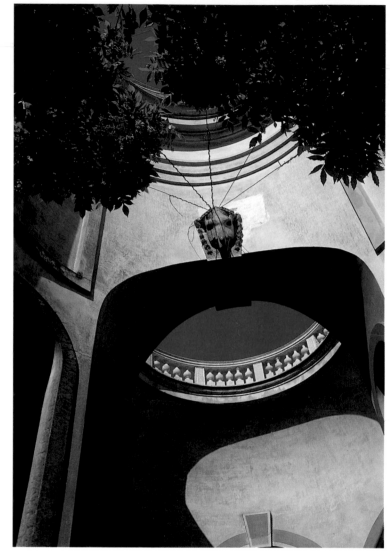

ABOVE *Two views of the Villa Pisani: herms on what Wharton described as the 'majestic façade' (left) and the orangery 'built in the airy and romantic style of which the Italian architect has not yet lost the secret' (right).*

OPPOSITE *Outside the Padua Botanic Garden, only a few minutes' walk from the Prato della Valle: a little canal (left) and one of the statues flanking the bridges (right), which, Goethe reported, are 'colossal statues of Popes and Doges, together with smaller ones erected by guilds, private individuals and foreigners to famous men who either taught or studied here'.*

More like a Versailles palace than a villa of the *villeggiatura*, which Wharton tells us 'may be regarded as a good example of a stately Venetian garden', is 'the great villa built at Stra on the Brenta . . . for Alvise Pisani, procurator of St Mark's, by the architects Prati and Frigimelica. In size and elegance it far surpasses any other house on the Brenta.' Commissioned around 1718, it was actually built *c.* 1735–40. Later Napoleon bought it but stayed there for only one night. This is the garden upon which Wharton modelled that belonging to the fictitious Duke of Pianura, evocatively described in her novel *The Valley of Decision*.

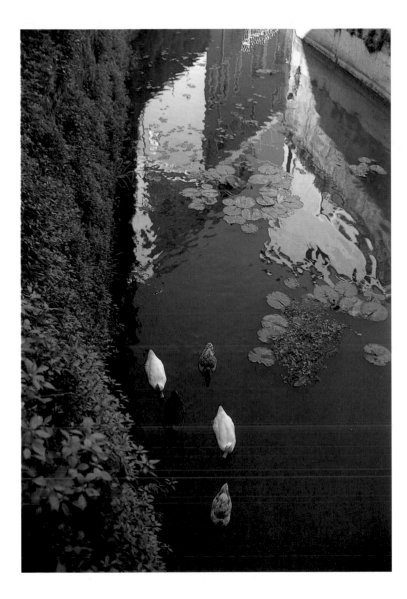

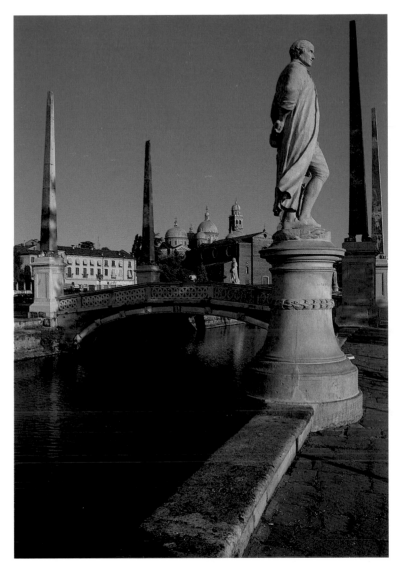

Wharton found the university town of Padua 'one of the most picturesque cities of upper Italy; and the seeker after gardens will find many bits along the narrow canals . . . Indeed, one might almost include in the gardens the beautiful Prato della Valle, the public square with its encircling canal crossed by marble bridges, its range of baroque statues of "worthies" and its central expanse of turf and trees.'

One of Padua's 'worthies' was Petrarch, whose concept of the garden as a retreat, exemplified by his garden in Provence, was to be a fundamental influence on Renaissance garden makers. He left

Padua to write his last sonnets in a hermitage high up in green, volcanic hills in the village of Arqua. 'Amidst the Euganean hills,' he wrote, 'not more than ten miles from Padua, I have built myself a small but pleasant dwelling, surrounded by an olive grove and a vineyard.' Wharton visited the house, which was decorated with frescoes to his muse Laura, who was married and as unobtainable as Dante's Beatrice. Petrarch died the day before his seventieth birthday sitting in his chair, which, together with his inkstand and his stuffed cat, became part of a shrine to the poet, and a place of pilgrimage as beloved as Dante's tomb in Ravenna.

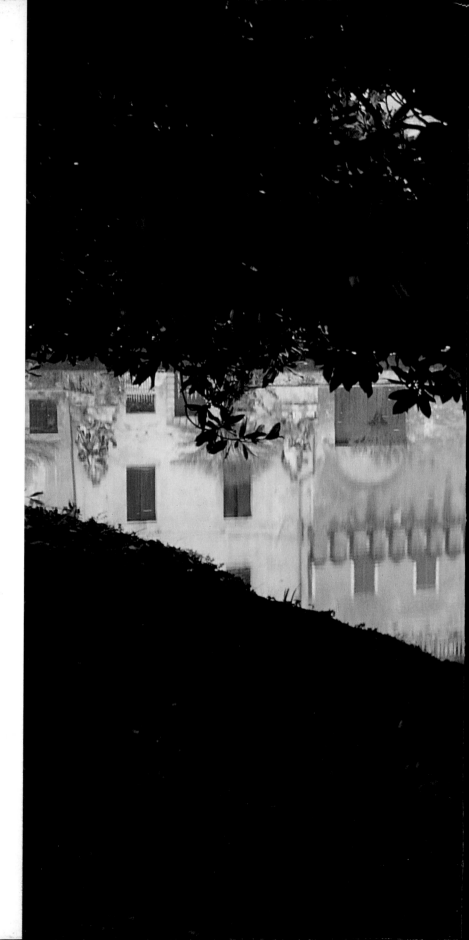

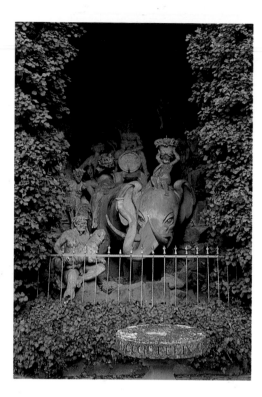

Wharton and Berry sent another postcard to Henry James:
    'Without the Worm the Beaks are growing starker,
    The more so in This Room; and if Petrarca
    Could live again he'd sing: "We want the aura
    Of Henry more than all the lure of Laura!"'

It is said that Petrarch climbed Mount Ventoux for the sake of the view and was the first Western man to do so. When he looked out from his hill towards Venice, his view took in the lower reaches of the Euganean hills surrounded by swampland that stretched to Venice. It was three centuries before the landscape before him would be exploited by garden architects – in, for instance, Valsanzibio, only a few miles away, and a few miles further, the Castle of Cataio, an 'extraordinary edifice', Wharton observed, 'built for the Obizzi of Venice about 1550 . . . said to have been copied from the plans of a castle in Tartary brought home by Marco Polo.'

The Castle of Cataio reflected in the still waters (right) and its 'huge artificial grotto' (above), as Wharton described it, 'with a stucco Silenus lolling on an elephant, and other life-size animals and figures, a composition recalling the zoological wonders of the grotto at Castello'.

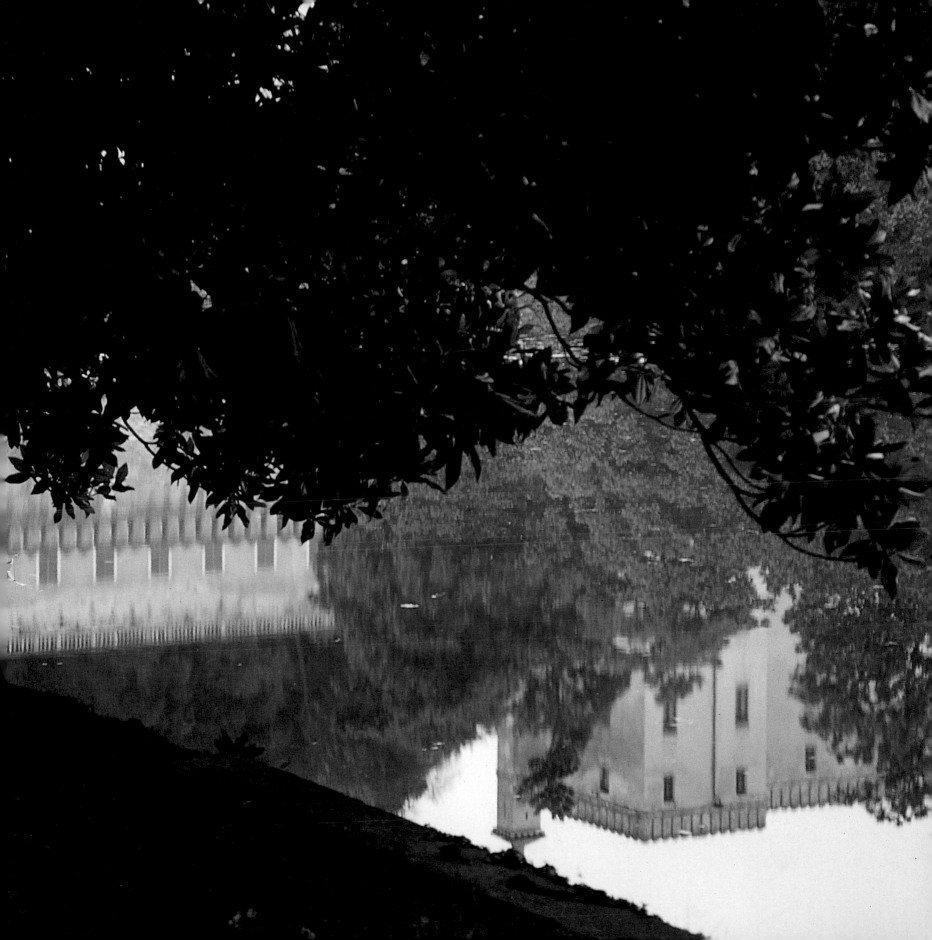

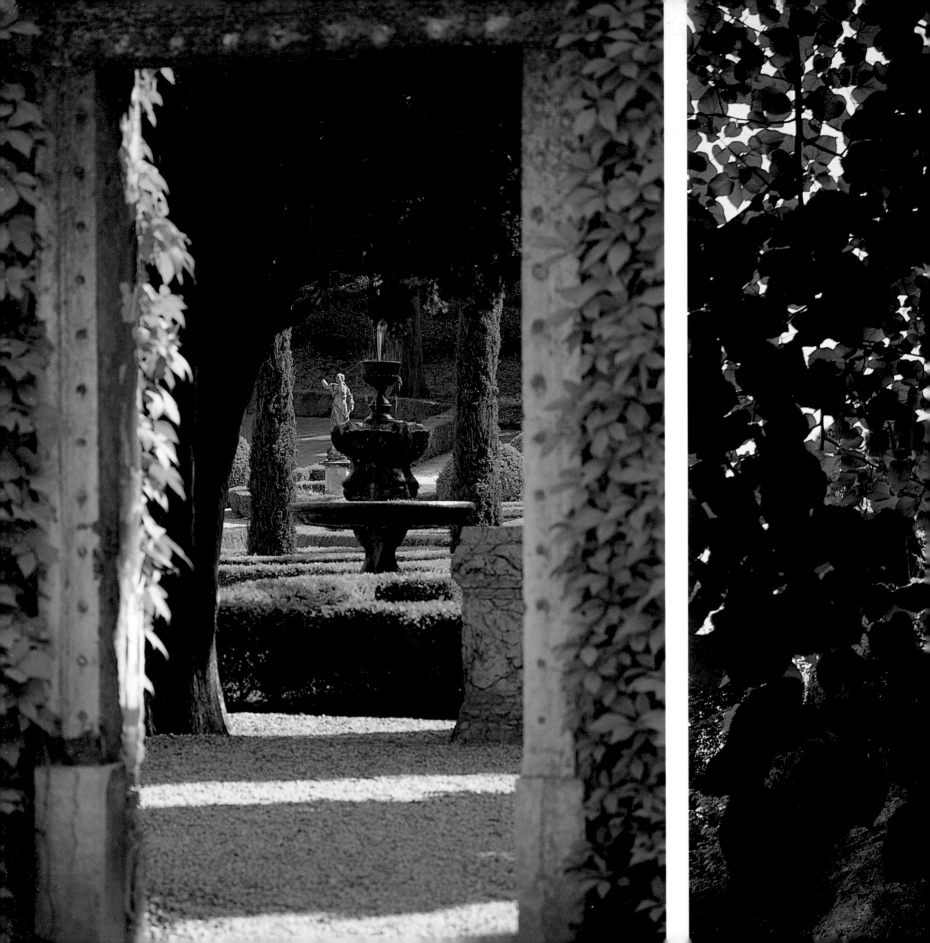

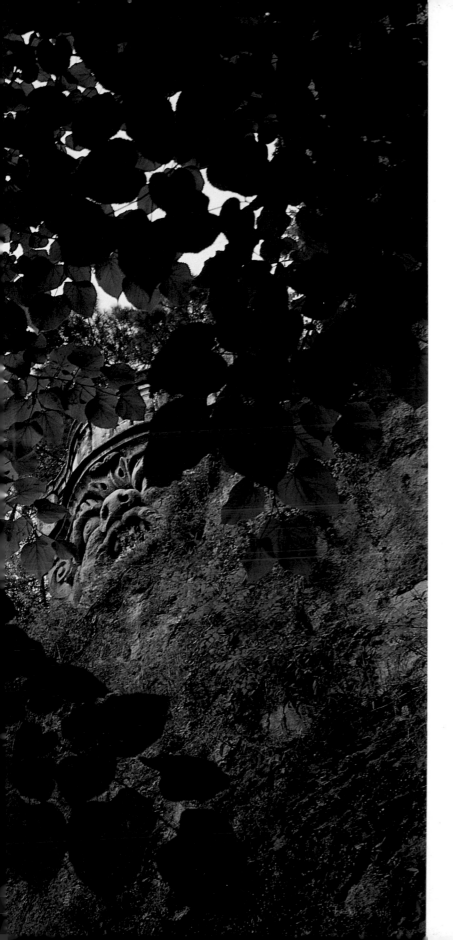

GIUSTI GARDENS

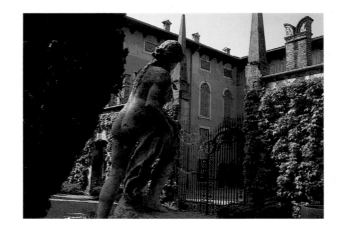

'DRIVING ACROSS THE BRIDGE along a dull and dusty street, the carriage stops at a stuccoed house with painted architecture, not much better than the rest. But when the heavy entrance doors are swung back, an enchanted vista holds the traveller spellbound – the deep, refreshing green of an avenue of cypresses half a millennium old, leading to a precipice crowned by the foliage of a higher garden. For pure sensation there is nothing in Italy equal to this first glimpse through the Giusti gateway.'

This rousing introduction to the Giusti Gardens was written by Sir George Sitwell, whom Edith Wharton had inspired to make an Italian pilgrimage even more comprehensive than her own. Because this green oasis in the middle of Verona was included on the itinerary of the Grand Tour travellers, which took in the balcony from which Shakespeare's Juliet was said to have been wooed by Romeo, the Arena and the Tombs, it was, observed Wharton, 'better known to sightseers than any other garden in northern Italy'. She appreciated the gardens' 'charm and the dusky massing of their cypresses', although she deemed them unimportant to students of Italian garden architecture as they 'preserve few traces

Stonework and verdure in the Giusti Gardens: trees and hedges, statuary and fountain, glimpsed through a doorway (far left); the mascherone *above the grotto, intended to frighten the visitor looking up at it through trees (left); a statue alongside a 'goodliest cypress' adorning the entrance to the* palazzo *from the garden (above).*

of their original design'. The Murray guidebook, normally full of quirky detail, gives a perfunctory entry in its 1866 edition, saying that the 'gardens are well laid out and the view of Verona is very fine'; but the author of the 1899 edition, published four years before Wharton's visit, warmed to the place, noting that the 'beautiful gardens open to strangers (small fee), are planted with cypresses, some of great age'.

The gardens had been open to the public as early as the fifteenth century, long before Agostino Giusti transformed it in about 1570 into his celebrated Renaissance gardens – of which neither the original plans nor the exact date survive. Like Dante, the Giusti family left behind the war between the Guelphs and the Ghibellines in Tuscany and established themselves in Verona early in the fifteenth century, and these origins explain the Tuscan-style terracing of the gardens. Agostino Giusti, made prosperous by his mills, was an erudite collector of Roman artefacts and inscriptions, and a *cavaliere* of the Venetian Republic. In recognition of the sophisticated style of his gardens, which was probably unknown in Verona at the time, the Giusti family was given the epithet 'del Giardino' in the early 1700s.

It was invariably the cypresses that caught visitors' imaginations; some of them were 700 years old, planted before the Giusti, who added to them. As the centuries unfolded, the cypresses grew in stature, eliciting admiring hyperbole in direct proportion to their size. In 1611, Thomas Coryat, in *Crudities*, found 'two rows of lofty cypresses, 33 in rank'. Thirty-five years later John Evelyn recounted, 'at the entrance of this garden grows the goodliest cypress I fancy in Europe, cut in pyramid [obelisk] it is a prodigious tree both for breadth and height, entirely covered, and thick to the base'. Charles de Brosses also found the trees 'prodigiously high and pointed' on his 1739 visit, and by 1786, when Goethe arrived, the cypresses had 'soared into the air like awls' (pointed tools for making holes in wood). By the twentieth century Sir George Sitwell claimed they were 'as tall as the tower of Verona and older than the oldest

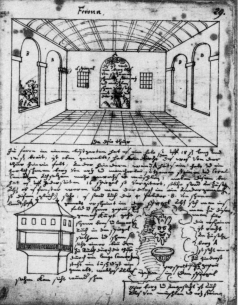

palaces'; and the avenue of cypresses, he said, had such 'a grave and haunting beauty that it might have led to the place of the oracle, to the garden of Plato, the tomb of Dante, the cavern where sleeps the Venus of the ancient world'.

In fact, this avenue led past a difficult little maze on the right to something even more memorable: a grotto surmounted by a fierce *mascherone* (mask) – of the type used above fireplaces in nearby Valpolicella and Vicenza, and recalling Bomarzo's Mouth of Hell – which emitted tongue-like flames on special occasions such as the 1581 production of Tasso's *Aminta*, which was staged here for the first time. Carved out of the tufa and designed to arouse all the senses, the grotto had distorting mirrors, and was decorated with mother-of-pearl shells, coral and seashells, brought over to Venice from Cyprus. It was, said Coryat, 'moistened with delicate springs and fountains conveyed by lead pipes' and 'sweet-tasting waters'. In the north-west of the garden was an acoustic stalactite grotto with echoing corridors.

After the sensual experience of the grottoes the visitor climbed up the circular stairs of a turret – probably at first the only means of getting up there, as the gardens were planned to unveil the view gradually, along a predetermined path to the terraces carved out of the cliff above, which were once as renowned as the cypresses. A belvedere marks the lookout point, directly above the *mascherone*, which gives a fine view over Verona. All the travellers, though, found it much more exciting to be able to see Mantua, Parma and the Alps 'though at a great distance' than the splendid view of Verona by the Adige River, directly below them.

ABOVE *Henrich Schickhardt's 1598 drawing shows the main grotto with square mirrors on either side of a fountain and frescoed windows.*

RIGHT *The 'enchanting vista' described by Sitwell: an avenue of cypresses leads to the* mascherone, *its fiery look – it was designed to spit out flames – enhanced by winter shadows, and the grotto beneath.*

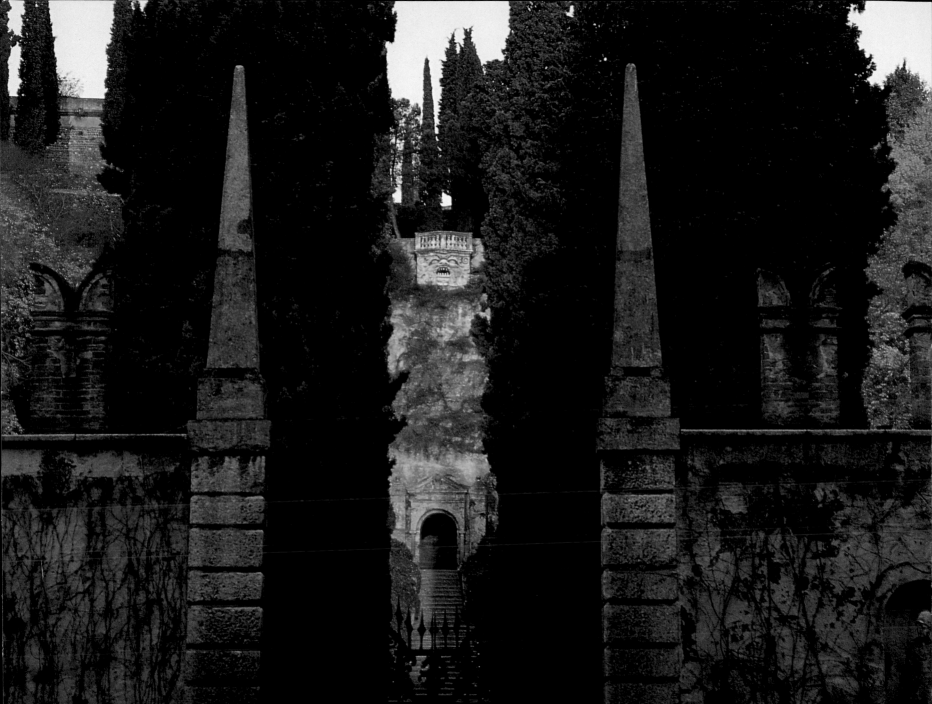

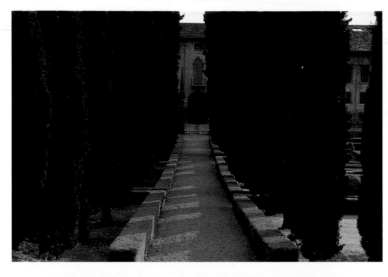

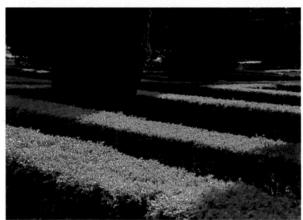

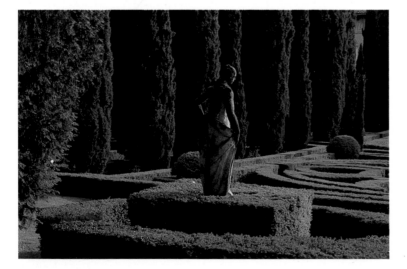

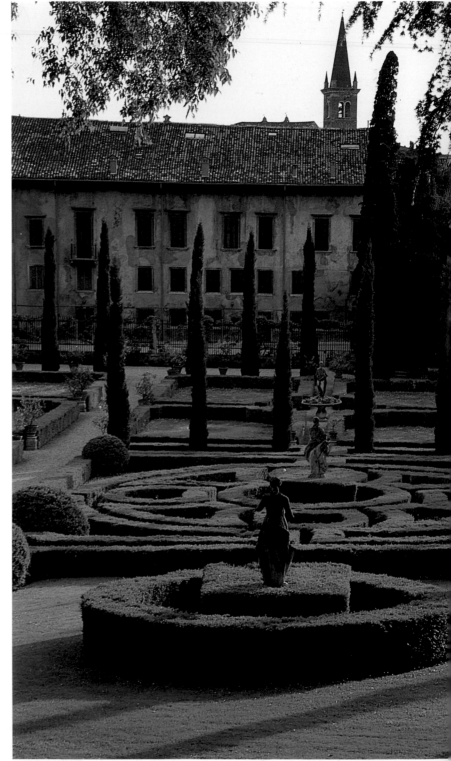

'The more permanent materials of which [the Italian garden] is made – the stonework, the evergreen foliage, the effects of rushing or motionless water – all form part of the artist's design. But . . . the inherent beauty of the garden lies in the grouping of its parts – in the converging lines of long ilex walks, the alternation of sunny open spaces with cool woodland shade, the proportion . . . between the height of a wall or the width of a path.'

The Giusti Gardens exemplify Wharton's definition of the components of the Italian garden's 'total impression of charm': in their sense of line (apart from the curves that replaced their original geometry), as in the cypress alley leading to the palazzo (far left, top); in their foliage, as in the parterre (far left, centre); and in their stonework, such as the pagan deities presiding over it (far left, below). The cypresses, looking like awls, the tall windows of the palazzo and the tower (left) echo the verticals in the fabric of Verona's architecture.

RIGHT *The gardens were designed so that the patterns of the parterre would be revealed when the visitor looked down from the turret.*

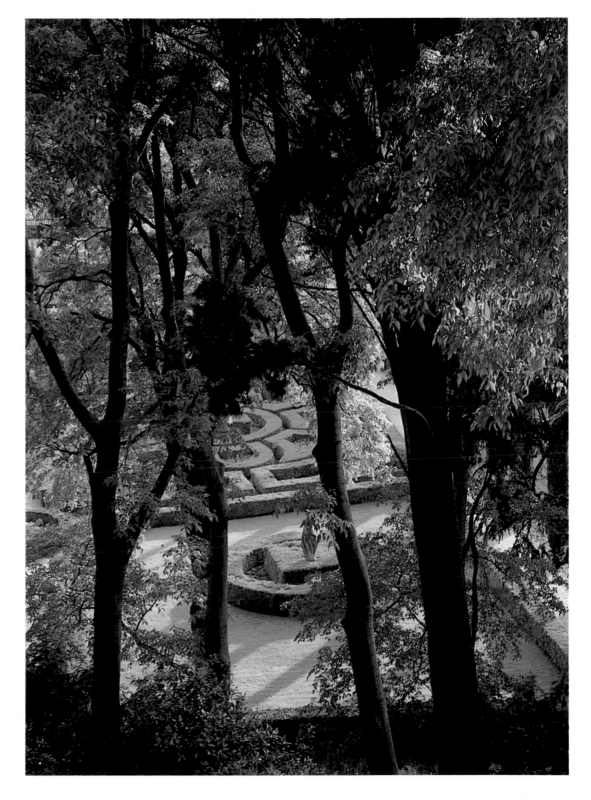

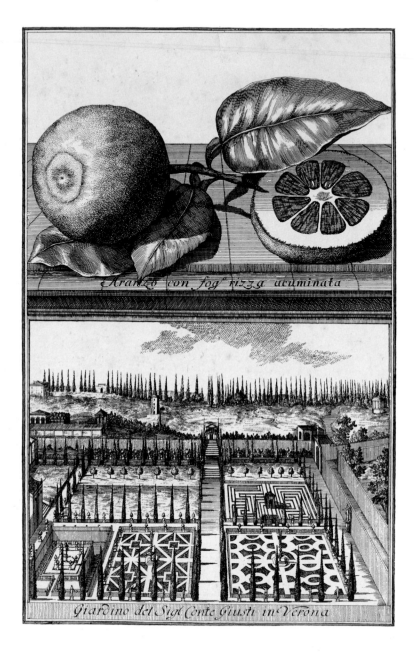

Araniz̃o con fogˡ rizza acuminata

Giardino del Sigˡ Conte Giusti in Verona

ABOVE *J. C. Volkamer introduced a citrus collection into the garden. His illustration of 1714 shows the squares of the parterre, surrounded by cypresses, before they were taken out by Trezza.*

OPPOSITE *The fountain brings music to the gardens, an appropriate addition, for they were dedicated to the Muses and Agostino Giusti was a music lover. They were also dedicated to the Genius of Mirth and to Flora.*

Looking down from the upper storeys of the villa also gave a bird's eye view of the parterre below – whose prospect changed through the centuries. Early in the 1700s the visitor would have seen the comprehensive *agrume* (citrus fruit) collection introduced by the German gardener and illustrator J. C. Volkamer and admired terraces planted with 'curious knots and fruits of divers sorts – figs, oranges, apricots and cypress trees'. Thomas Coryat, who provides this description, was taken round the gardens by 'Count Augustus Justus' (Agostino Giusti) himself. He also remarked on a 'wild riot' of cypresses, which both Sitwell and de Brosses were to compare to the 'scene of a witch's sabbath'. Until the early 1800s the square parterres were planted in the geometric patterns of the Renaissance, each square enclosed by cypresses. The parterres altered completely in the 1800s when the gardens were romanticized by architect Luigi Trezza – and the geometric shapes were replaced with French-style horseshoes and circles. He also removed many of the cypresses so that the statues he brought into the middle of each square could be admired from the house without obstruction.

Goethe was one of the last travellers to see the gardens in their original state. He picked some cypress branches and sprays of caper blossom, and walked through Verona wondering why he was being stared at, unaware that in Italy cypresses are always carried by mourners. The alterations to the gardens continued throughout the nineteenth century. 'Probably no garden was less suited to landscape style but landscaped the Giusti garden was,' commented Georgina Masson. The maze was dug up and the upper terraces transformed into winding walks. Then in the 1950s there was a return to the original. Although the grottoes are still closed, the present Giusti, Count Niccolò, has recently replanted the original maze, which flummoxed Charles de Brosses, who related how 'I, always the simpleton, foolishly entered and I was there for an hour in full sun fuming and ranting unable to find my way out until the people of the house came and pulled me out.'

The Giusti Gardens are a calm green haven of peace from the thundering traffic that lies just outside their heavy portals, making their music – of the fountain and the arias that drift across the gardens from the nearby music school – even sweeter still. And can their evocative atmosphere and delightful-sounding fountains be heard somewhere in the compositions of two of their exceedingly musical visitors – Mozart and Fauré?

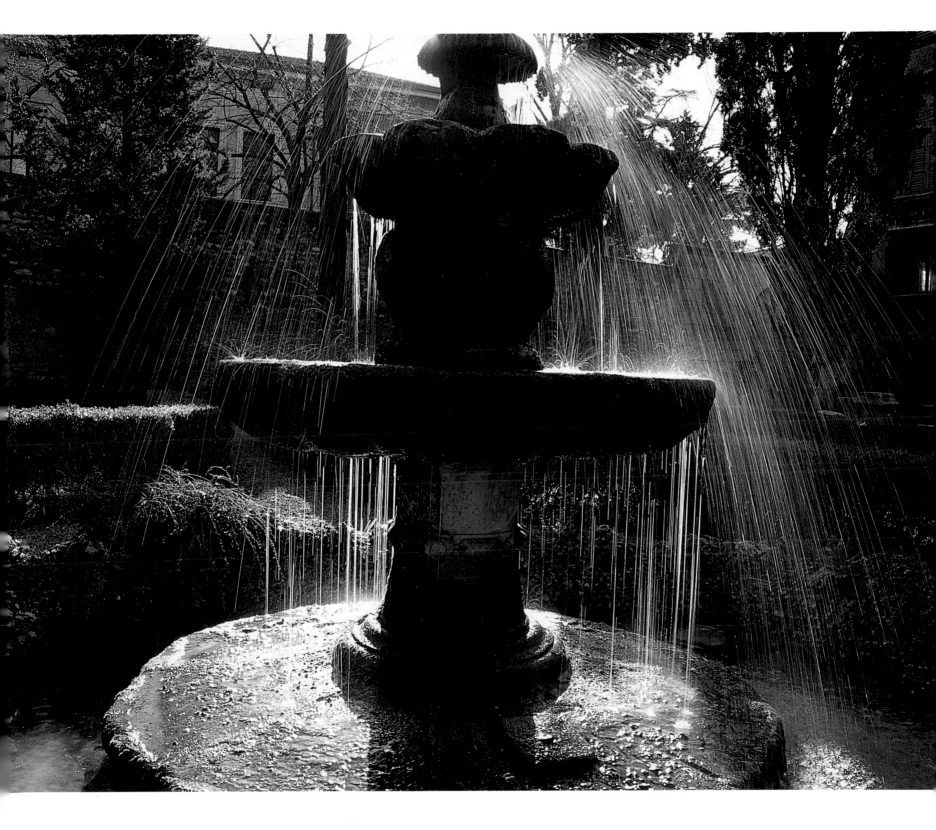

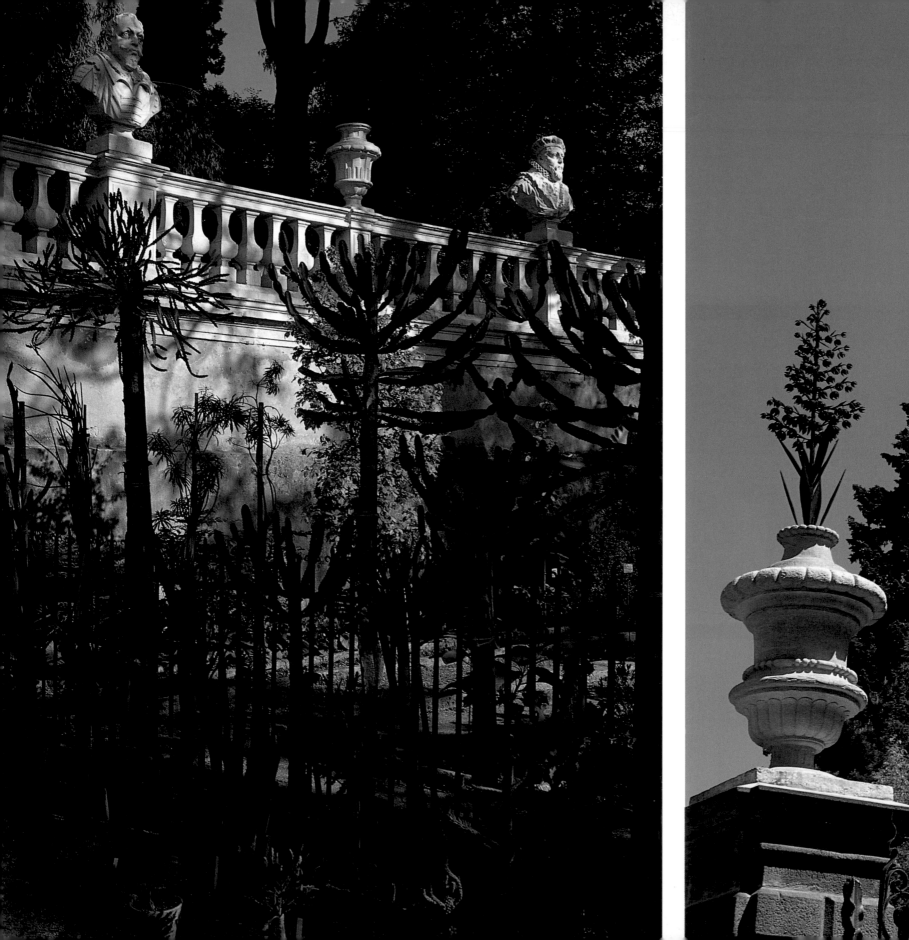

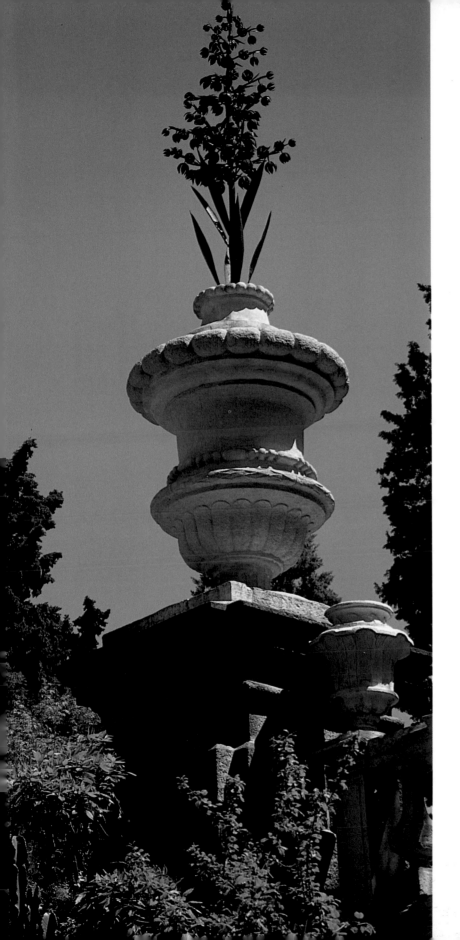

PADUA BOTANIC GARDEN

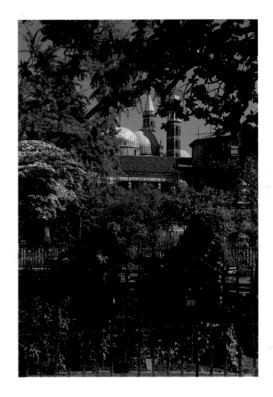

THE OTHER CITY GARDEN OF RENOWN IN THE VENETO, scarcely less old than the Giusti Gardens, is the distinctively round and entirely flat Botanic Garden of Padua; it is supposed to be the oldest botanic garden in the world. Only a stone's throw from the Prato della Valle, and surrounded by Padua's 'narrow canals', it is further enhanced by the spectacular backdrop of Padua's landmark basilica, Sant' Antonio, lately obscured by the current Italian craze for construction. The garden reverberates with the sound of energetic drilling, as deafening as the excited shrieks of the Italian schoolchildren who pour into the grounds daily.

ABOVE *The basilica of Sant' Antonio, which provided a dramatic setting when the garden was first planted, is barely visible today.*
FAR LEFT *A balustrade tops the wall that encloses the* hortus cinctus.
LEFT *Vases containing ironwork yuccas are the garden's hallmark.*

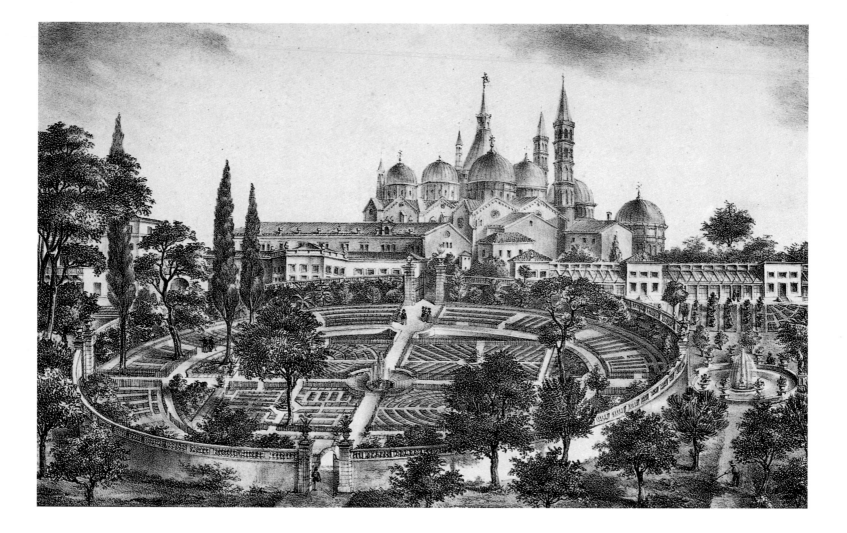

The Padua Botanic Garden was conceived and planned by the Venetian nobleman Daniele Barbaro, and his ideas were executed by the architect Giovanni Moroni da Bergamo, in 1545, for the purpose of serious botanical study to accompany the founding of the first chair of science at Padua University. Its most celebrated 'student' was Goethe, who here met up with his 'palm', which was famously to inspire his essay on the morphology of plants. It is not only the garden's celebrity plant, but also the oldest, since a fungal infection brought about the demise of the previously oldest incumbent, *Vitex agnus-castus* (the chaste tree), twenty-five years ago, still mourned by the garden staff as if it were yesterday. Younger by a substantial eighty years, Goethe's palm is housed like a giraffe in a tall greenhouse built protectively around it.

Edith Wharton was always delighted to find a garden that 'kept something of its ancient savor'; and inside the walls it is exactly as she described it: 'a large circular space enclosed by a beautiful old brick wall surmounted by a marble balustrade and adorned alternately with busts and statues'. The whole of the *hortus cinctus*, the circular garden, has a wide bed running along its circumference, and, in the middle, a square divided into four quadrants bisected by two alleys oriented to the cardinal points, marking the entrances to the garden. This square is the *hortus simplicium*, the Garden of Simples, which at first grew only medicinal plants from which to study pure remedies from nature. Initially, each of these quadrants was intricately designed in a different graceful geometrical star or circle pattern, laid out with stone-edged beds in which a different species of medicinal herb was grown. Each bed was identified numerically on a master plan – a concept that was both decorative and scientific. The very unsimple designs with which the 'simples' were arranged have been changed over the years but the basic layout remains the same.

Into this *hortus simplicium* came John Evelyn, having walked across the Prato della Valle. He was so enchanted by the different species that he 'gave order to the gardener to make me a collection of them for an *hortus hyemalis* (also *hortus siccus*) by permission of the Cavalier Professor of Botany'. The dried plants accompanied him as he laboured over the Simplon Pass astride a mule on his return to England.

In 1704 the four entrances to the garden were made more ornate by new gates topped with urns 'planted' with flowering yuccas fashioned in metal. To match these embellishments a marble balustrade was added, topped with busts of the many curators of the garden. The fountain to the east gate is dedicated to the Four Seasons and the wise King Solomon; the fountain to the south gate to Theophrastus – the student of Aristotle, best known for his ironic seminal studies into 'character', but also the author of the nine-volume *Historia Plantarum* as well as a further six volumes on the aetiology of plants, *De Causis Plantarum*.

Outside the *hortus cinctus* was an arboretum, the planting of which began in 1760; and many of its trees, including magnolias and *Ginkgo biloba*, are still there. When Goethe arrived twenty-six years later he found it a 'cheerful garden', with many plants staying in the ground all through the winter if planted near the brick walls. 'But towards the end of October, the place is roofed over and kept heated during the short winter months.' Greenhouses and a botanical theatre were built early in the nineteenth century.

Coming from Weimar in Germany, Goethe had never seen such variety, and noted that 'to wander among a vegetation which is new to one is pleasant and instructive. It is the same with familiar plants as with other familiar objects: in the end we cease to think about them at all. But what is seeing without thinking? Here, where I am confronted with a great variety of plants, my hypothesis that it might be possible to derive all plant forms from one original plant becomes clearer to me and more exciting.' His careful study of the peculiar structure of the *Chamaerops humilis* palm prompted his theory that all plants derive from the germ of a 'primal plant', which he was forever hopeful of finding.

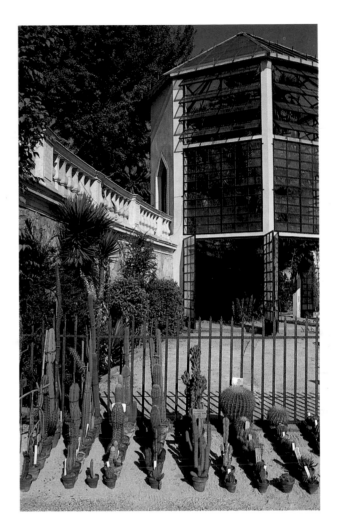

ABOVE *The hexagonal greenhouse containing Goethe's palm,* Chamaerops humilis *var.* arborescens, *echoes the shape of the garden's central fountain. Close to the east gate cacti and succulents enjoy a bake in the sun.*

OPPOSITE *In Andrea Tosini's lithograph of 1835 the domes and spires of Sant' Antonio appear like a panoramic stage set behind the garden. 'The wall', Wharton wrote, 'is broken by four gateways, one forming the principal entrance . . . the other three opening on semicircles in which statues are set against a background of foliage.' Originally, the walled garden was laid out as a complicated mosaic, impossible to maintain, but much else of the original structure – the square, divided into quadrants within an enclosed circular space – survives.*

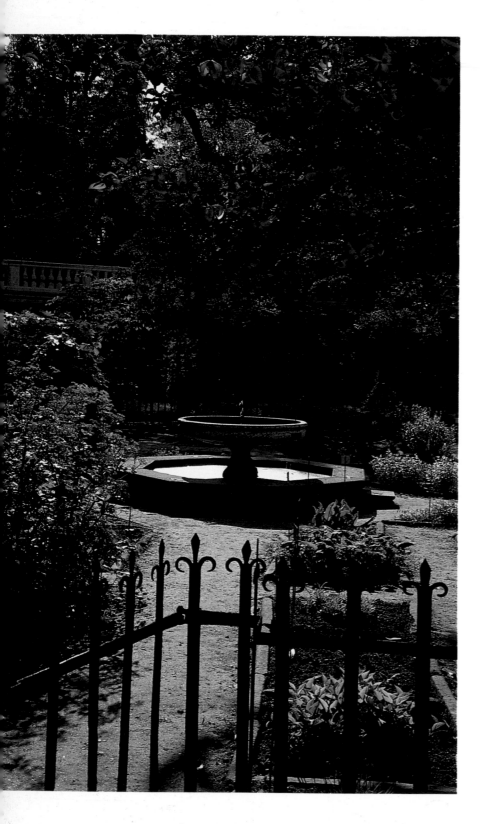

Over the years, the garden was steadily enriched with plants from all over the world, especially those countries with strong political or commercial links with the Veneto. The establishment of a library, herbarium and laboratories have enabled the garden to play an important role in the introduction and study of many exotic plants.

In addition to the 'simples', the garden contains a wide variety of rare specimens and plant collections. Majestic swamp cypresses (*Taxodium distichum*) and a magnolia thought to have been planted in the eighteenth century are among the rare and long-surviving trees. There are poisonous plants whose degree of toxicity is indicated, Alice in Wonderland style, by the number of black crosses on their labels. Indigenous plants from the Euganean hills include tree heathers and broom, while olives and holm oaks represent the Mediterranean maquis. Aquatics flourish, such as *Victoria cruziana*, the giant water lily from the quiet backwaters of the Amazon, which develops its enormous floating foliage platters alongside tanks containing lotus (*Nelumbo nucifera*) and water lilies grown to decorate the pool beneath the Fountain of Theophrastus. Glasshouses built in the early nineteenth century are home to orchids, ferns and carnivorous plants.

There is also a garden for the blind, with textured and aromatic plants, labelled in braille. For the deaf and hard of hearing the garden is a peaceful haven. It closes at six o'clock, just as the drilling stops outside.

LEFT *A fountain within one of the quadrants of the Garden of Simples. 'In the garden itself the beds for "simples"', Wharton noted, 'are enclosed in low iron railings, within which they are again subdivided by stone edgings, each subdivision containing a different species of plant.'*

OPPOSITE *Since its beginnings as a garden for medicinal plants, the Padua Botanic Garden's collection has been expanded to include a vast number of species from all over the world. These include a peony collection (top), seen here beside the stone-edged beds noted by Wharton; Chinese palm trees, Trachycarpus fortunei (centre), planted in the alley leading to the west gate; and aquatic plants (below), including Cyperus papyrus and tropical and exotic water lilies grown in ponds fed by an artesian well – all immaculately tended by the gardeners.*

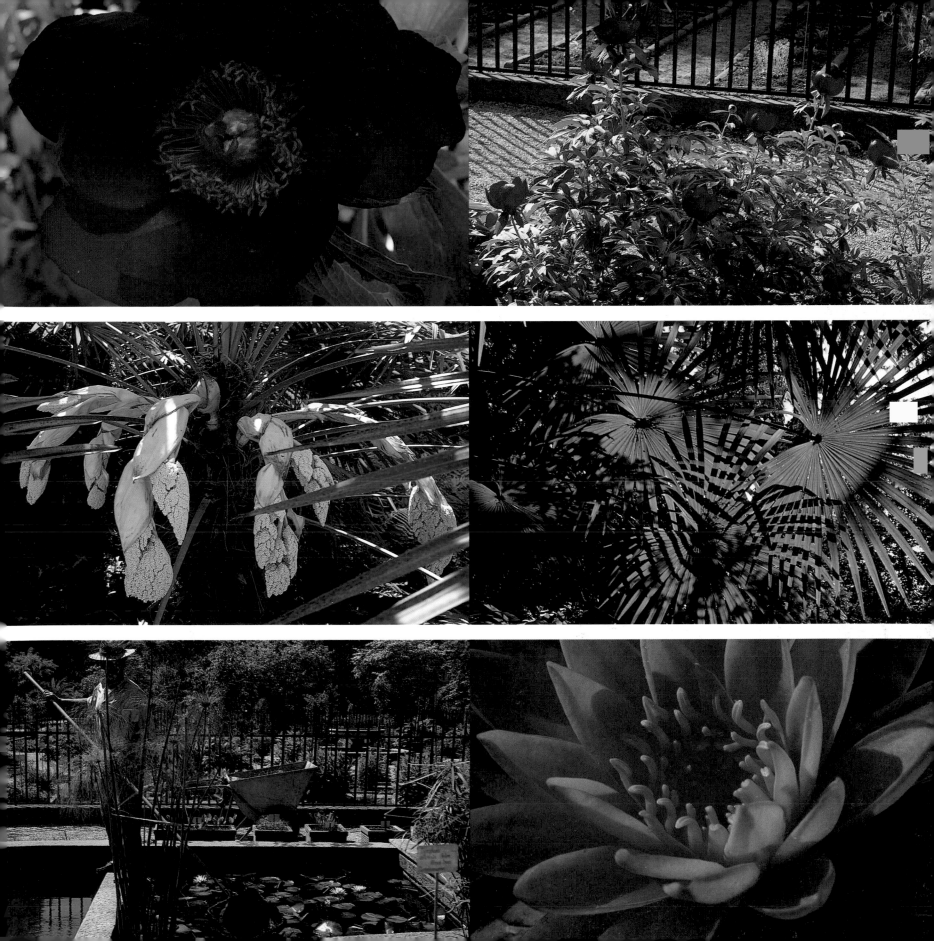

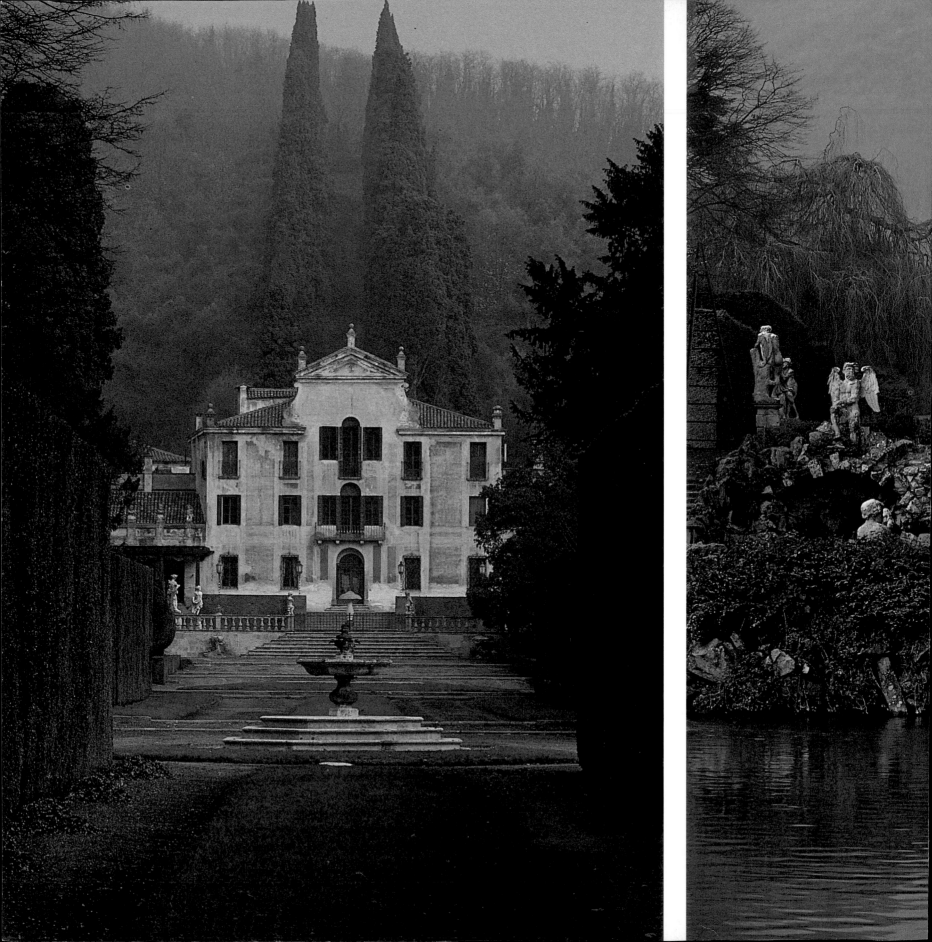

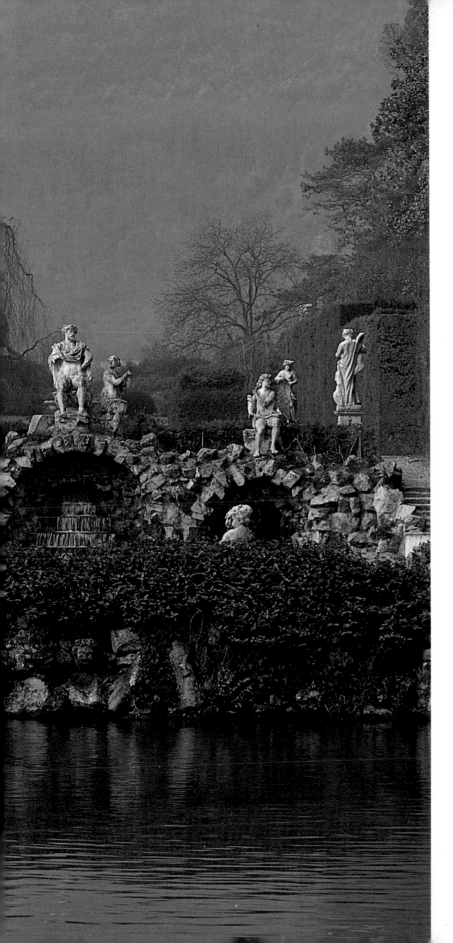

VALSANZIBIO

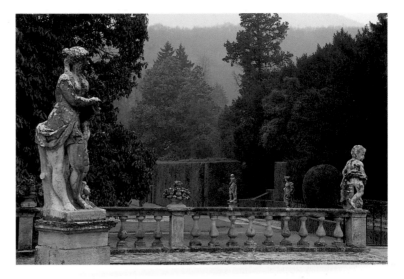

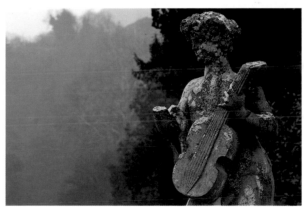

The villa sits at the top of the north-south axis of the garden at
Valsanzibio, facing the Fountain of Pila and the Fountain of the Mushroom.
A double avenue of cypresses carries the eye beyond the house to the top of
the hill (far left). From the villa's balustraded terrace there is a view over the
tapis vert bordered by beech hedges (top). On the terrace (in the centre of which
is the Fountain of the Mushroom) are four statues, two of which are visible
here: on the left is Abundance and, holding a violin, is Pleasure (above).
The garden's second axis runs from east to west and is formed by a
prospettiva d'acqua, which culminates in the Fountain of the Winds,
presided over by Aeolus, Zephyr, Borea and Deiopea (left).

THE 'LOVELY INTRICATE GARDENS' of Valsanzibio are amongst the few that Edith Wharton mentions in her autobiography, written thirty-five years after her visit. Just how intricate they really are she could not possibly have known. They were spun into a complex allegorical web nearly 350 years ago and their meaning lost with time and the passing of the garden from one family to another. The present owner, Count Fabio Pizzoni Ardemani, was eight years old when his parents bought the property in 1929, and since inheriting it from his elder brother in 1985 he has devoted himself to the complete restoration of the garden and all its fountains and to unravelling the clues to its broader and deeper meaning. It is to him that this sphinx-like garden has finally revealed her secrets.

The property of Valsanzibio comprises a valley and the surrounding lower reaches of the Euganean hills. It dates back to the fourteenth century, when it was owned by various families, including the famous Venetian Contarini; since then its boundaries have shrunk and expanded with the vicissitudes of marriages, inheritances and changes of fortune. But the real story of the garden as we know it today began in 1630, when the plague hit Venice, wiping out a large percentage of the population, and the Venetian nobleman Zane Francesco Barbarigo removed his family to the safety of their country estate at Valsanzibio. This prompted him to enlarge the villa and begin to think about developing the garden, which at the time consisted only of a *giardino segreto* in front of the house. The rest of the property was devoted to orchards, woodland and two *peschiere* stocked with fish. His elder son, Gregorio, became a priest and renounced his right of inheritance in favour of his much younger brother Antonio, who idolized him.

Gregorio Barbarigo was a childhood friend of Cardinal Fabio Chigi, and when Chigi became Pope Alexander VII in 1655, he asked Barbarigo, by then Bishop of Padua, to become his secretary. During his years as secretary to the Pope, Barbarigo commissioned a Roman architect, possibly Bernini's brother, to design a garden for him next door to the Pope's garden at the Quirinale, which he named the Garden of the Four Fountains – now a road of the same name. Obviously passionate about water, he asked the same Roman architect to design him a garden at Valsanzibio, with water as its theme – abundantly provided by sources in the hills. Without ever having visited the site, the architect drew up plans according to Barbarigo's instructions and specifications. An oil painting of this

idealized garden shows how elaborate it was.

In accordance with strict laws of proportion, twenty-four squares made up the configuration of the garden. The Barbarigo brothers, Gregorio and Antonio, who worked closely together and corresponded voluminously on every aspect of the garden, proceeded with its execution around 1660. It was inaugurated nine years later. Based on the three essential elements of the Italian garden – water, stonework and evergreens – the biaxial design consisted of a north-south axis which descended from the hills, through the villa, continuing as a long *tapis vert*, hedged by beeches, to the end of the garden. Punctuated with two fountains and water jets, this avenue had a principally 'evergreen' character. Valsanzibio was one of the earliest gardens to put into practice the laws of perspective that had been developed in Renaissance painting and the *tapis vert* avenue became progressively narrower as it left the house to make it seem longer.

An east-west axis, which ran like a transept, took water as a theme, and, incorporating the two fishponds which had been dug two centuries before, embellished them with statues. The scheme was further punctuated with fountains, water tricks and cascades that rose gently in succession and carried the eye into the hills. This ensemble formed a *prospettiva d'acqua* which featured a water theatre given depth and distance. On either side of these two avenues, each of the garden 'squares' had a different theme or purpose, inspired by features from the gardens of Imperial Rome. These included a maze, a *leporarium* (where rabbits were kept), aviaries and a theatre-in-the-green. Along the boundary, the 'squares' were sometimes joined together when more land was required for orchards or game reserves.

Taken superficially, the garden could be viewed, as Wharton deemed it, as 'one of the most beautiful pleasure grounds in Italy', but it is more than that: Gregorio Barbarigo wove a symbolic tale into the architectural fabric of his garden. Both the themed 'squares' and the statues are strategically placed, each one a message bearer identified by an inscription and positioned to relate to the whole. In no other garden has Wharton's guiding maxim of discovering 'the meaning of things and their relation to each other' been expressed with more subtlety and sophistication.

At the time Gregorio and Antonio Barbarigo made the garden, the Church was in the throes of conflict with Renaissance ideals propounded by the Neoplatonists, who looked to classical Greece

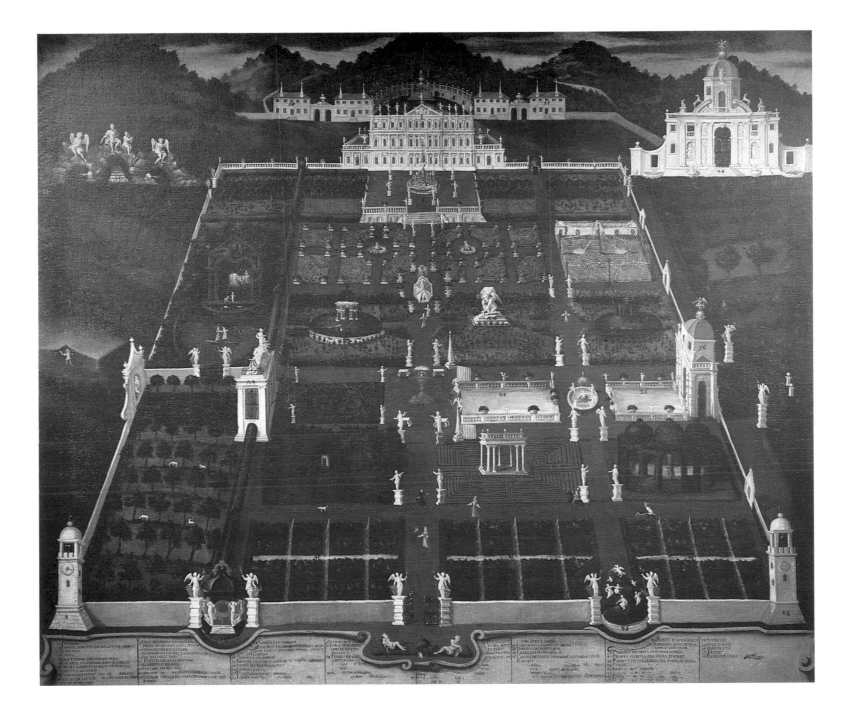

An idealized seventeenth-century painted plan of the garden by an unknown artist shows the position of its main features, although the whole of the bottom half and the left-hand arch were never built. The garden's complicated Christian message is told in its carefully considered layout and its statues and fountains, which were designed to be seen in a specific order. Diana's Gate, once the garden's main entrance, is below the fishponds. Below them is the labyrinth. A large statue of Time is visible at the fulcrum of the garden and near it is the leporarium, inhabited by rabbits in warm weather.

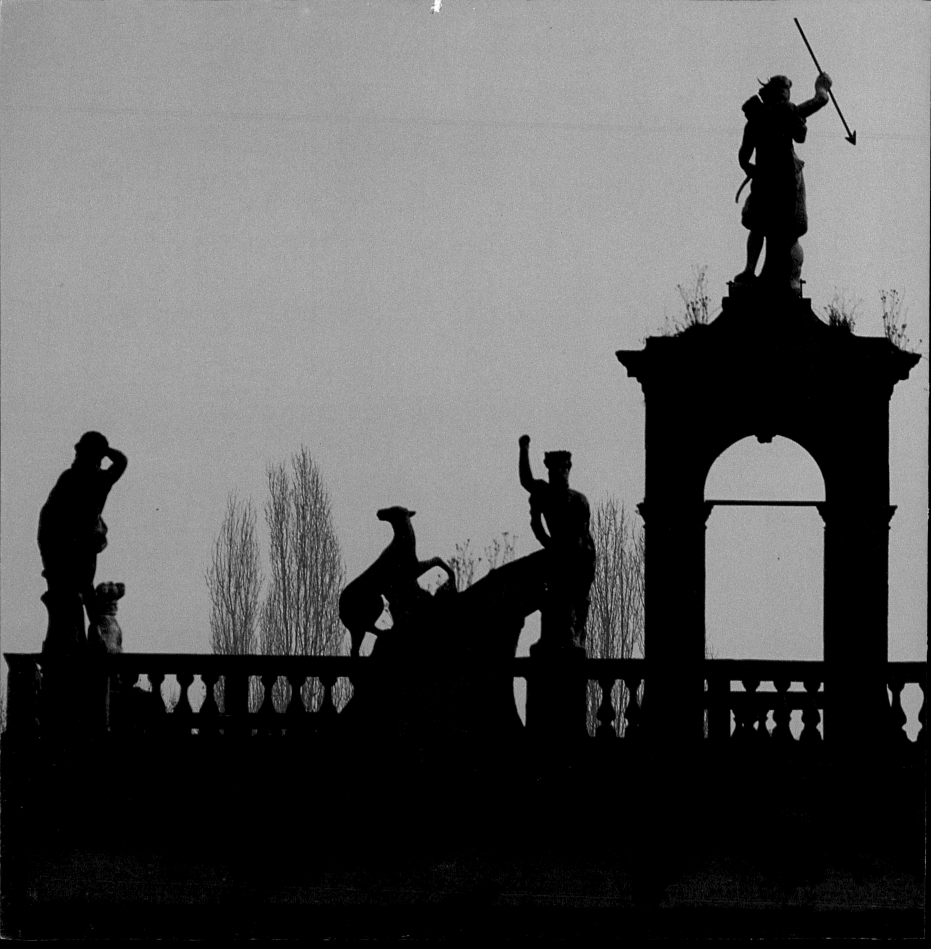

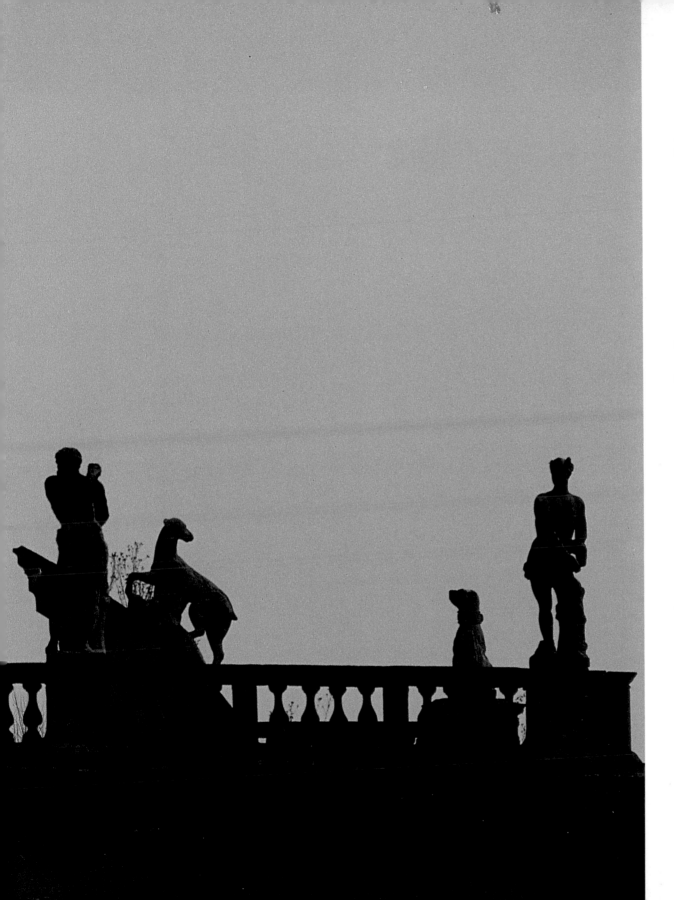

Visitors in the sixteenth and seventeenth
centuries would have entered the garden
from the river through Diana's Gate, designed
to give a magnificent first impression and lead
the eye through to wonder beyond. On top of
the gate are statues of Apollo, Jupiter, Diana,
Hercules and Mercury (all false gods),
two greyhounds and two bull mastiffs.
The golden statue of Fame that once crowned
it blew off in a hurricane. The gate is as a
starting point in a journey from the pagan
to the Christian world.
The garden's message is given in a sonnet
engraved on the scalinata. The first verse
echoes a similar poem inscribed on the pedestal
of a sphinx at Bomarzo; the middle two verses
refer to the seven planets, mentioned in Dante's
Divine Comedy *as a prelude to Paradise; and
the last reflects the attainment of Paradise.*

❧

You that curious arrive and every part
explore to find beautiful things and rare
observe and tell if one does really appear
that by nature its all and not by art

Here distributes a brighter SUN its dart
VENUS more beautiful leaves the sea right here
Here the MOON has mutations much more clear
His fury MARS cannot till here impart

SATURN once here his offspring no more
crunches
Here JUPITER succours serene and wide
To all his frauds here MERCURY renounces

Here always smiles but never tears arise
The lightening of the court here never bounces
The hell is there and here is Paradise.

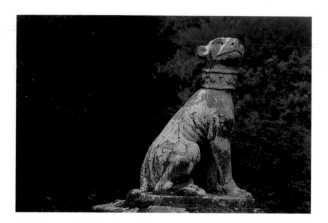

A bull mastiff on top of Diana's Gate turns his
head away from the north (representing Martin
Luther and the Reformation) towards the south
(the Vatican in Rome). Diana's Gate (below) is
the starting point for the prospettiva d'acqua
(right). In the foreground, two river gods pour
water into Diana's Bath, which then flows
through the circular Fountain of the Rainbow and
continues to the Fountain of the Winds beyond.

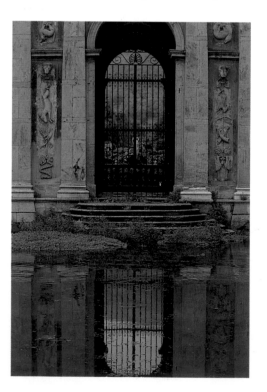

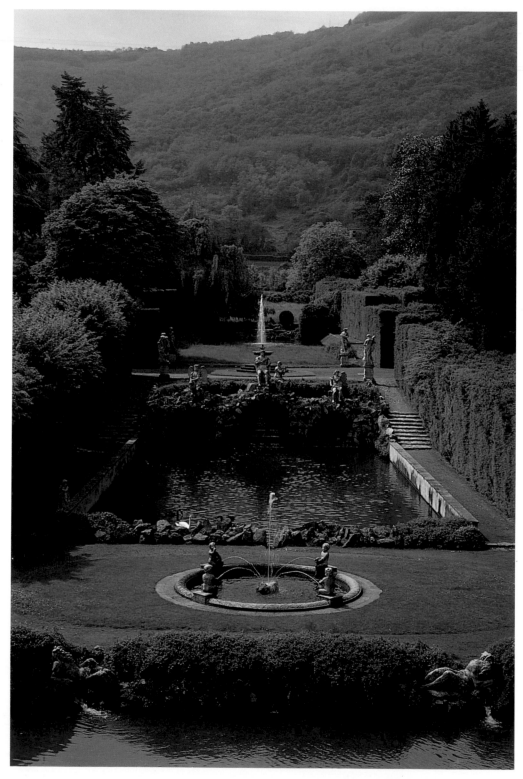

and Rome for inspiration. The Counter-Reformation associated ancient Rome and its mythological gods with the pagan world. In 1566 Pope Pius V had many of the pagan statues removed from the Belvedere Court at the Vatican. Yet at the same time, only a few miles away from Villa Lante, the most flagrantly pagan garden in Italy was being created by an iconoclastic aristocrat, Vicino Orsini. Its grotesque monsters and horrifying scenes represented a frightening, disturbing and bizarre underworld, which visitors stumbled through by an unprescribed and uncharted route, eventually reaching a temple at the top of a valley. The garden's message was that Redemption was through love, not God. This was the garden of Bomarzo, which needless to say did not please the Catholic Church.

Valsanzibio was conceived as the antithesis to Bomarzo, in deliberate homage to San Carlo Borromeo. Gregorio Barbarigo and San Carlo, although born one century apart, were both Bishop of Bergamo for a time, and this gave Barbarigo the opportunity to study Borromeo's uncompromising doctrines. Barbarigo held him up as an example of virtue, and like him founded a seminary. His original wish was to become a monk, and this is represented by the 'hermitage' across from the labyrinth. So self-effacing was he that he twice refused an offer of the papacy. Only too well aware of the deeply subversive Bomarzo, and in homage to his hero, Barbarigo animated his garden with the spirit of Christianity.

The first stanza of the sonnet inscribed on the *scalinata* of Valsanzibio sets out the meaning of the whole garden and is, to the last syllable, a deliberate parody and play on the words of the verse on the pedestal of the sphinx which greets the visitor at the entrance to Bomarzo. Whereas Bomarzo represents a haphazard wandering through an underworld that explores the dark forces of life, where there is no clear path and you may or may not find your way out, the path in Valsanzibio is clearly set out: the further you move away from the fallibility of pagan mythology exemplified in Diana's Gate at the entrance to the garden, the more sophisticated and intelligent the experience becomes until you reach the *scalinata*, which are on the threshold of Paradise, represented by the Fountain of the Mushroom. Before you reach Paradise there is a final obstacle of two leopards – a reference to one that almost caused Dante to turn back at the end of his journey. However, they have been temporarily distracted by their thirst so you can slip through to the upper terrace while they drink the water dripping from the basins.

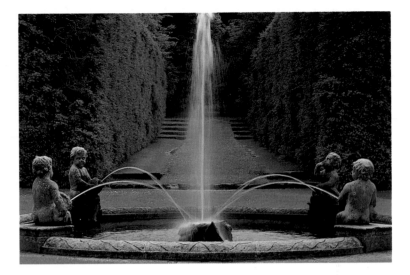

At the Fountain of the Rainbow (above), originally called the Fountain of the Swan because there was a swan at its centre, visitors could turn from the prospettiva d'acqua to the labyrinth hidden behind the hedge. As an allegory of life's experiences, those who choose the right path – that of virtue – will find their way through the maze. On their exit, they will find the Fountain of Pila and (below) statues of Mercury and Argus (in the foreground), a many-eyed giant shepherd who represents human wisdom and stands guard over his captives. Mercury symbolizes Gregorio Barbarigo himself. As the mediator between the human and the divine, he lulls Argus to sleep with his music, enabling people to pass him as he dozes. Thus, the Church triumphs over the pagan world.

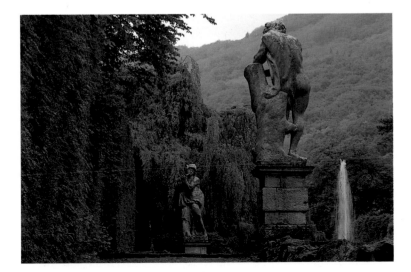

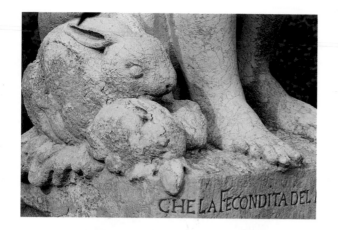

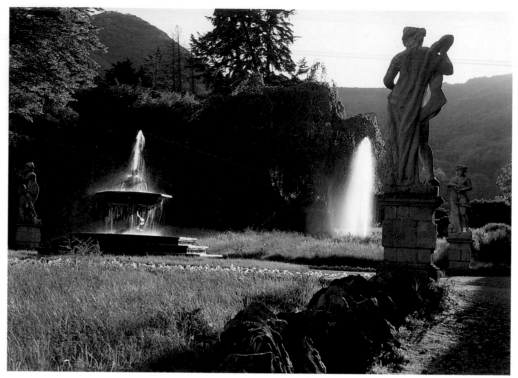

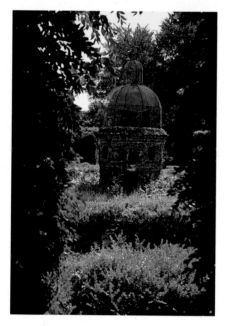

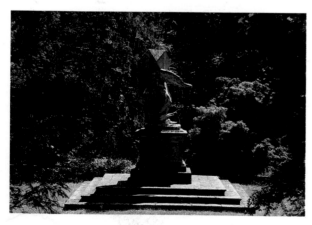

THIS PAGE *Health and Fecundity complete the group of statues surrounding the Fountain of Pila (above). Fecundity, who represents the perpetuation of human life through earthly reproduction, is personified as a woman with rabbits at her feet (detail left, top). The theme of rabbits is echoed in the* leporarium *positioned nearby, in which live rabbits hop about an island (left centre). The statue of Time (left below), referred to as Saturn in the sonnet, serves as a counterpoint to Fecundity, reminding the spectator that human mortality can only be transcended through cultivation of the spiritual. He leans on an hourglass, his wings spread, but he is anchored to the ground by the weight of the block on his shoulder. He turns his face away from the pagan (represented by the view towards Diana's Gate) towards the Church (symbolized by the villa and its Paradise terrace).*

FACING PAGE *The Putti Fountain (top), the source of playful* scherzi d'acqua, *is the last pagan obstacle to be negotiated before the ascent of the* scalinata *that represents the final stage in the journey. The words of the sonnet that provides the key to unlock the mystery of the entire garden are inscribed on its steps (far right centre). At the foot of the staircase, the thirsty leopards guarding Dante's peaceful Paradise, represented by the upper terrace, drink from dripping basins (far right below).*

The Fountain of the Mushroom (right below) sits in the centre of the terrace, symbolizing the ecstasy brought by enlightenment. The theme of pleasurable attainment is amplified by statues on the terrace that represent Quiet, Joyfulness, Pleasure, Virtue, Abundance, Free Will, Solitude and Beauty.

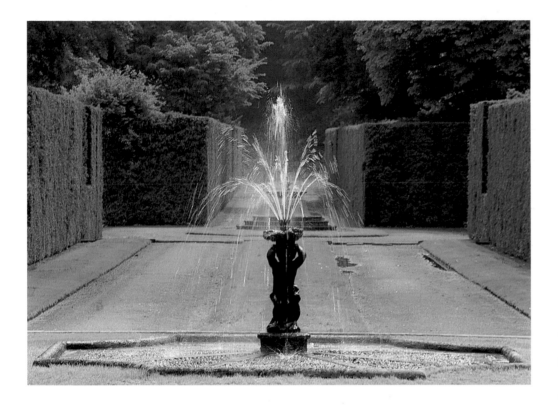

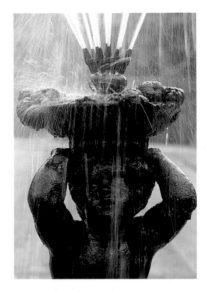

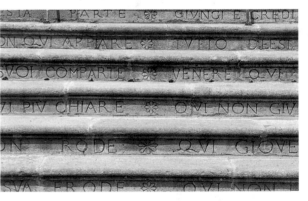

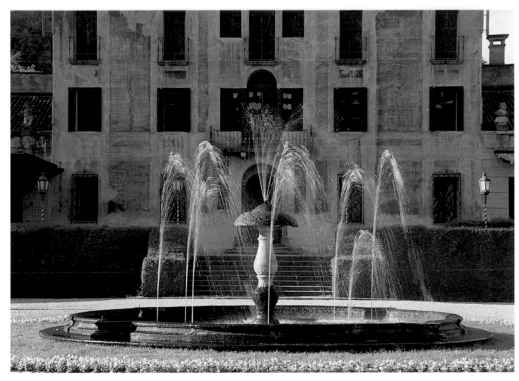

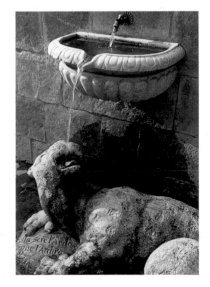

VILLA CUZZANO

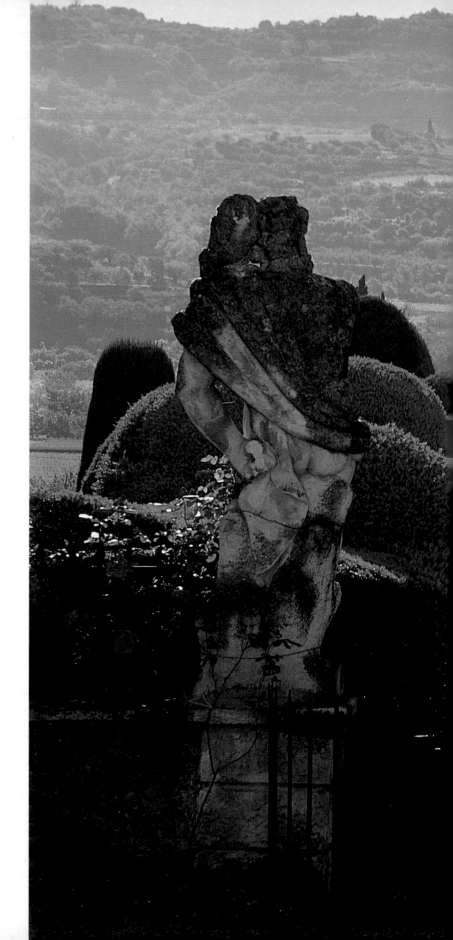

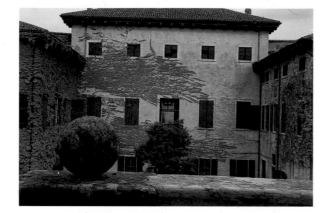

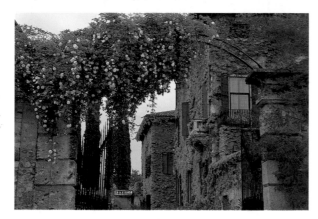

The view to the courtyard from the little church at Villa Cuzzano (top) pleased Edith Wharton, who commended its 'careful placing . . . exactly on an axis with the central saloon of the villa, so that, standing in the chapel, one looks across the court, through this lofty saloon, and out onto the beautiful hilly landscape beyond. It was by such means that the villa-architects obtained, with simple materials and in a limited space, impressions of distance, and sensations of the unexpected . . .' The chapel was built by the Allegri family to commemorate San Carlo Borromeo's visit on his way back from the Council of Trent in 1563.

The archway overhung with Rosa banksiae (above) leads the eye past the two wings of the villa to the view beyond. From the parterre, the tapis vert culminates in cypresses, which, like everything Italian, have developed their own character with time. Once the drive went between them and up to the gate, where it stopped; now it winds round the villa.

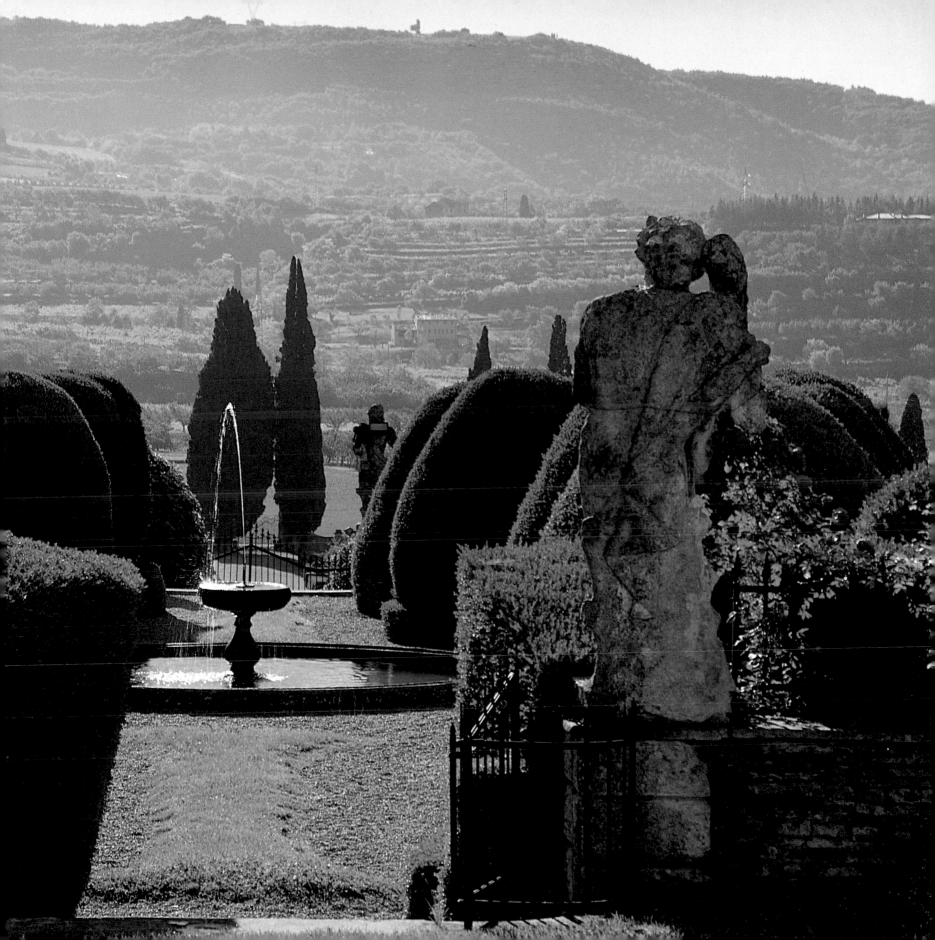

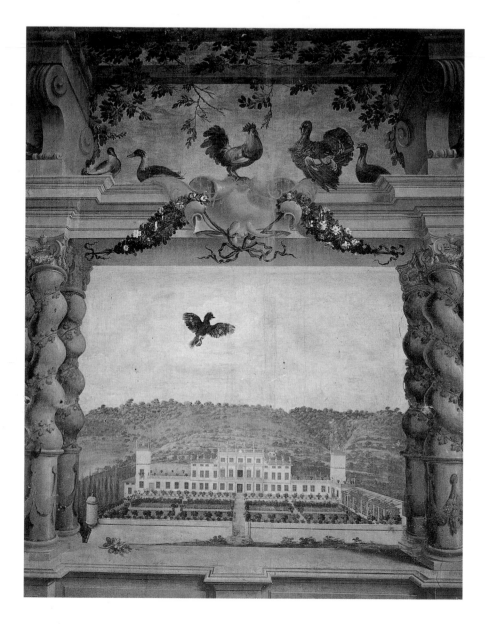

ABOVE *An eighteenth-century fresco in the villa shows that the parterre had a geometric layout before it was transformed with swirling* broderies.

OPPOSITE *The villa is flanked by twin turrets, reminiscent of the Villa Aldobrandini. From the grassy terrace in front there are views over the parterre and the farmland beyond. Sir Geoffrey Jellicoe remarked that as the parterre is the sole interest of the garden it 'becomes rich and complicated'. It requires much maintenance: gardeners hoe the gravel in the time-honoured way and old wood is cut from inside the topiary to regenerate growth.*

EDITH WHARTON WAS DELIGHTED TO DISCOVER that only seven miles (11.25 kilometres) away from the transformed Giusti Gardens, just north of Verona, students of Italian garden architecture would find 'a beautiful old house standing above a terrace garden planted with an elaborate *parterre à broderie*': the Villa Cuzzano.

The parterre is the principal focus in the garden of this agricultural property, and it was made as decorative and dramatic as possible. Designed to be viewed from above, the best vantage point from which to admire the swirling design of its *broderie*, it was also meant to be enjoyed at ground level from the grassy terrace that runs between the parterre and the villa.

Its arabesque design was far removed from the strict geometric forms of Roman parterres and probably owes something to the example of French gardens. The curving shapes also melted into the flowing lines of the vineyards that followed the contours of the undulating landscape surrounding it. Completely open to the landscape, the garden, observed Sir Geoffrey Jellicoe, following Wharton twenty years later, was like 'a great airy salon'. There was space everywhere.

The estate has produced olive oil and wine since the fifteenth century. The original battlemented palace was replaced by the present villa, built to the design of the architect and sculptor G. B. Bianchi towards the middle of the seventeenth century. The Allegri family sold it in 1842 to Giovanni Antonio Arvedi of Verona, whose descendants still own it today. Like the Barbarigo, the Arvedi also had a religious, vigorously anti-pagan acolyte of San Carlo Borromeo. In this instance it was a nun, the daughter of Giovanni Arvedi, Lucidalba, who founded her own order, the Arvediane, which she housed in another of the family's villas. When their numbers dwindled to five, her order was absorbed into a larger one. She condemned all the mythological statues that stood in the niches of the courtyard and on top of the balustrade of her father's villa as 'pagan' and had them thrown into the river. They were subsequently found lying on the riverbed and were retrieved and restored to their original positions around the villa.

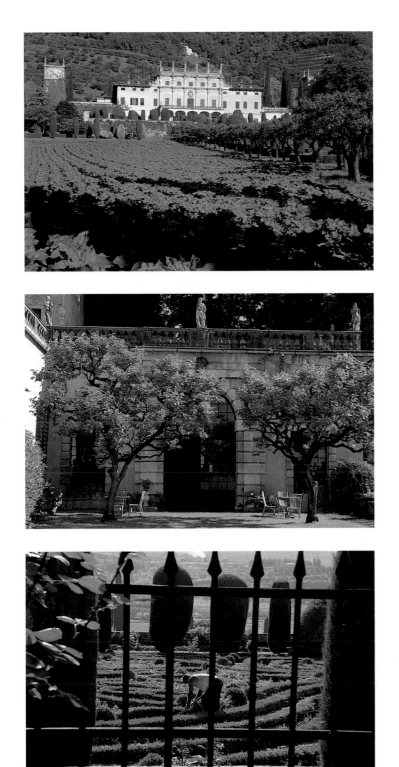

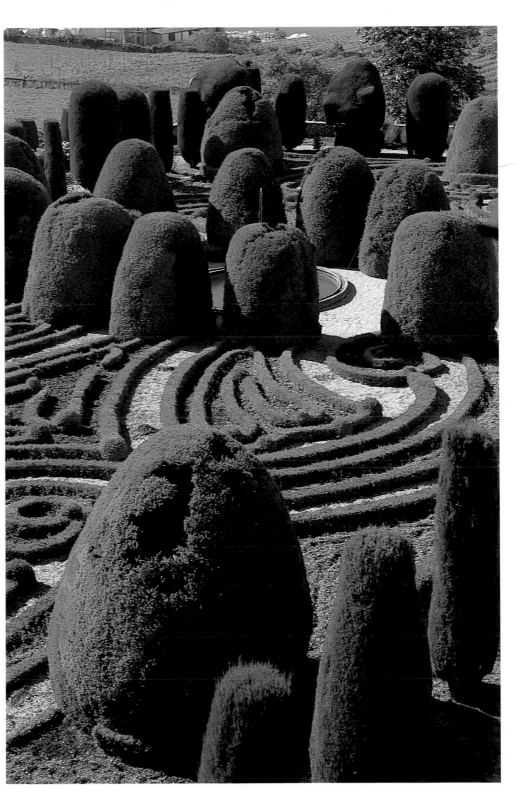

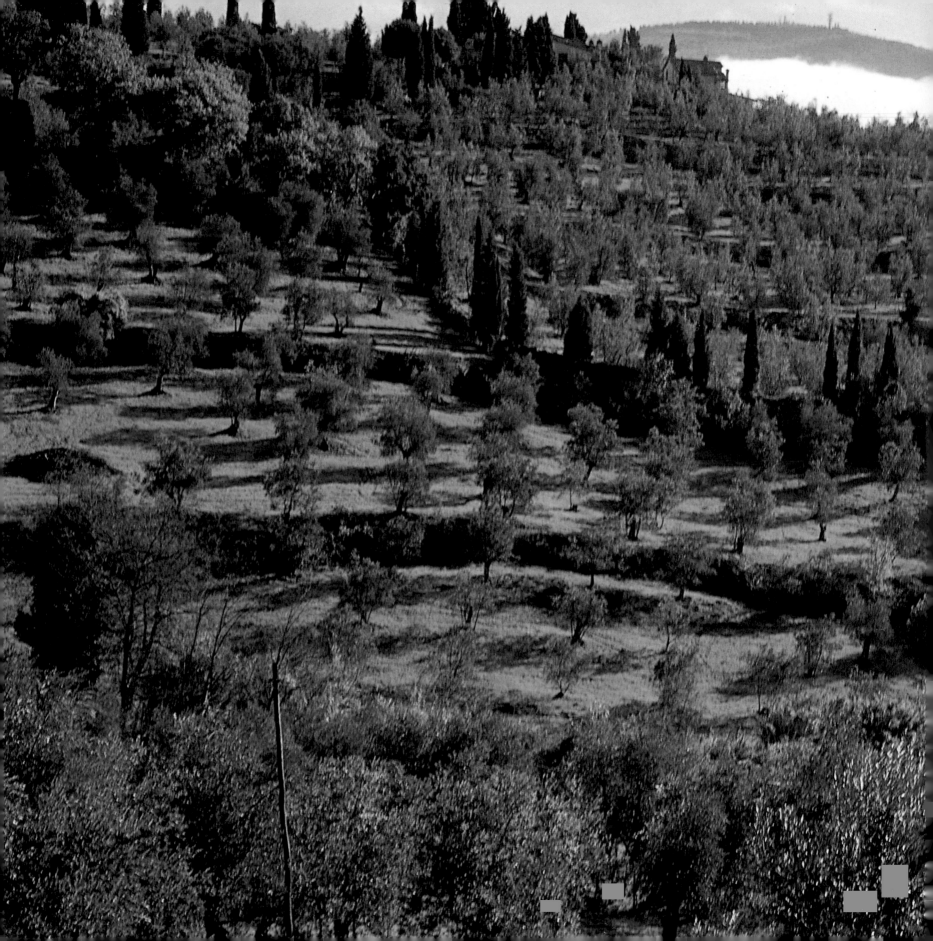

GARDENS NEAR FLORENCE

OR CENTURIES Florence has been celebrated for her villa-clad hills,' wrote Edith Wharton. 'According to an old chronicler, the country houses were more splendid than those in the town, and stood so close-set among their olive orchards and vineyards that the traveller "thought himself in Florence three leagues before reaching the city".' She went on to explain: 'It is perhaps owing to the fact that Florence was so long under the dominion of one all-powerful family that there is so little variety in her pleasure-houses. Pratolino, Poggio a Caiano, Cafagiuolo, Careggi, Castello and Petraia, one and all, whatever their origin, soon passed into the possessorship of the Medici . . .'

If the Florentines' history is anything to go by, without the Medici Florence may not have had any gardens at all and would not have made so significant a contribution to the early Renaissance. The Florentines were volatile, fickle in loyalties but never in grudges. An incident of scorned love, whose reprisal was murder, set off the war between the Guelphs and the Ghibellines which divided Florence into two camps, lasted decades and drove Dante, a Guelph, into exile, never to return.

The Medici family rose to power in the fifteenth century through their influence over the Vatican, cultivating their position as the Pope's bankers and tax collectors, and controlling the Vatican's valuable alum mines. By and large the Medici made enlightened use of their wealth, but none were as illustrious and as cultured as Cosimo the Elder and his grandson Lorenzo the Magnificent. Cosimo the Elder, born in 1389, fifteen years after Petrarch's death, eagerly responded to the panegyric hymns to nature of Petrarch and Boccaccio (Florentine poet and author of the *Decameron*), derived from their passion for the countryside and Plato's ideas about life. He instigated the humanist movement, in which nature, philosophy and gardens became one

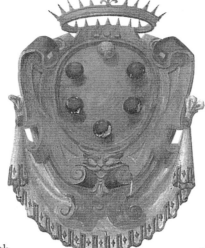

and by pruning his own vines he established the Medici tradition of doing much of their gardening themselves. Like Pliny, he regarded his garden as a place to cultivate his soul. 'Yesterday I arrived at Careggi,' he wrote to a friend, 'not so much with the object of improving my gardens as myself . . . do not forget to bring with you the book of our friend Plato . . . for there is nothing that I desire so ardently as to find out the true road to happiness.'

The essential elements of the Italian garden found their way to Florence and Rome through Greece, where they had been introduced from Persia. The Greek Xenophon had visited the fabulous gardens of the oriental kings, where he found water, plane trees, aromatic shrubs and fruit trees. These and other elements were incorporated into Greek gardens, and made cerebral when Plato taught philosophy in the garden of his Academy. Lorenzo the Magnificent revived Plato's idea by founding a school in a garden in Florence for promising young artists.

Ruling like benevolent despots, the Medici family presided over Florence's political and cultural fortunes more or less continuously for over three hundred turbulent years, weathering the plots that were constantly afoot to overthrow them. No sooner were they thrown out, than a movement was under way to reinstate them. Successive civil wars between the most powerful Italian states – Naples, Venice, Milan and the Vatican, all attempting to swallow up one another or fight off French, Spanish and Turkish invasions – created chaos and unspecified acts of barbarism, tolerated and often perpetuated by patrons of some of the greatest art ever produced. Only the yoke of the Medici could prevent total anarchy while at the same time promoting Florence's artistic character.

It was inevitable that the treachery and high drama that was part of Florentine daily life would be expressed elsewhere. In a

PREVIOUS PAGES *The view from across terraced olive groves from the Villa Gamberaia perfectly illustrates Wharton's point that 'It is . . . typical of the old Tuscan villa that the farm or* podere *should come up to the edge of the terrace on which the house stands.' Morning mist has yet to lift from the valley beyond.*
OPPOSITE *A rainbow over Florence. The Medici family, whose coat of arms is shown here (above), were always under a thundercloud, opposed by many, such as Savonarola, who ranted about 'the sword of the Lord in a darkened sky over Florence'.*

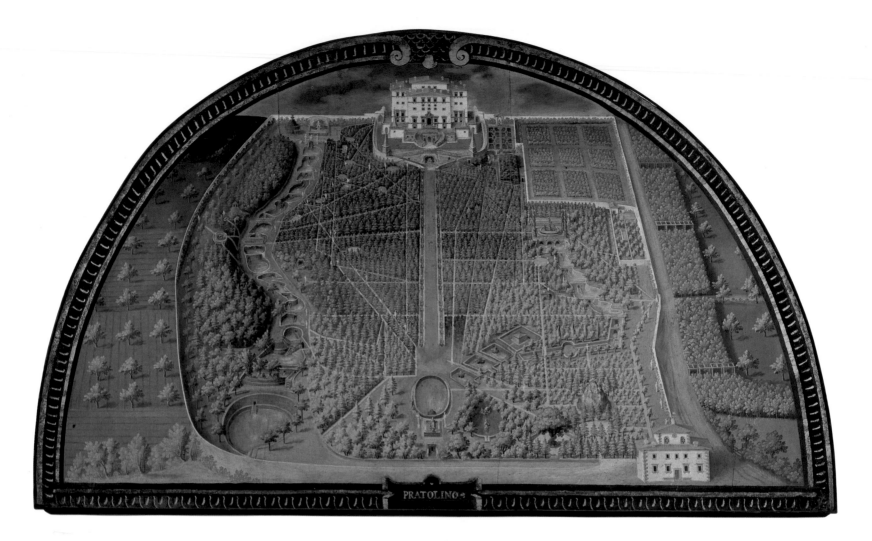

PRATOLINO

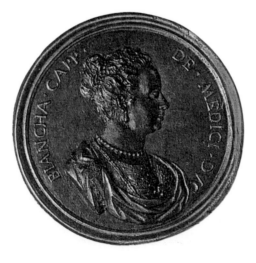

Commissioned by Grand Duke Francesco I de' Medici for the amusement of Bianca Cappelli (right), Pratolino, as Giusto Utens's lunette of 1599 (above) shows, was designed by Buontalenti around a central axis: a long avenue extending from the palace on the crest of a hill to the bottom of the park. It celebrated water in a most inventive way. John Evelyn describes 'a large walk at the sides of whereof gushes out of imperceptible pipes . . . this canopy or arch of water was I thought one of the most surprising magnificences I had ever seen, and exceedingly fresh during the heat of summer'. 'At the end of the walk', Montaigne recalled, 'is a fair fountain discharging itself into a great basin through a marble statue, carved in the similitude of a woman starching linen. Below is another vessel to contain the hot water for making the starch.' Giovanni Guerra's drawing of 1604 (opposite, above) shows a pergola of water.

But in 1819 the villa's foundations, the waterworks and all but one of the grottoes were destroyed, and the statues were broken up, stolen or used to fill cisterns. The only surviving feature is Giambologna's statue of the Apennines (opposite, below), which Evelyn described as 50 feet (15 metres) tall 'having in his body a pretty square chamber, his eyes and mouth serving for the windows and doors'.

society infused with deception, the Florentines, and the Medici in particular, were no less inventive in elaborate plots to murder one another. It was said that the cuckolded husband of Isabella de' Medici (Grand Duke Francesco I de' Medici's sister) pretended to kiss her one evening while accomplices lowered a rope from the ceiling and strangled her. The rope was pulled up again and he raised the alarm, claiming that she had died of apoplectic seizure. A thwarted plot to murder Pope Leo X was to apply poisoned bandages to his anal fistula. Another scheme involved setting a barrier of swords and daggers just below the surface of the water where Duke Cosimo I de' Medici plunged into the River Arno every day for his swim. The Florentines were also renowned for their sense of occasion and theatrical scenery, seen in the fantastic triumphal arches they made to welcome brides; in the fake cathedral façade made for victorious Pope Leo X; and in the pageants at the Boboli Gardens, unmatched for invention and wizardry.

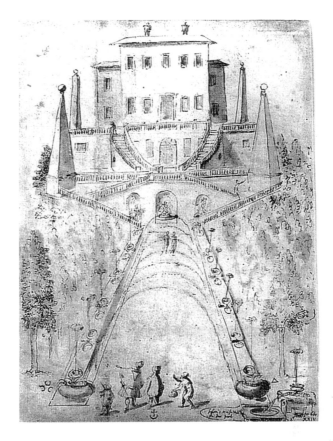

The Medici applied all their wit, trickery and sense of drama to their garden designs. And in no garden was the spirit of machination and imagination better employed than at Pratolino, which the Grand Duke Francesco I commissioned from Buontalenti from 1569 to amuse his mistress Bianca Cappelli (who later became his second wife). Amongst the first Mannerist gardens to reflect the desires of the owner in its design, as opposed to slavishly obeying classical laws of proportion and seeing the garden solely in relation to the house, it was conceived around the natural contours of the land, as an entirely magical place.

Built only twenty years after the Villa d'Este at Tivoli, Pratolino, which was fed by twelve springs, also celebrated water in a most inventive way. Jupiter sat at the top of the garden in his guise as a god of rain; water shot out from his thunderbolt and flowed down in cascades and pools. 'The Gardens', wrote John Evelyn, 'are delicious and full of fountains. In a grove sits Pan feeding his flock, the Water making a melodious sound through his pipe & Hercules whose Club yields a Shower of water, which falling into a huge Conch has a naked woman riding on the backs of dolphins.' One of the grottoes was described by Montaigne: 'Not only is music and harmony made to sound by water power; statues move and doors open, animals dive and drink by a single movement, the whole grotto can be filled with water, and all the seats will squirt water over your breech.' Alas, the ingenious Pratolino was razed to the ground in 1819 because it was too expensive to maintain.

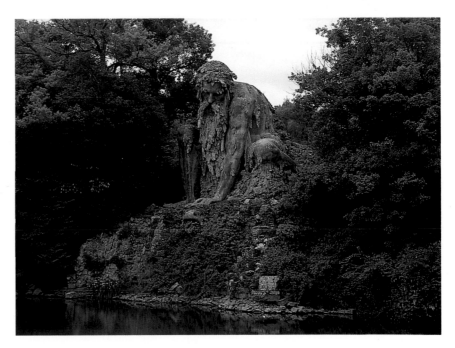

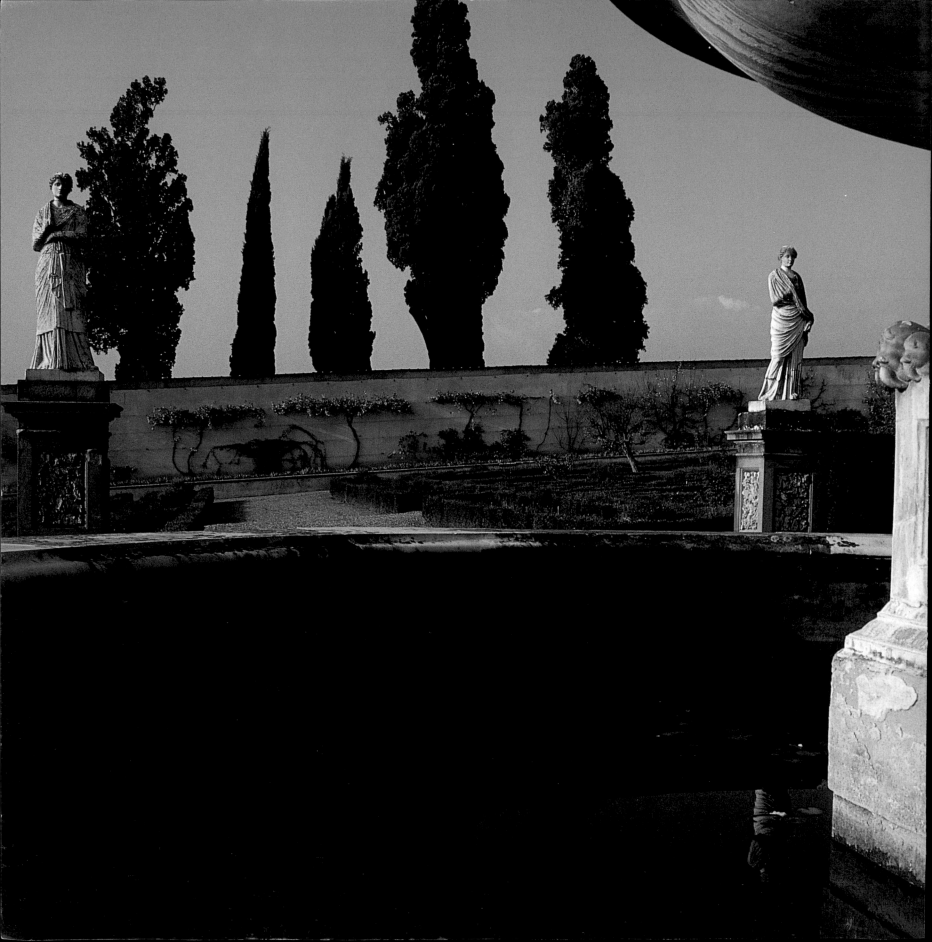

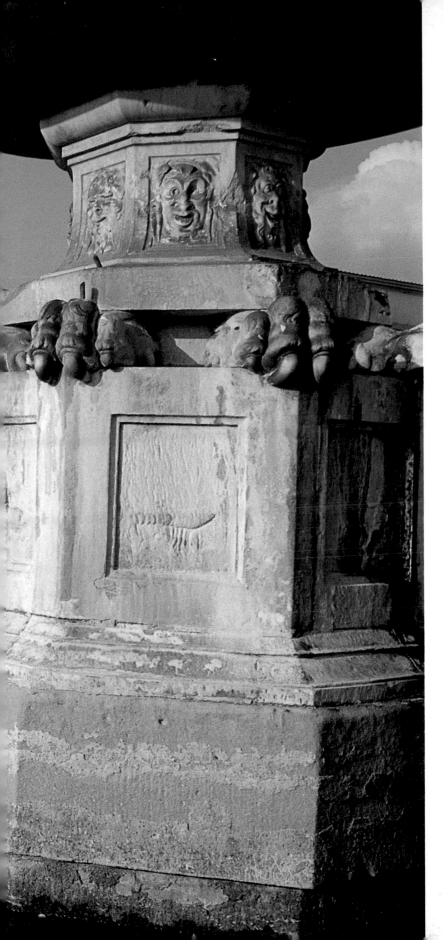

VILLA CASTELLO

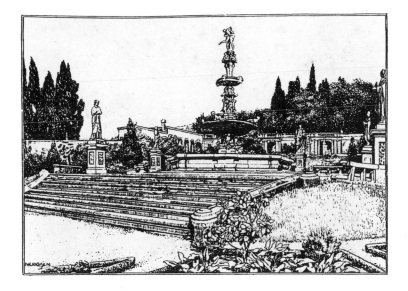

'Wide steps', noted Wharton, 'lead up to the first terrace, where
Il Tribolo's stately fountain of bronze and marble stands surrounded by
marble benches and statues on fine rusticated pedestals.' This was the
Fountain of Hercules (left), the centrepiece of the garden's fountains. Only
the base, including the lion's claws on which seven marble putti once sat,
remains. The top, now gone, was made by Giambologna and Ammannati,
using Tribolo's models, and can be seen in Nelly Erichsen's 1901 illustration
(above) from Florentine Villas by Janet Ross. The fountain was built in three
tiers. One was decorated with goats symbolizing Duke Cosimo I, with spiral
tails instead of hind legs, who spat water into the basin; another had putti
queezing out of the mouths of geese water which ran over the rim of the basin.
It was crowned with a representation of one of Hercules's many labours, the
truggle with the giant Antaeus, who was invincible only if he touched earth.
Hercules lifted him into the air, as the Duke lifted water from the earth, and
his life, as water, was crushed out of Antaeus's body and flew out of his
mouth in an enormous jet. Janet Ross tells us that the fountain was
'surrounded with statues of ladies and gentlemen of the Medici family; but
their drapery is so tightly drawn round them in stiff straight folds that
they resemble far more one's idea of Roman senators and their wives'.

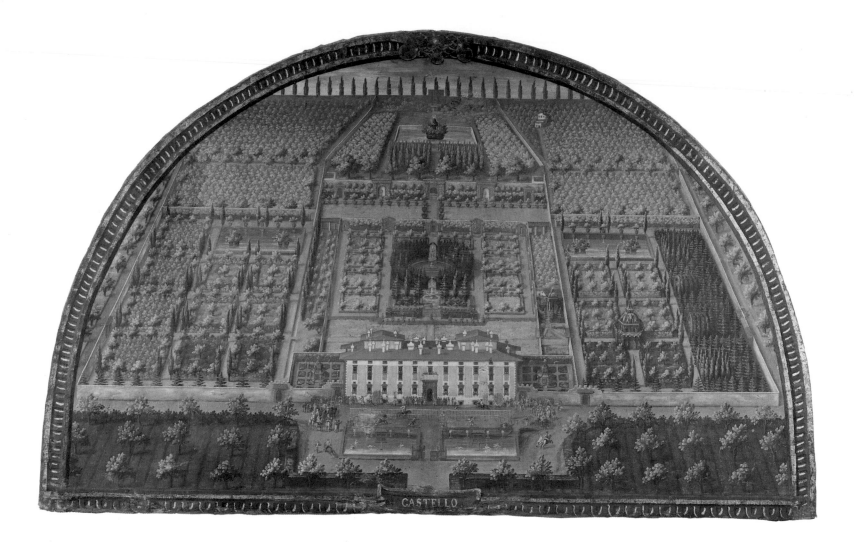

CASTELLO

The garden was to be a topographical representation of a miniature Tuscany from the top of the Apennines to the Arno valley – given life and fertility by Duke Cosimo I. Utens's lunette of 1599 shows how Tribolo's varied and ingenious use of water began at the very top of the garden with a lake. From this the water descended into a Lemon Garden, whose retaining wall contained a grotto flanked by two statues, never completed, celebrating the sources of the water for the garden: the Rivers Arno and Mugnone, personified, with water pouring from their mouths and wrung from their beards. Their fame as river sources was, however, later eclipsed by Ammannati's great statue of the Apennines (opposite), sculpted after Tribolo's death and personifying their perennially snowy heights. Water that sprang from a cap on top of his head continually dowsed him with cold water and kept him shivering.

THE VILLA CASTELLO, situated on the lower slopes of Monte Murello, 3 miles (4.8 kilometres) out of Florence, was bought in 1477 by a young relation of Cosimo the Elder and Lorenzo the Magnificent, Lorenzo di Pierfrancesco de' Medici, with his brother Giovanni. Lorenzo di Pierfrancesco was the greatest patron of Botticelli, who is said to have painted *Primavera* in celebration of Lorenzo's imminent May marriage. It seems that Botticelli's inspiration for his flowery mead in his *Primavera* was a description from Boccaccio's *Decameron*, which, though based on the Villa Palmieri in Florence, greatly resembles the garden that was to be made at the Villa Castello: 'In the midst of this garden was something which they praised even more than all the rest: this was a lawn of very fine grass, so green that it seemed nearly black, coloured with perhaps a thousand kinds of flowers. This lawn was shut in with very green citrus and orange trees . . . and in the midst of this lawn was a fountain of very white marble most marvellously carved. A figure standing on a column in the midst of this fountain threw water high up in the air, which fell back into a crystal-clear basin with a delicious sound . . .'

The transformation of the garden from the flowery mead of Boccaccio and Botticelli did not take place, however, until the next century, after the Medici had experienced the trials and tribulations of the siege of Florence, the mad monk Savonarola, conspiracies and weak leadership, which all contributed to their banishment from Florence in 1494. Lorenzo di Pierfrancesco took the Medici arms off the walls of the Villa Castello and changed the family name to Popolano. It was Duke Cosimo I de' Medici who made the Medici illustrious again and the garden of the Villa Castello their flagship.

Duke Cosimo I was baptized by his great-uncle and godfather, Pope Leo X, to 'revive the memory of the wisest, the bravest and the most prudent man yet born to the house of Medici' and chosen as duke in 1537. Water was the new Duke's element. 'A man is not powerful until he is as powerful by sea as by land,' he declared as he ordered a fleet of galleys to be built, which in 1571 would prove extremely useful to Pope Pius V in his Battle of Lepanto against the Ottomans. The Duke further expressed his affinity with water by building two enormous aqueducts into Florence, providing the city's citizens with clean drinking water. And so it followed that the two great gardens which he initiated, the Villa Castello and the Boboli Gardens in Florence, would celebrate his aqueducts and naval achievements.

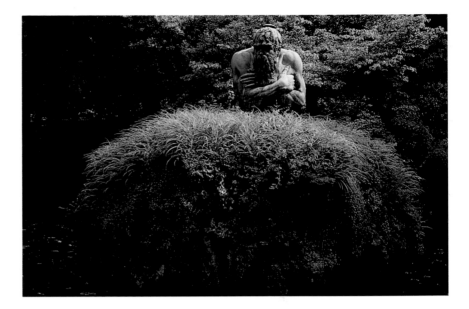

Almost immediately after his election, Duke Cosimo I called upon his favourite sculptor, Niccolò Tribolo, to bring water to the top of the slope, and to devise a garden around sculpture and fountains. It was to be one of the earliest Renaissance gardens with a coherent iconographical scheme. Two aqueducts were needed to provide enough water and pressure to service Tribolo's elaborate plan of fountains, grottoes, water jets, sculpture, fishponds and canals. Had it all been carried out, it would have extended by another mile and a half and would have been, proclaimed the architect Vasari who took over the garden following Tribolo's death in 1550, 'the most magnificent and ornate garden in Europe'. However, much of the garden has since been destroyed by thoughtless alterations.

The water descended from a lake at the top of the garden, through a Lemon Garden directly below it (well protected from north winds), whose retaining wall contained a grotto flanked by two statues: one of Fiesole pouring water into a vase held by the River Arno, the other of Monte Asinaio pouring water into a vase held by the River Mugnone. These were the two main sources of water for the garden. The niches in the retaining wall were decorated with stalactites to reinforce their wild and rustic origins. From the grotto the water continued into the neighbouring Labryinth Garden, which had a Fountain of Venus in its centre. Immediately below the labyrinth was the Fountain of Hercules.

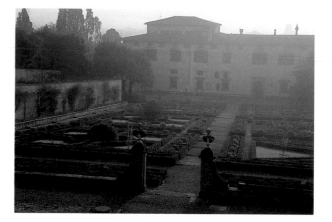

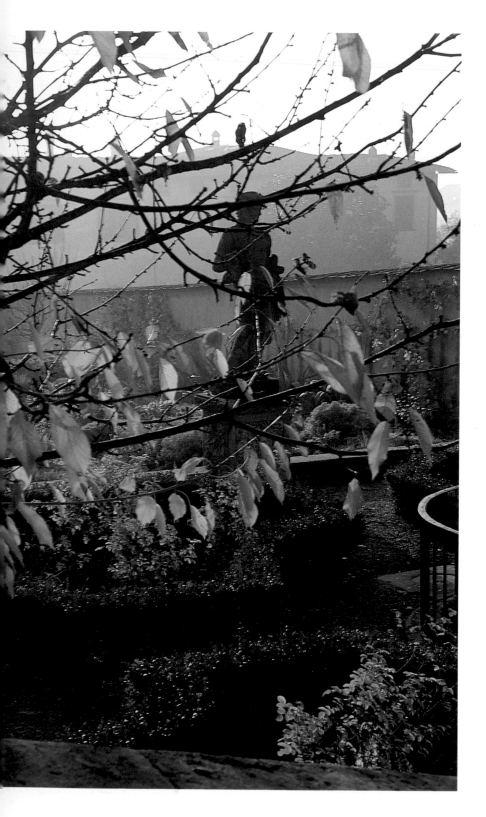

It was said that this fountain was without precedent at the time. It was built in three tiers, crowned with a representation of Hercules struggling with the giant Antaeus. For the volume and the pressure necessary for its amazing effects, a whole aqueduct had to be built to bring water from the Medici-owned Villa Petraia further up the hillside. Edith Wharton objected to the 'preternatural whiteness' of the sculpture, which was meant to stand out in stark contrast to the *bosco* at the top of the garden and the dark green of the cypresses, which had been dug up when she saw it. The water then passed into the fishponds at the front of the villa, already there when the garden was laid out, and was meant to have continued to the Arno, in an entirely novel way, as a pair of canals on either side of an avenue of mulberry trees.

As the French botanist Pierre Belon noted when he visited the garden in 1546, providing the fountains made the plants possible. The Lemon Garden became home to 600 varieties of citrus fruits, and the Duke himself planted roses, the flower of Venus, outside the labyrinth. The box parterres were planted with fruit trees and the walls espaliered with pomegranates and oranges. Outside the inner walls, to the east of the garden, was a *giardino segreto* containing medicinal herbs, sent from the botanical gardens of Pisa – which Duke Cosimo I founded – and Padua.

The garden at the Villa Castello took nearly forty years to build, and during that time Duke Cosimo I became preoccupied with making the Boboli Gardens; but after his second marriage in 1570 (his first wife died in 1562), he retired to the Villa Castello, where he took up the cultivation of jasmine for his remaining years until his death in 1574.

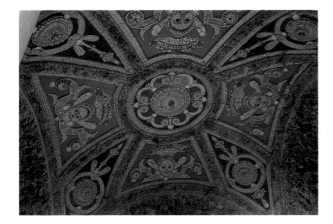

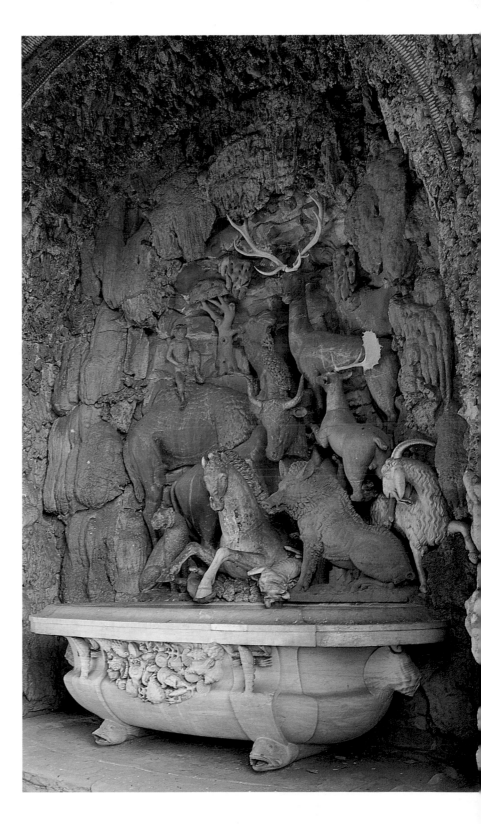

OPPOSITE *One of the parterres to the side of the villa (left), beyond which lies the giardino segreto (far left). A statue of Aesculapius, the god of healing, stands in the centre of the giardino segreto, a garden of medicinal herbs – on the right-hand side of Utens's lunette (page 110).*

ABOVE AND RIGHT *The use of the grotto in Italian gardens, Wharton reflected, 'is a natural development of the need for shade and coolness, and when the long-disused waterworks were playing, and cool streams gushed over quivering beds of fern into the marble tanks, these retreats must have formed a delicious contrast to the outer glare of the garden'. She described how in the one at Castello, 'As is usual in Italian gardens built against a hillside, the retaining-wall at the back serves for the great decorative motive', within an opening in which is 'one of those huge grottoes which for two centuries or more were the delight of Italian garden-architects. The roof is decorated with masks and arabesques in coloured shell-work, and in the niches of the tufa of which the background is formed are strange groups of life-sized animals.' In one niche, in a basin carved with fish and shells (right), was a menagerie of horse, fallow deer, dromedary and other animals. In the other niches were a hierarchical collection of animals that symbolized associations with the Medici. A unicorn, for example, who purifies water by dipping his horn into it, represented Duke Cosimo I, bringing health to Florence through the gift of pure water; a rhinoceros was associated with Duke Alessandro, after whose assassination Cosimo I had been made duke. A giraffe recalled a gift from the Sultan of Babylon to Lorenzo the Magnificent which had excited so much interest it was sent round to the convents to gratify the curiosity of the nuns. 'The creature . . . pokes its nose into every peasant's basket,' wrote Tribaldo de' Rossi, 'and is so gentle that it will take an apple from a child's hand. But it died . . . and everybody was sorry for the beautiful spotted giraffe.'*

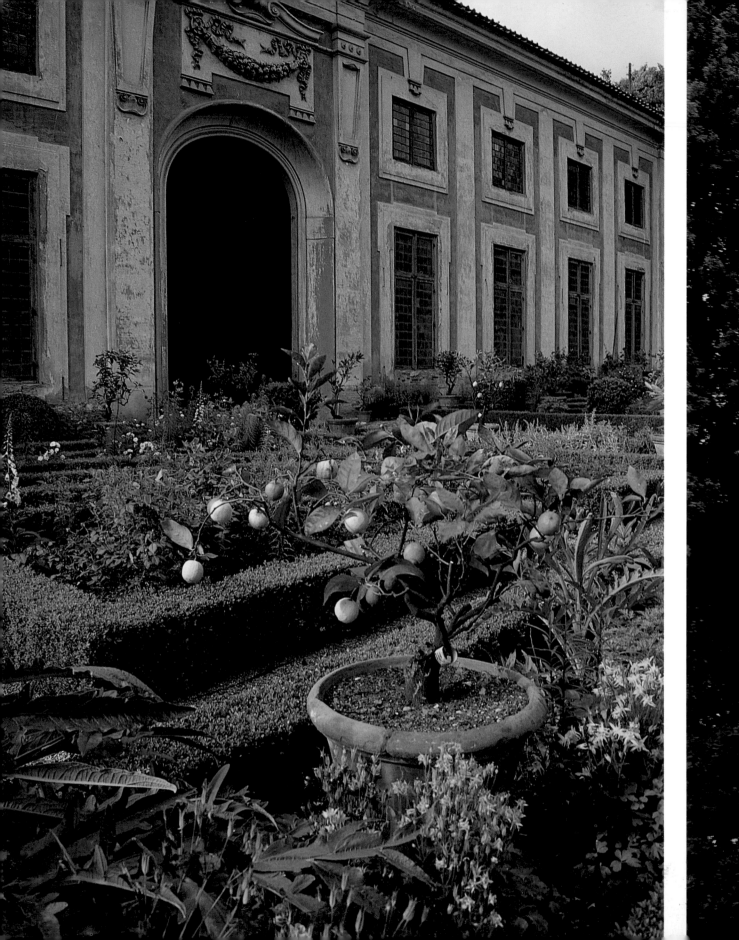

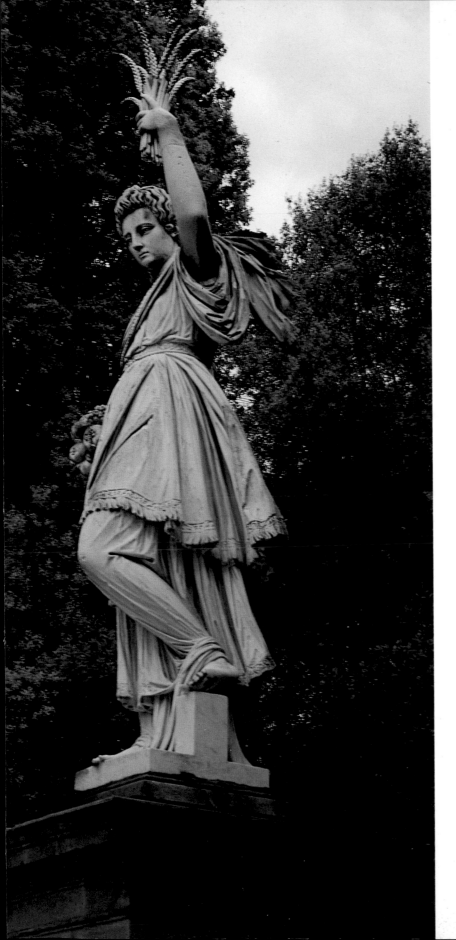

BOBOLI GARDENS

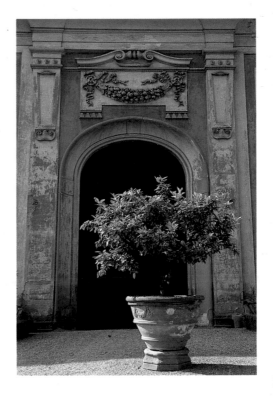

ABOVE AND FAR LEFT *By 1785 Grand Duke Pietro Leopoldo of Lorraine had transformed what was previously a little zoo and animal keeper's house into a hothouse for orange and lemon trees from the island garden of the Isolotto, and created a garden in front of it. The mint and cream building was designed by Zanobi del Rosso.*

LEFT *This statue was supposed to have been modelled on Joanna of Austria, who married Grand Duke Francesco I de' Medici, but she died before it was completed. It was then decided that it would be transformed into a symbol of Abundance, to flatter the Grand Duke's reign. It was taken over by Giambologna, who made a lifesize wax model of Joanna's face, but he also died, in 1608. Work was resumed twenty-eight years later by Giambologna's pupil Tacca, who left the wax model out in the August sun and it melted – so nobody knows whose face is on the statue. It was finally erected in the Boboli Gardens in 1636, after a plan to mount it on top of a marble column in St Mark's Square was abandoned when the supporting beam rotted and the column fell over and broke.*

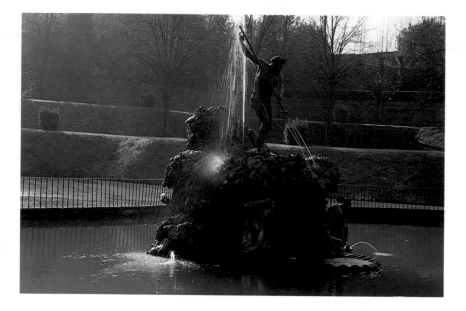

DUKE COSIMO I DE' MEDICI married the very wealthy Eleonora de Toledo, daughter of the Viceroy of Naples, and she, feeling restricted by the small terrace of the Palazzo Vecchio, wanted a large garden to walk in and enough room to grow her rare plants and flowers. In 1549 she bought the Pitti Palace and started developing the Boboli Gardens on the steep hillside behind it. The building, which had been planned, according to Machiavelli, to be the 'most imposing palace yet built by a private citizen', had sat unfinished for 100 years, abandoned by the Pitti family after the death of Luca Pitti in 1472. After eleven years of supervising the garden, Eleonora, aware of her failing health, insisted on moving into the still unfinished palace in 1560, where she died only two years later.

In keeping with Medici tradition, Duke Cosimo I and his wife took a great interest in plants and gardens. As well as having initiated the sophisticated garden at Villa Castello, Duke Cosimo I is credited with creating a garden of medicinal herbs in Florence as well as founding Pisa's School of Botany. His special passion in the Boboli Gardens was the planting of several orchards of dwarf fruiting trees.

To lay out the Boboli Gardens, behind the Pitti Palace, Duke Cosimo I and Eleonora called in Niccolò Tribolo, who was still working on the Villa Castello after ten years. Tribolo conceived what has remained the nucleus of the gardens, although his scheme

was considerably embellished and extended in the seventeenth century. He took advantage of the meadow and the natural horseshoe shape that the hills made behind the palace, created during the years when it had served as a quarry. The hillside was planted in symmetrical blocks of evergreen trees – cypress, fir, holm oak, laurel – that would form a dark background to a colossal fountain he was planning to build and set in the middle of the *prato*. The whiteness of the centrepiece set against a dark forested canopy echoed a description in Boccaccio's *Decameron*, which also inspired Villa Castello. The fountain was to consist of an enormous granite basin supporting the white statue of Oceanus – the father of the river gods, recalling Duke Cosimo I as ruler of the waves and water, the essence of life. He would be accompanied by three river gods, representing the three ages of man. Similar to the pond at the Villa Castello, the terrace above it was to be a simple rectangular *peschiera* with a simple narrow-stemmed cylix fountain, but that was the extent of the architecture. All around, the hills were to be planted as *boschetti*.

In the summer of 1550 Tribolo set off for Elba to find the piece of granite needed for the basin of the fountain – over 19 feet (6 metres) in diameter – but died on the way back. His plans for the gardens, however, were carried out, first by Bartolomeo Ammannati and later the tremendously inventive Bernardo Buontalenti, whose flair and sense of surprise was everywhere in the Pratolino garden and in the grottoes he would devise for the Boboli Gardens, describing the Great Flood.

In the 1560s, Ammannati created harmony between the building and the gardens by adding two wings to the palace, which echoed the horseshoe shape of the amphitheatre. The courtyard this created was where the early theatrical displays that have made the Boboli Gardens famous were performed. In 1565 Grand Duke Cosimo I's son Francesco, who would later make Pratolino, celebrated his marriage to Joanna of Austria with a pageant of floats telling the story of the gods' genealogy – one of which inspired Neptune's Fountain, now in the centre of Tribolo's *peschiera*. The marriage of Duke Cosimo I's younger son, Grand Duke Ferdinando I, who would later develop the Villa Petraia, with Christine of Lorraine (granddaughter of Catherine Sforza de' Medici) in 1589, was even more sophisticated, with ingenious devices – exploding volcanoes and fire-eating dragons – as its climax, and the whole courtyard flooded to a depth of 5 feet (1.5 metres) for a pageant

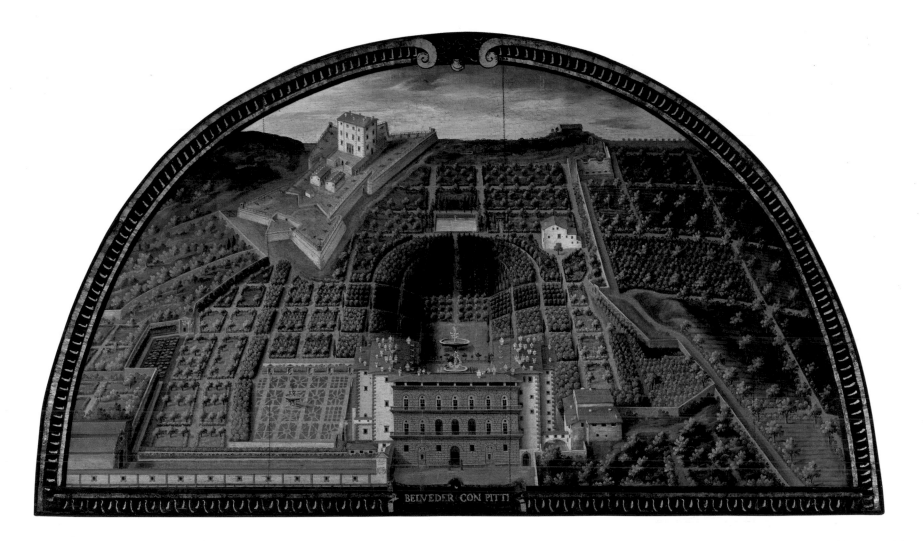

BELVEDER CON PITTI

OPPOSITE *The statue on Neptune's Fountain was made by Stoldo Lorenzi for Duke Cosimo I de' Medici. It was based on a chariot of the Triumph of Neptune – one of twenty floats for the pageant of the genealogy of the gods held for the wedding of his son Francesco to Joanna of Austria on 21 February 1566. This Neptune is unlike the usual reposing river gods: he is deliberately hurling the water from his trident – it shoots out on wet days – down the hill. The tritons and naiads are part of the original fountain, and also by Lorenzi, but the rocky island was installed later in the seventeenth century.*

ABOVE *'The most important, if not the most pleasing, of Tuscan pleasure-gardens lies', wrote Wharton, 'within the city walls. This is the Boboli garden, laid out on the steep hillside behind the Pitti Palace. The plan of the Boboli garden is not only magnificent in itself, but interesting as one of the rare examples, in Tuscany, of a Renaissance garden still undisturbed in its main outlines.' Utens's 1599 lunette shows how 'Behind the fountain, and in a line with it, a horseshoe-shaped amphitheatre has been cut out of the hillside, surrounded by tiers of stone seats adorned with statues in niches and backed by clipped laurel hedges, behind which rise the ilex-clad slopes of the upper gardens. The amphitheatre is one of the triumphs of Italian architecture. In general design and detail it belongs to the pure Renaissance, without trace of the heavy and fantastic barrochismo which, half a century later, began to disfigure such compositions in the villas near Rome. Indeed, comparison with the grotesque garden architecture of the Villa d'Este at Tivoli, which is but little later in date, shows how long the Tuscan sense of proportion and refinement of taste resisted the ever-growing desire to astonish instead of charming the spectator.'*

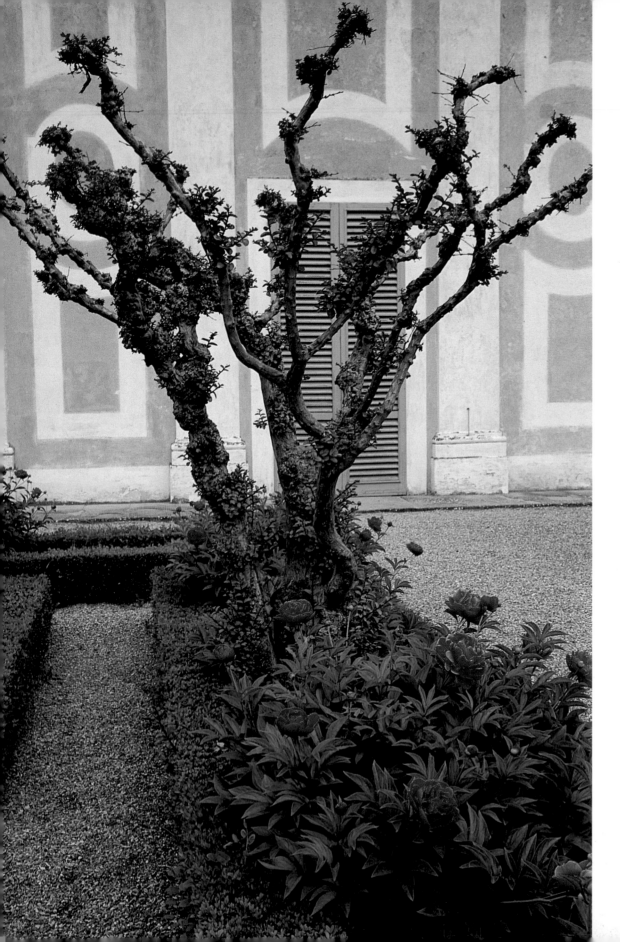

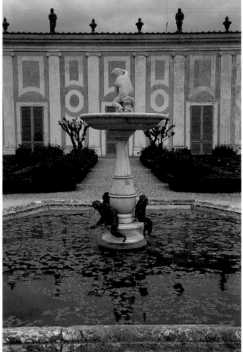

At the very top of the hill is the Garden of
the Cavaliere, next to the rampart Michelangelo
built along the city walls during the 1529 siege.
A house in the style of a fort, built for Cardinal
Leopoldo de' Medici, was replaced in the
nineteenth century by this elegant casino (left),
first used as a school for younger Medicis and
now a porcelain museum. The impish monkey
fountain (above) is attributed to Giambologna
because it resembles the birds he created in the
grotto at the Villa Castello (now in the Bargello
Museum in Florence). Evelyn saw on his 1644 visit
'a fort standing on a hill, where they told us his
highnesse Treasure is kept (I saw in this Garden
a rose grafted on an Orange Tree): much
topiary work and columns in architecture
about the hedges'.

RIGHT Roses now grow in the Garden
of Madama, planted with dwarf fruit trees
by Duke Cosimo I.

scene of eighteen galleys manned by heroic Christians, storming a Turkish fort.

In the seventeenth century, when the bold breadth of Roman garden design made its presence felt, the Boboli Gardens were substantially enlarged and two main axes established. The first, already created by Tribolo, was elongated to its furthest point at the top of the hill, where an enormous statue of Abundance provided the focal point. The second involved a long cypress avenue called the Viottolone, leading to the newly created island garden of the Isolotto and out again to the fabled city entrance, Porta Romana, where it could go no further. This new area was developed by different architects over a period of 150 years from land annexed from the Borgoli family – for whom the garden was named, but to whom the loss of land caused such anguish that their ghosts haunt the Isolotto. On either side of the Viottolone there were labyrinths, *ragnaia* and small gardens created to house the various horticultural enthusiasms of the Medici. Grand Duke Francesco I, for example, introduced mulberry trees to Tuscany in the Boboli Gardens and Grand Duke Ferdinando a large collection of potatoes. John Evelyn, on his 1644 visit, found the garden 'full of all variety, hills, dales,

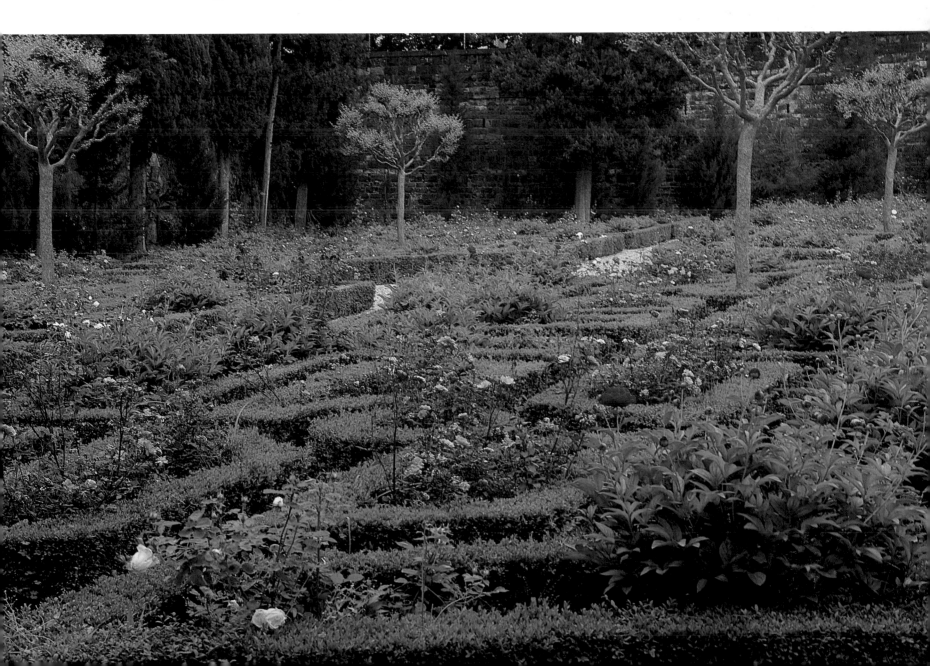

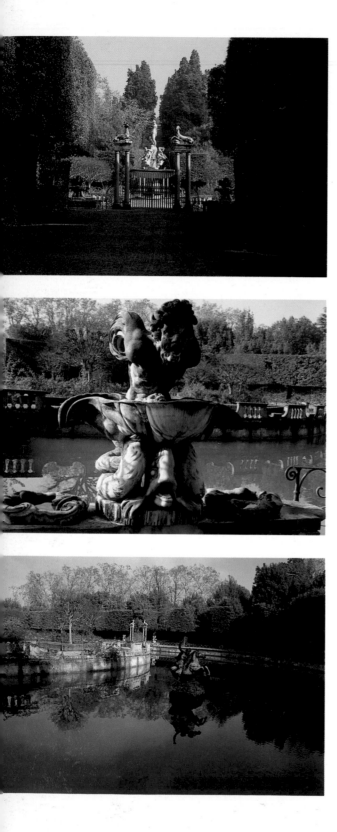

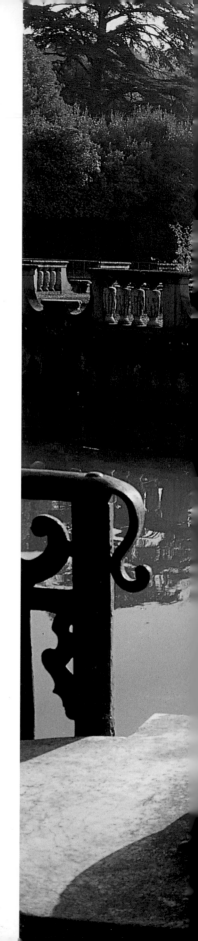

rocks, groves, aviaries, vivaries, fountains (especially one of five jettos, the middle basin being one of the longest stones that I ever saw)'. This was Tribolo's, now on the Isolotto.

The amphitheatre, which Edith Wharton praised as 'one of the triumphs of Italian garden design', was enlarged in 1599. The *boschetti* were removed, as was Tribolo's Fountain of Oceanus, in 1646 to the safety of Isolotto, and six tiers of seats were installed. The pageants continued on an even grander scale, with a horse ballet to celebrate the marriage in 1661 of Grand Duke Cosimo III de' Medici and Marguerite Louise d'Orleans. Sir Geoffrey Jellicoe gave a rousing description: 'When all Florence went to the Pitti and the spirit of pageantry and spectacle was abroad, then was the time that Boboli stirred . . . huge wooden erections illuminated by bonfires and torches, dancing would take the place of show . . . Far into the night the gardens would throb to the rhythm of seething, surging masses – the same rhythm of madness that sixty years before had for one moment been beaten out by Savonarola, and the next had turned and destroyed him.'

The lack of personal charm that Wharton found was certainly made up for in public service. In 1932, after a flag-throwing ceremony in the amphitheatre, Hitler and Mussolini are said to have driven down the Viottolone in a convertible. During the Second World War, the meadow of the amphitheatre was ploughed up to grow vegetables and the area behind the Isolotto, now a children's playground, served as an emergency cemetery. The *limonaia* temporarily gave refuge to paintings when the River Arno flooded in 1966 and now serves as a workshop to restore statues. The garden also became a repository for statues brought from other Medici villas – the dismantled Pratolino, for example, whose wonderful statue of a washerwoman apparently lies in pieces in a hidden forgotten area off the main cypress alley.

The Isolotto, a water and lemon garden, was designed by Alfonso Parigi in 1618, based on the Maritime Theatre of Hadrian's Villa in Tivoli. Amongst its fountains are the Fountain of the Harpy (left, centre) and Giambologna's Fountain of the Ocean, in the middle of the island (right), resting on Tribolo's basin, which arrived from Florence pulled by twenty-five pairs of oxen. Andromeda sits on a pedestal in the water, her feet in chains. Perseus (left, below) rides to her rescue. The gate to the Isolotto (left, top) was presided over by capricorns, representing Duke Cosimo I's zodiac sign; the Viottolone rises up behind it.

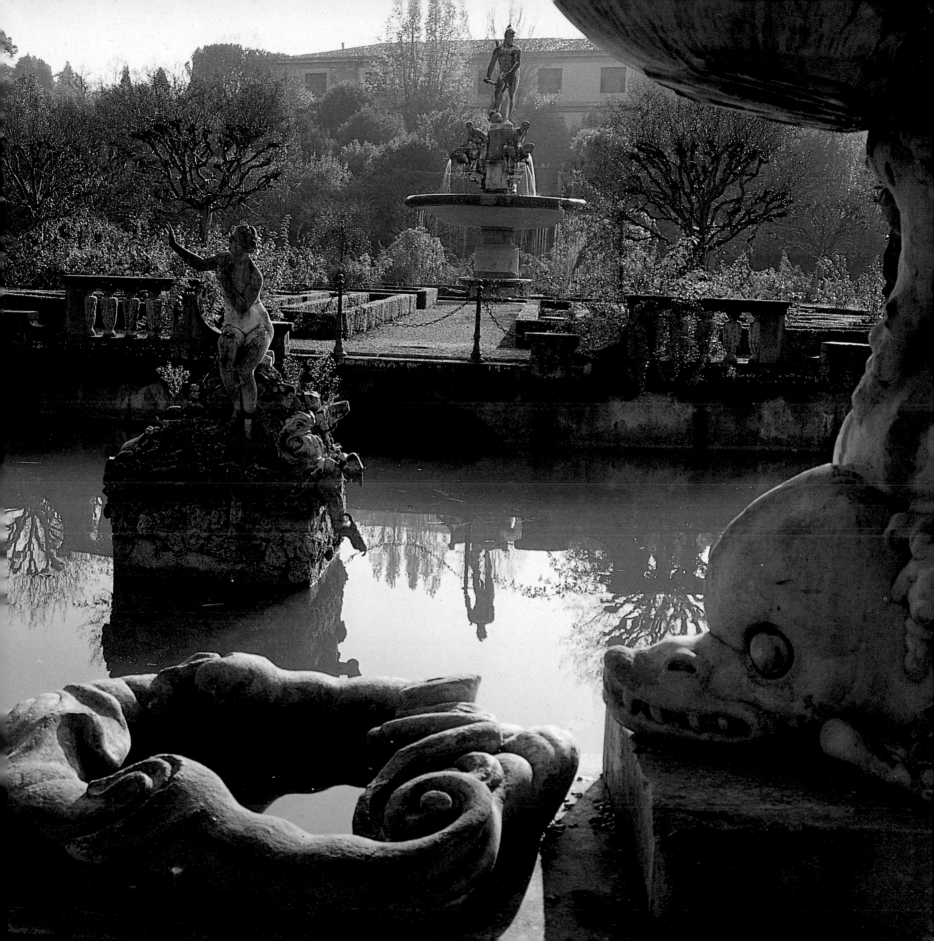

VILLA PETRAIA

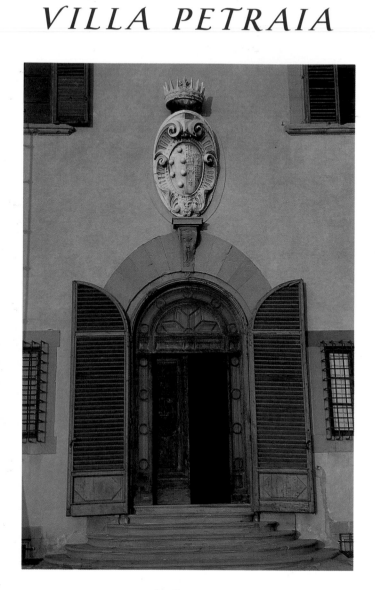

Ownership of the Villa Petraia is easily identified by the Medici insignia
(above), which was emblazoned on everything they built, including monks'
privies. The 'balls' are thought to be either cupping glasses or pills, representing
doctors or medics – hence the name Medici, or, more fancifully, the dents made
by the blows their ancestor, the brave knight Averado, sustained on his shield
while defending peasants against a monster. The number of 'balls' on the
emblem was never fixed. The six here, topped by the ducal crown, belong to
Grand Duke Ferdinando I. Looking across the peschiera and the parterre on a
misty November day, at dusk, the garden is at its most magical (right).

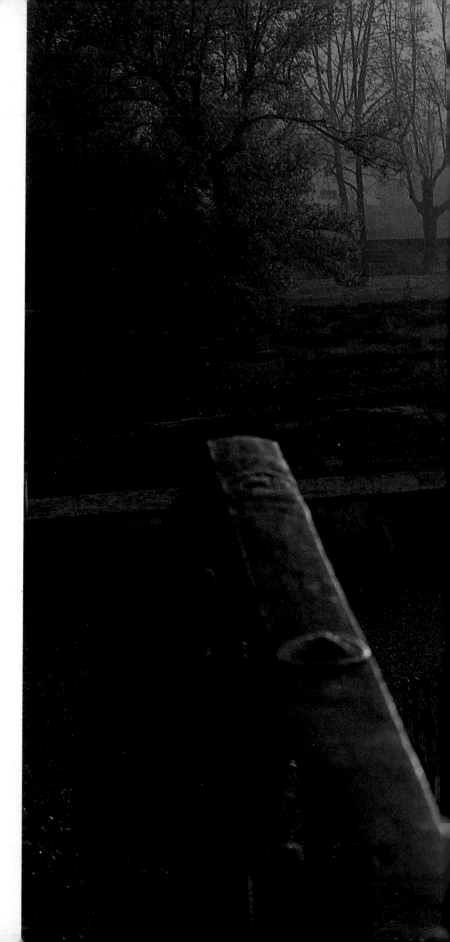

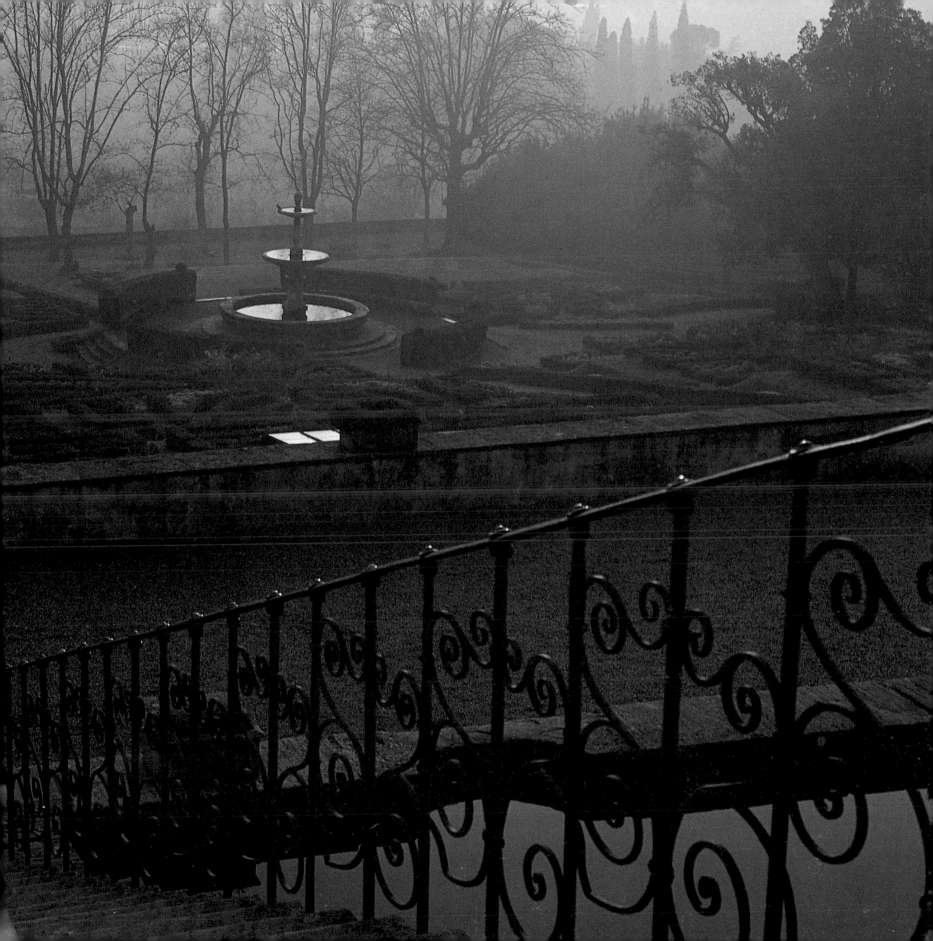

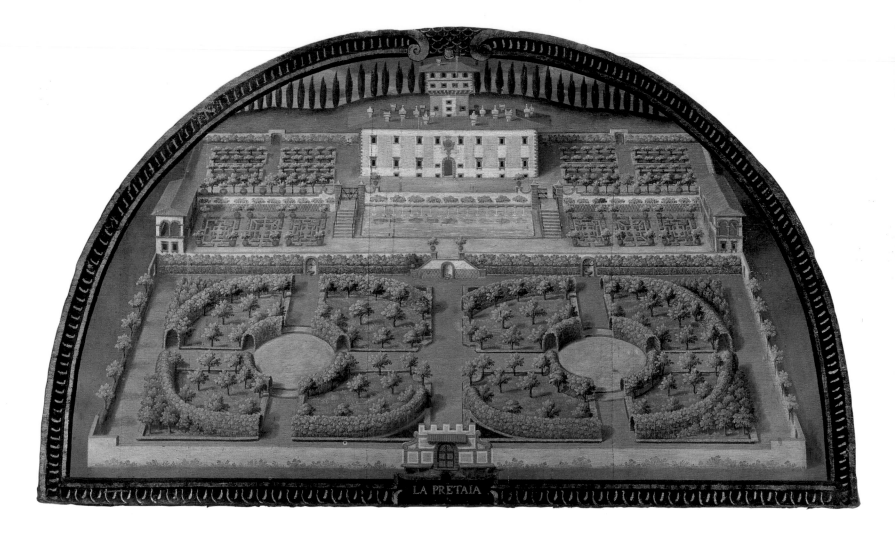

LA PRETAIA

'At Petraia', noted Wharton, 'the gardens are less elaborate in plan than at Castello . . . like the other Florentine villas of this quarter, where water is more abundant, Petraia has a great oblong vasca, or tank, beneath its upper terrace.' The garden originally consisted, as portrayed (above) in 1599 by Utens, of three terraces with geometric configurations, planted on either side with symmetrically arranged rows of fruit trees and, in the middle, parterres. On the lowest terrace were two large squares, subdivided into four compartments planted with circular pergolas with boschetti in the corners. On the middle terrace enormous aviaries were erected for Grand Duke Ferdinando I's fine collection of pheasants. When Florence became the temporary capital of Italy in 1865 the villa became a royal residence and Vittorio Emanuele II and his second wife Countess Mitafiori spent much time there, often dining al fresco on a platform set high up in an ancient ilex, still there today, on the left-hand side of the upper terrace. The house, which Wharton described as 'a simple structure of the old-fashioned Tuscan type, built about an inner quadrangle', has gone except for the 'very beautiful tower', as has most of the original garden. A small nineteenth-century loggia (opposite, top and below) stands in place of one of the aviaries. Only the vasca (opposite, centre) is left: a cooling presence on hot days, its surface mirroring the sky and the clouds that pass across it, and responding to the changing light and atmosphere.

FROM THE TERRACE OF VILLA PETRAIA, Ariosto wrote:

> To see the hills with villas sprinkled o'er
> Would make one think that even as flowers and trees
> Here earth tall towers in rich abundance bore.
> If gathered were they scattered palaces
> Within a single wall, beneath one name,
> Two Romes would scarce appear so great as these.

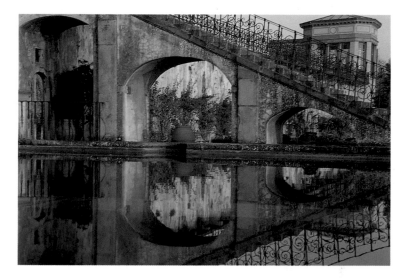

The villa whose view moved Ariosto to such eloquence was built as a fortress in the fourteenth century by the wealthy Strozzi family, rivals of the Medici. Only the tower remains. Marking the connection between the families, it was modelled on Florence's Palazzo Vecchio, which housed the *signoria* (the Florentine senate), of which the Strozzi and the Medici were prominent members.

Palla Strozzi became involved in the Albizzi conspiracy to overthrow Cosimo the Elder and after the latter regained power, he confiscated Strozzi's Villa Petraia in 1427 and banished him to Padua. He sold it to the Salutati family, brilliant managers of the Medici bank in Rome and fellow humanists, who did much to increase the Medici fortune. In 1568, however, Duke Cosimo I bought the property back and gave it to his son Ferdinando, who was a cardinal but had to secularize himself when his elder brother Francesco died without an heir: he became Grand Duke and two years later married Christine of Lorraine.

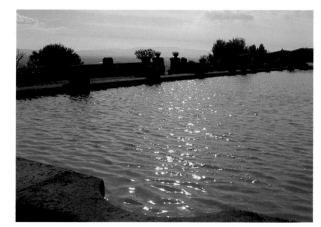

Buontalenti, who had finished the Villa Castello and Boboli Gardens after Tribolo's death, was commissioned to build a new villa on the foundations of the old fortress and lay out the gardens around it. Both the Villa Castello and the Villa Petraia were built on the foothills of Monte Morello less than a mile from each other, and at one time had an ilex tunnel that connected them. But unlike the Villa Castello, with its complex symbolism and water schemes, the Villa Petraia had a very simple garden based on geometry and symmetry that initially did not include a single fountain.

However, by the time Edith Wharton visited it, its *pièce de résistance* was the Fountain of Venus – symbol of Florence – brought from the Villa Castello in 1780. It stood in the Upper Garden, or Figurine Garden, but was not part of the original design and now does not even form a part of the garden. The statue was removed several years ago, ostensibly for restoration, but it is so valuable that it is now going to be housed inside the villa's courtyard, which is decorated with frescoes celebrating Medici history. The long *vasca* or *peschiera* is the only original feature remaining, and the best.

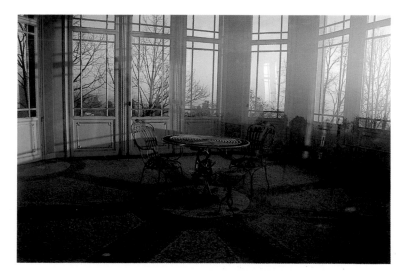

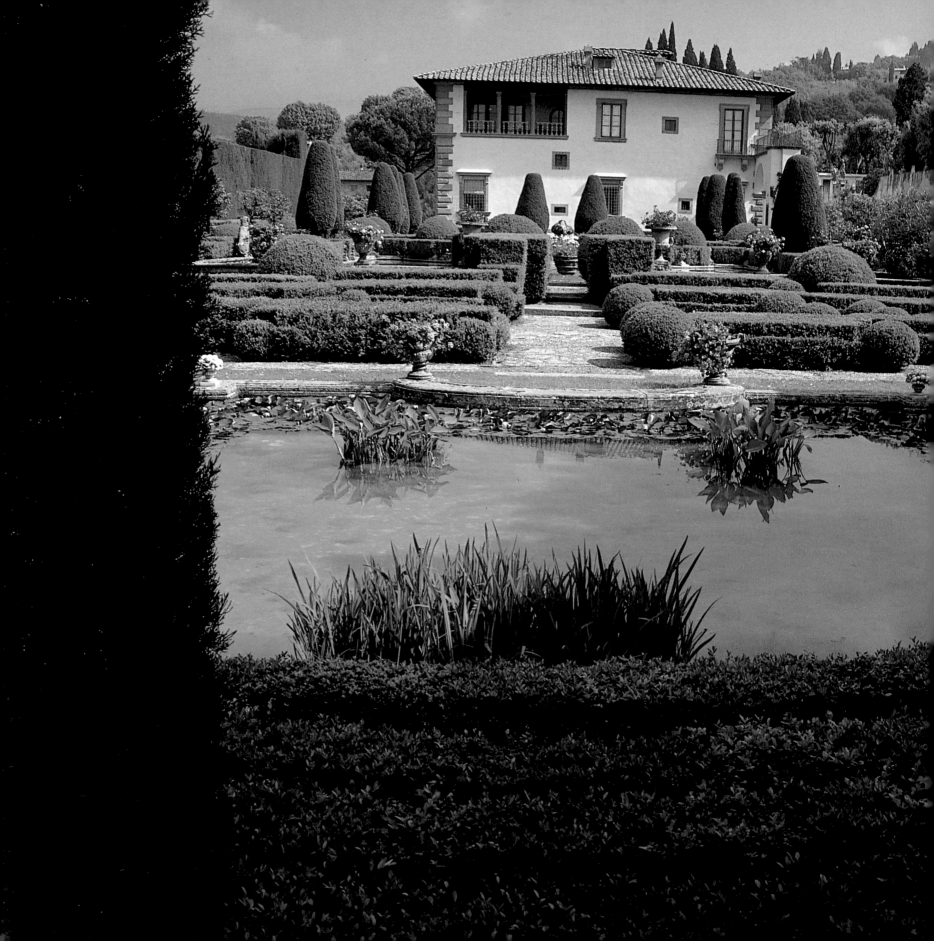

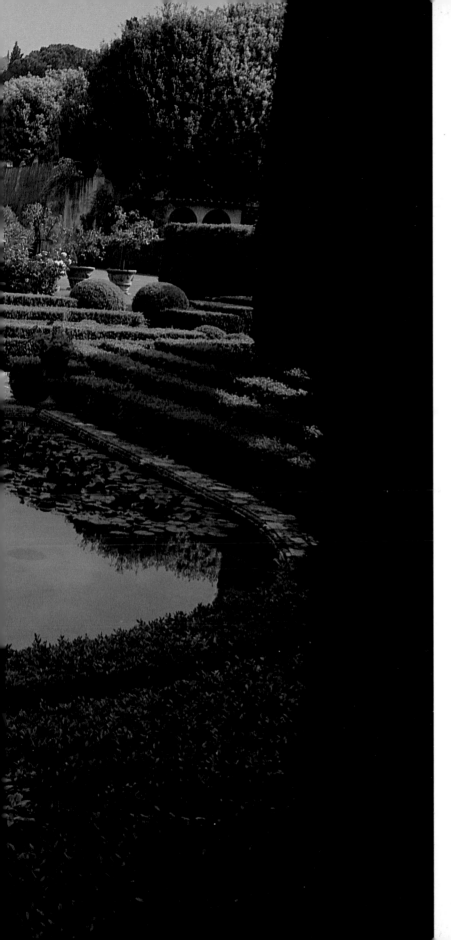

VILLA GAMBERAIA

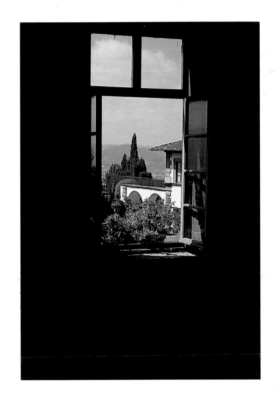

EDITH WHARTON waxed most lyrical about the Villa Gamberaia. Its great appeal, which shines out of her – and every – account, is that it is 'probably the most perfect example of the art of producing a great effect on a small scale'. It is a garden people can relate to because it was tailored for a family of means but not great wealth, while at the same time successfully combining all the features and 'sensations' of the classic Italian garden. 'It was a garden that varied with every aspect – playful, stately and simple', enthused Sir Geoffrey Jellicoe: 'more Italian than the Italians themselves'.

The Villa Gamberaia, seen from the Water Garden and from the limonaia, is typical of the severe restrained Tuscan architecture. At the turn of the century, it was bought by Princess Giovanna Ghyka, whom Bernard Berenson described as 'a narcissistic Rumanian lady who lived mysteriously, in love with herself perhaps and certainly with her growing creation, the garden of Gamberaia'. Originally an orchard, the Water Garden was the idea of Princess Ghyka's inseparable companion, Miss Blood.

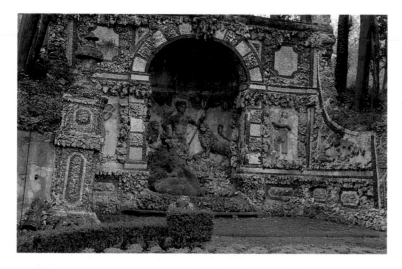

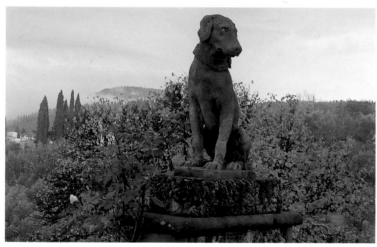

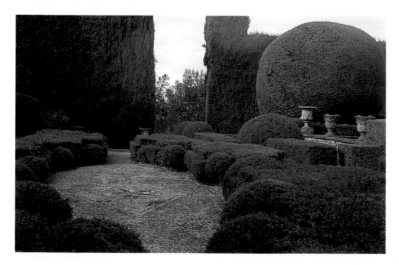

The villa is perched on the ridge of a hillside just outside Florence, overlooking the Val d'Arno and the village of Settignano, where Boccaccio lived in the fourteenth century, also famous for spawning a number of famous Renaissance sculptors. Art must be in the air, for the art historian and collector Bernard Berenson chose to make it his home when he bought his villa, I Tatti, there.

The villa started off modestly in the fourteenth century as a small convent of Benedictine nuns, and derives its name, meaning 'place of the crayfish', from the lake near by where the locals went to catch *gamberi* (crayfish). Each successive owner has improved and built upon the achievements of the last. In 1610 Zanobi di Andrea Capo built the villa but the architect is unknown. He died nine years after its completion and the villa passed into the joint possession of his two nephews, who bought the neighbouring villa of La Doccia, which became the rented home of Berenson before he bought I Tatti. One died five years later, but the other, Andrea di Cosimo Lapi, lived at the Villa Gamberaia for fifty-nine years.

The initial impetus was to bring water to the villa, which was a lengthy process and not without complications. His plans must have been quite ambitious from the start, for he solicited water rights from his neighbours and obtained permission to make conduits through neighbouring land to access this water, arousing the ire of one widow who accused him of purloining her water. She started suing him in 1636 and apparently a dispute is still going on. Once he had his water, Andrea di Cosimo Lapi embarked on a garden that now had so much water it could grow virtually anything, but bankrupted himself in the process. Janet Ross described it as 'one of the most characteristic seventeenth-century gardens in the neighbourhood of Florence, with grottoes inlaid with shells of different kinds and various coloured marbles, statues, vases, fountains and *jeux d'eaux* of every description'. He planted the cypresses, laid out the bowling green (there is some dispute about this) and the property passed to Antonio and Piero Capponi.

Before it was bought by Princess Giovanna Ghyka in 1900, for many years it was let out 'in lodgings for the summer' and when Wharton saw it shortly after she observed that 'it doubtless owes to this obscure fate the complete preservation of its garden-plan . . . before the recent alterations'. Princess Ghyka, sister of Queen Natalie of Serbia, loved the garden obsessively, sharing it with her companion, Miss Blood. They 'cultivated their garden', said Harold Acton, 'as Voltaire proposes in *Candide*, without heeding the outer

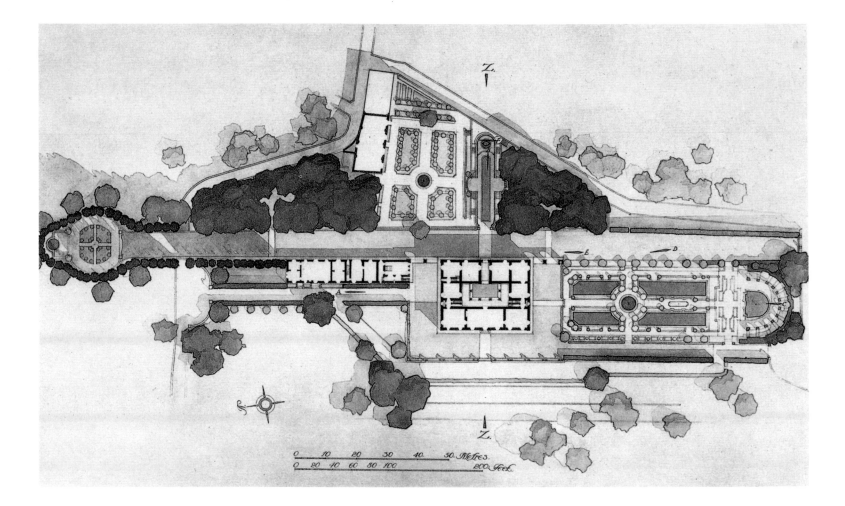

The nymphaeum (top) is at the base of a hill, similar to a cave, overhung by a cypress wood – or those at the Villa Castello and the Giusti Gardens. Neptune is in the middle, next to a lion, a symbol of Florence; musicians adorn the walls. Stone dogs and lions were often seen on the parapets of old Florentine gardens and here (centre) is one of the 'solemn-looking stone dogs' described by Wharton. At the end of the garden is an exedra of clipped cypresses (below), planted by Princess Ghyka; arched openings to open up the view were cut out of the cypresses by the present owner, Dottore Marchello Marchi, who bought the property from the Holy See after it was severely damaged during the Second World War.

This plan of the Villa Gamberaia from Sir Geoffrey Jellicoe's Italian Gardens of the Renaissance *shows the Water Garden and the cypress exedra on the far right, and the nymphaeum on the far left. Jellicoe said that its 'concept of domestic landscape is by general consent the most thoughtful the western world has known'. Wharton found it 'small but impressive'. Its plan, she said, 'combines in an astonishingly small space, yet without the least sense of overcrowding, almost every typical excellence of the old Italian garden: free circulation of sunlight and air about the house; abundance of water; easy access to dense shade; sheltered walks with different points of view; variety of effect produced by the skilful use of different levels; and, finally, breadth and simplicity of composition.'*

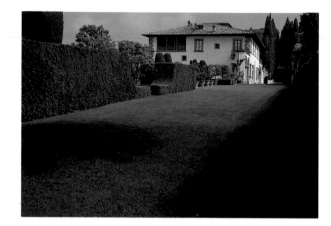

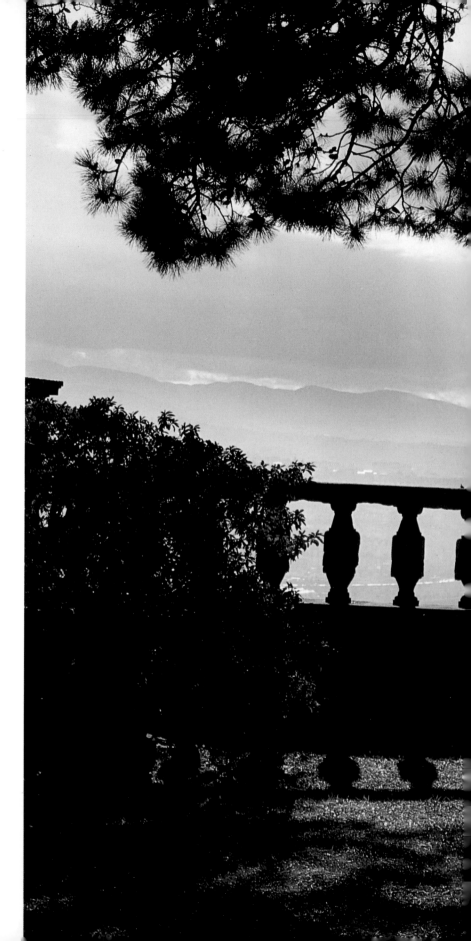

world'. Miss Blood is mentioned as a guest in Mary Berenson's diaries, but the Princess was somewhat of a recluse. The Marchese Origo recalled a rare viewing: 'Occasionally we visited the most beautiful, and certainly in my eyes the most romantic garden of all, that of the Villa Gamberaia, and I wandered about hoping that I might catch a glimpse of the place's owner, Princess Ghyka, a famous beauty who, from the day that she had lost her looks, had shut herself up in complete retirement with her English companion, refusing to let anyone see her unveiled face again. Sometimes, I was told, she would come out of the house at dawn to bathe in the pools of the water-garden, or would pace the long cypress avenue at night – but all I ever saw . . . was a glimpse of a veiled figure at an upper window.'

Visits to the garden were forbidden if the Princess was there, and even if she was away an appointment had to be made with her agent in Florence. It is entirely probable that Vernon Lee, who took Wharton to La Doccia, where she met the Berensons for the first time, also arranged and accompanied her to the Villa Gamberaia.

Princess Ghyka transformed the large parterre to the south of the villa into a water garden. 'This garden,' explains Wharton, 'an oblong piece of ground, a few years ago had in its centre a round fish-pond, surrounded by symmetrical plots planted with roses and vegetables, and in general design had probably been little changed since the construction of the villa. It has now been remodelled on an elaborate plan, which has the disadvantage of being unrelated in style to its surroundings; but fortunately no other change has been made in the plan and planting of the grounds.'

The garden contained most of the usual features of the

VILLA GAMBERAIA

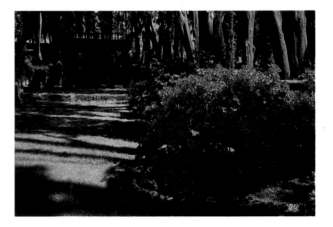

Renaissance garden – a grotto, a *tapis vert* (or a bowling green), a *nymphaeum*, a *bosco*, a *limonaia* – which were as masterfully positioned as pieces in a Chinese puzzle and the whole 3½ acres (1.4 hectares) was encircled by a stone wall and balustrade which traditionally broached its boundary walls. The features were arranged, in Wharton's view, as one might subdivide the rooms of a house, not just for utility, but also to make it more interesting.

'Aesthetic impressions were considered, and the effect of passing from the sunny fruit-garden to the dense grove, thence to the wide-reaching view, and again to the sheltered privacy of the pleached walk or the mossy coolness of the grotto – all this was taken into account by a race of artists who studied the contrast of aesthetic emotions as keenly as they did the juxtaposition of dark cypress and pale lemon-tree, of deep shade and level sunlight.' In many ways the Villa Gamberaia was a model garden: 'the real value of the old Italian garden-plan is that logic and beauty meet in it, as they should in all sound architectural work.'

ABOVE *Level sunlight casts long cool shadows on to the* tapis vert *and highlights a vibrant azalea in the* bosco.

FAR LEFT *Wharton described the 'long grass alley or bowling-green, flanked . . . by high hedges . . . [it] shows how well the beauty of a long stretch of greensward was understood . . . These bits of sward were always used near the house, where their full value could be enjoyed, and were set like jewels in clipped hedges or statue-crowned walls.' At one end the bowling green 'terminates in a balustrade whence one looks down on the Arno and across to the hills on the southern side of the valley' (left).*

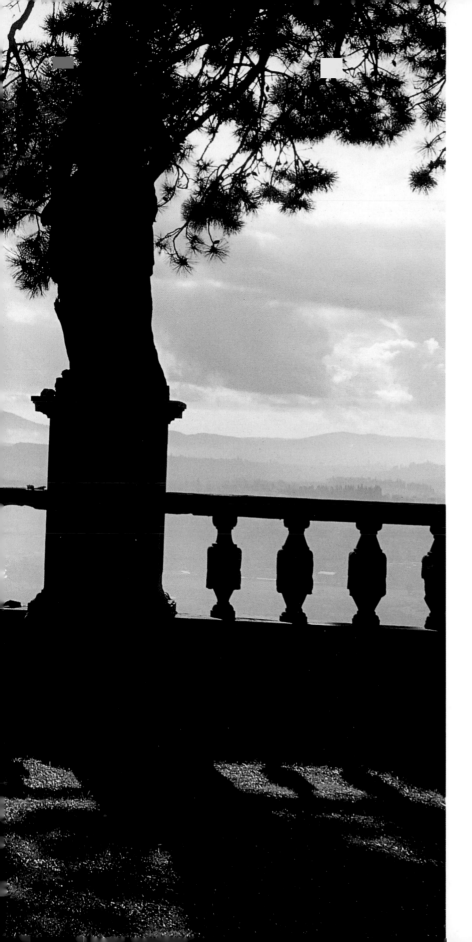

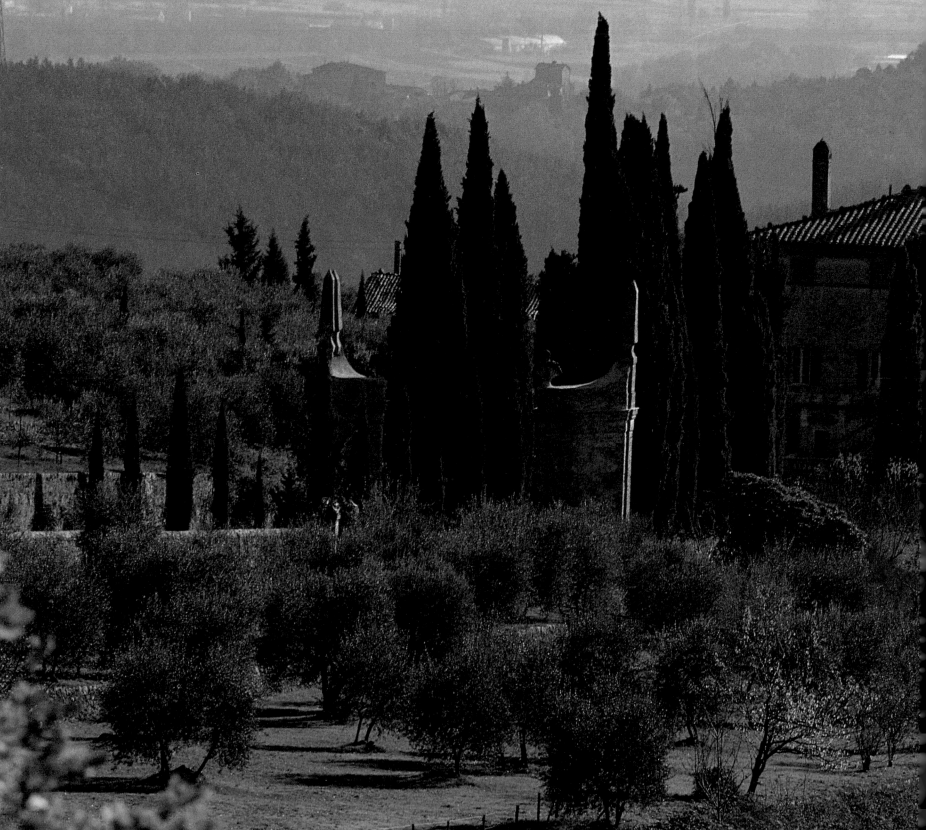

GARDENS NEAR SIENA

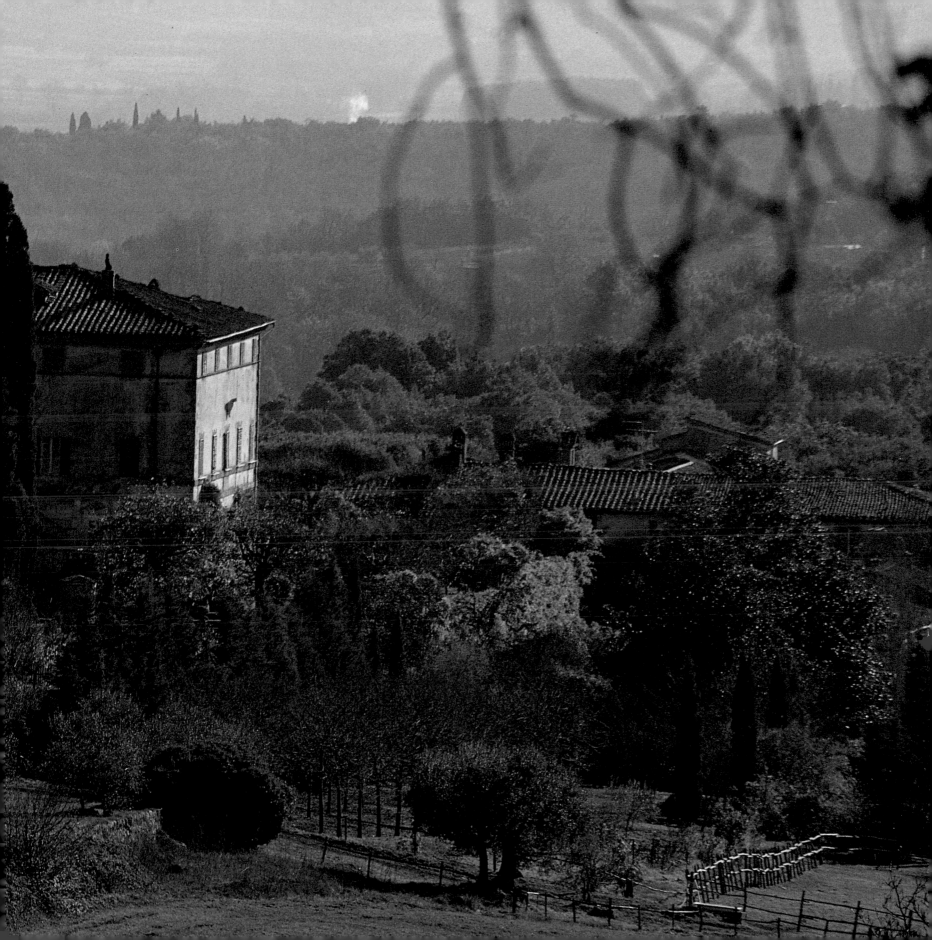

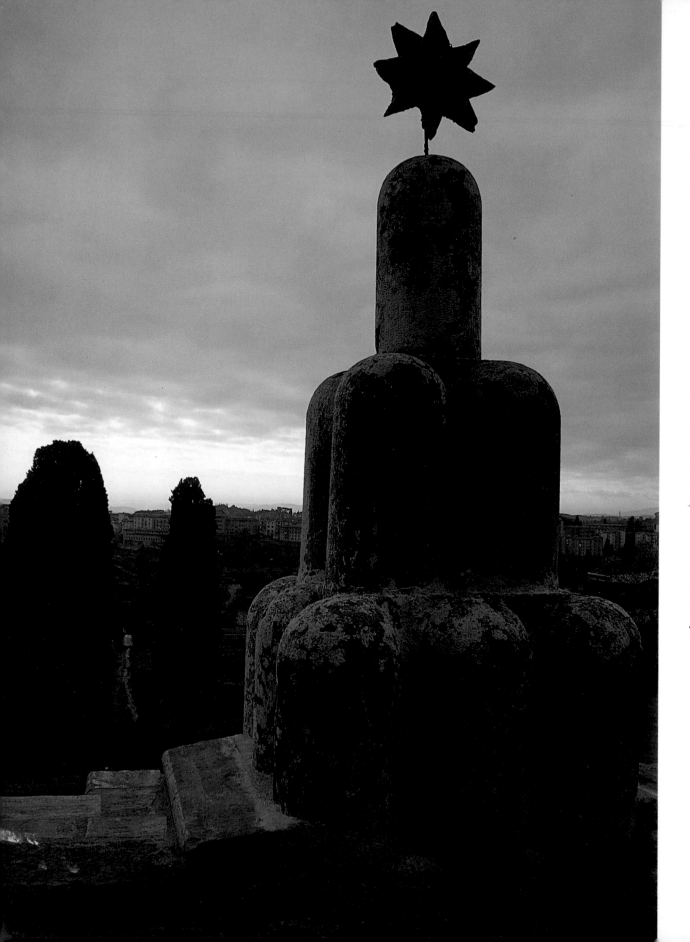

The distinctive heraldic device of the Chigi family presides over a view of the medieval city of Siena from the lowest terrace of their villa at Vicobello (left). Even the family is not sure whether their coat of arms represents the hills of Siena or the bullions of gold they made through banking. The Chigi were to Siena what the Medici were to Florence, and like them built many villas in the rolling Tuscan landscape of olive groves and vineyards where they sojourned for the months of the villeggiatura to escape the heat and bring in the harvest. Their favoured architect and painter was the brilliant Sienese-born Baldassare Peruzzi (opposite), who designed a whole clutch of Chigi villas, and whose severe exteriors belied the sumptuous decorations of his frescoed interiors. The influence of Peruzzi lived on after his death and, in the seventeenth century, the Chigi used their fortune and the style established by Peruzzi to transform a large farmhouse near Sovicille into one of the most glittering villas of Tuscany, the Villa Cetinale (previous pages).

To LEARN WHAT AN OLD TUSCAN GARDEN WAS, one must search the environs of the smaller towns, and there are more interesting examples about Siena than in the whole circuit of the Florentine hills', wrote Edith Wharton after she had embarked on a tour of these gardens, which she would also visit several years later with Vernon Lee. Of the three villas whose gardens are still in existence today, two were built by the merchant princes of the Chigi family. Vicobello was designed by the Sienese architect Baldassare Peruzzi, who did so much work for the Chigi that Carlo Fontana, who was commissioned to build the villa of Cetinale a century later, followed family tradition and took the characteristic Peruzzi villa as his model.

The Chigi were a bastion of Sienese banking and influence, comparable to the Medici of Florence. Their most illustrious art patron was Agostino Chigi, who founded the Roman branch of the bank. He had become fabulously wealthy through trade and been made treasurer to Pope Julius II. Peruzzi's first villa for the Chigi, Volte Alte, earned him the attention of Agostino Chigi, who commissioned him to build his renowned Villa Farnesina on the banks of the River Tiber, where he courted, flattered and indulged the Medici Pope Leo X, succeeding in wheedling the lucrative Elba alum mines monopoly away from the Medici. Perhaps this is why Duke Cosimo I de' Medici, taking time off his garden projects of Castello and Boboli, had no scruples about conducting his Siege of Siena in 1554–5, which more than halved its population and caused terrible suffering. It consigned Siena to its fate as a medieval outpost of Florence, where it was always known as 'Conservative Siena'. 'In Siena,' observed Henry James, 'everything is Sienese . . . Other places perhaps may treat you to as drowsy an odour of antiquity, but few exhale it from so large an area.'

The aura of the past also lingers in its smaller spaces. At a villa overlooking Siena are two features formerly often seen in Italian gardens – one renowned for its cruelty, the other for its charm. Wharton picked out the gardens of the Villa Gori, laid out in 1620,

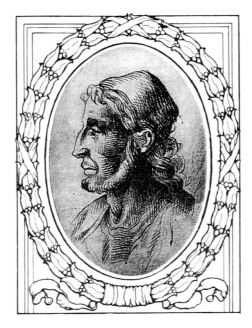

as 'though in some respect typically Sienese . . . in one way unique in Italy'. The two features survive much as she described them, each found at the end of the two 'antique alleys of pleached ilexes' that lead away from the villa. One ends up in the sinister world of the *ragnaia*, created to supply songbirds for the dinner table. 'The ancient tunnel of gnarled and interlocked trees, where a green twilight reigns in the hottest summer noon,' explained Wharton, 'extends for several hundred feet along a ridge of ground ending in a sort of circular knoll or platform, surrounded by an impenetrable wall of square-clipped ilexes. The platform has in its centre a round clearing, from which four narrow paths . . . are planted with stunted ilexes and cypresses, which are cut down to the height of shrubs. In these dwarf trees blinded thrushes are tied as decoys to their wild kin, who are shot at from the circular clearing or side paths. This elaborate plantation is a perfectly preserved specimen of a species of bird-trap once, alas! very common in this part of Italy.'

The other alley leads to 'a small open-air theatre which is the greatest curiosity of the Villa Gori', where Vernon Lee could hear 'a fully fledged nightingale singing from the solitary cypress projecting obelisk-wise above the stage'. After the flamboyant pageantry of the Medici gardens, the simplicity of the imaginative small, theatre-in-the-green drew a warm response from Wharton. 'No mere description of this plan can convey the charm of this exquisite little theatre, approached through the mysterious dusk of the long pleached alley, and lying in sunshine and silence under its roof of blue sky, in its walls of unchanging verdure. Imagination must people the stage with sylvan figures of the Aminta or the Pastor Fido, and must place on the encircling seats a company of *nobil donne* in pearls and satin, with their cavaliers in the black Spanish habit and falling lace collar which Vandyke has immortalized in his Genoese portraits; and the remembrance of this leafy stage will lend new life to the reading of the Italian pastorals, and throw a brighter sunlight over the woodland comedies of Shakespeare.'

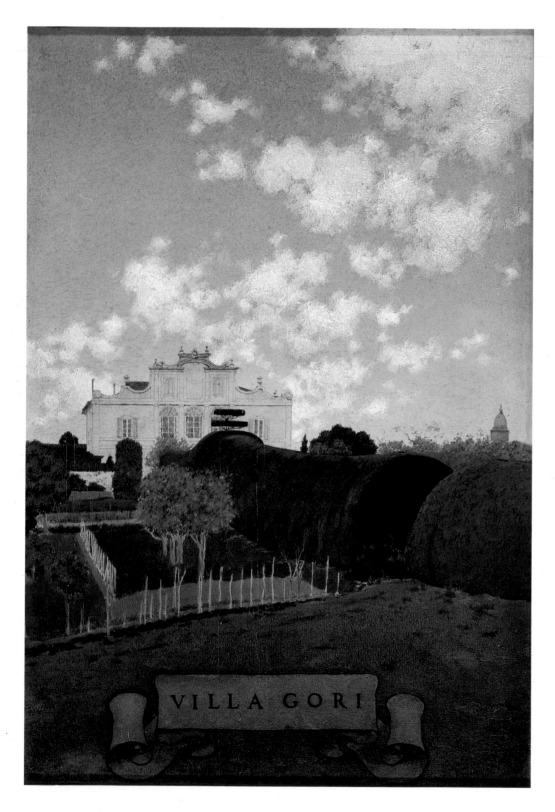

VILLA GORI

LEFT *Maxfield Parrish's illustration of the Villa Gori shows one of the two tunnels of clipped ilexes. This one led to the ragnaia, of which Vernon Lee wrote, 'However cheerful such domed walks of green look from the outside, this particular tonnelle [with] a dark murderous decoy mound instead of the sunny theatre at its end struck one as much blacker more gnarled and wholly evil . . . and here, no doubt, the only song would be that of the blinded decoy birds in their little cages, and the shrieks of the netted and limed victims.'*

OPPOSITE *The other tunnel leading from the villa – seen here with persimmons in the foreground – had a more pleasant exit, which Vernon Lee described as 'a uniquely perfect open-air theatre, whose stage and orchestra and side scenes of clipped cypress stand out a vivid golden green in the sunshine at the end of that blackness. The theatre is quite small and the speaking voice carries very easily.' Wharton embellished with more detail. 'The pit of this theatre is a semi-circular opening, bounded by a low wall or seat, which is backed by a high ilex hedge. The parterre is laid out in an elaborate broderie of turf and gravel, above which the stage is raised about three feet. The pit and the stage are enclosed in a double hedge of ilex, so that the actors may reach the wings without being seen by the audience; but the stage setting consists of rows of clipped cypresses, each advancing a few feet beyond the one before it, so that they form a perspective running up to the back of the stage, and terminated by the tall shaft of a single cypress which towers high into the blue in the exact centre of the background.'*

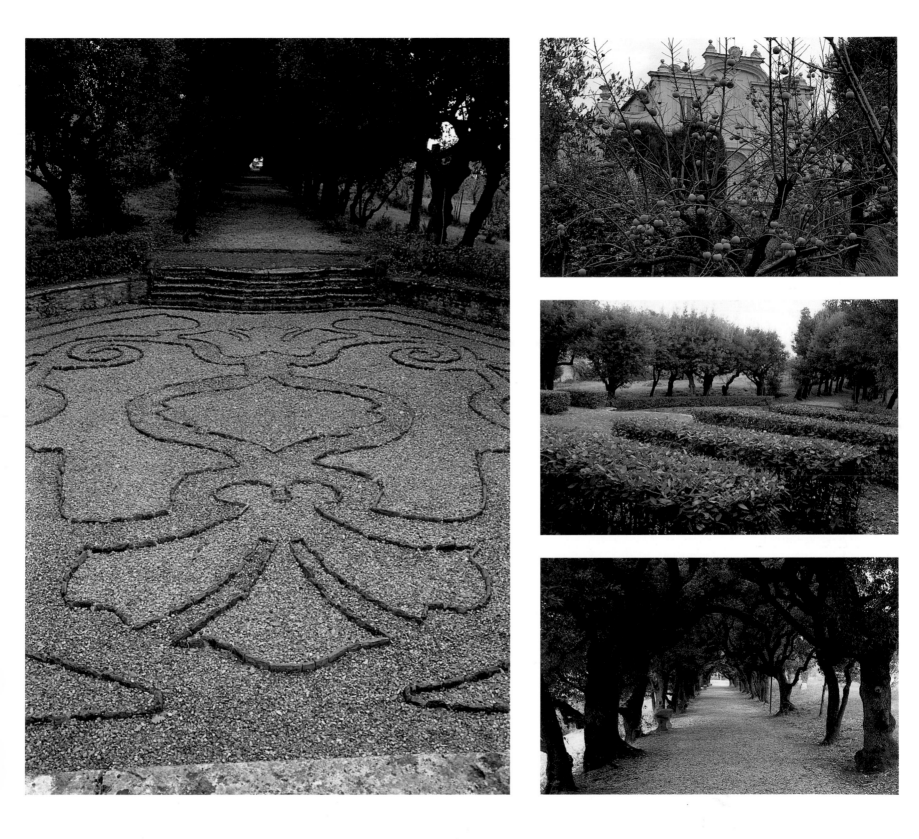

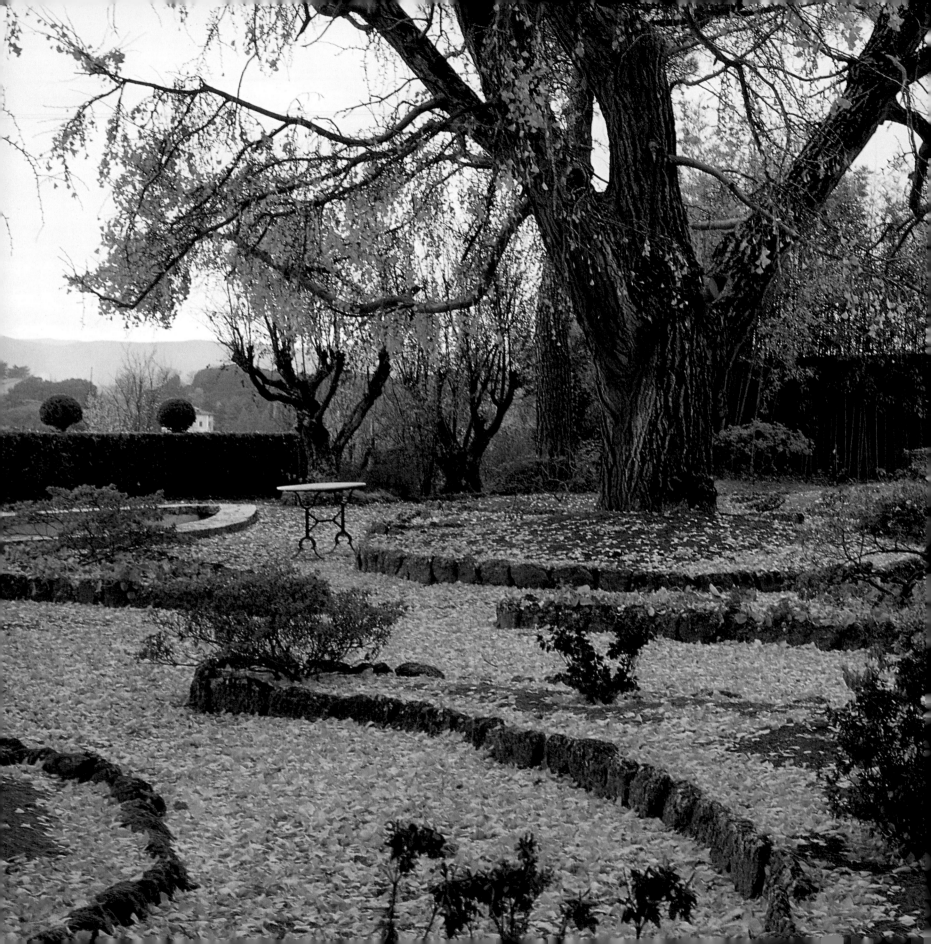

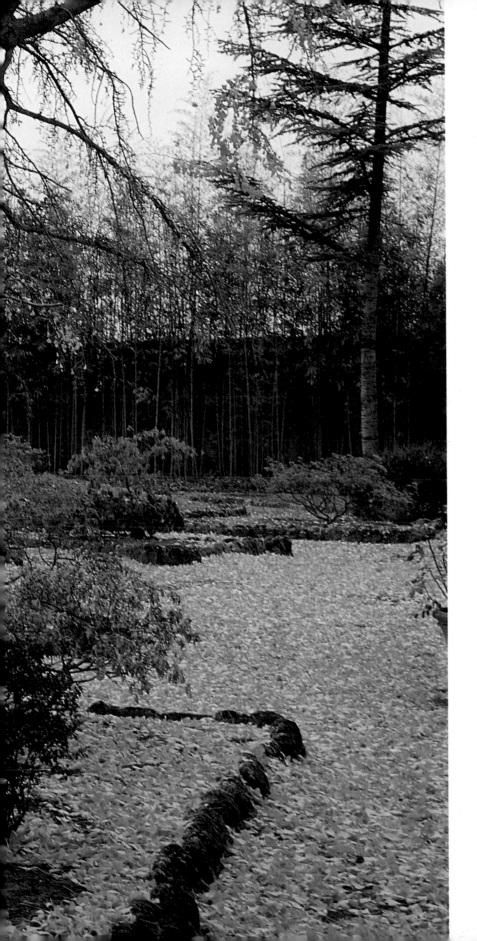

VICOBELLO

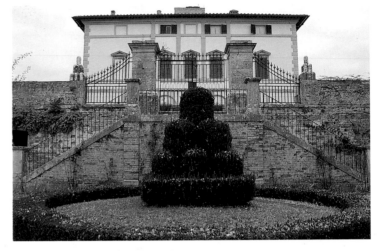

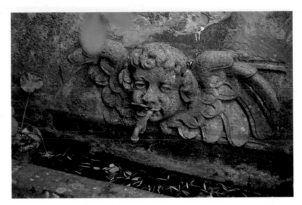

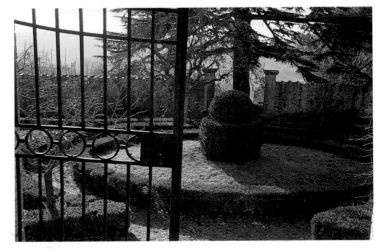

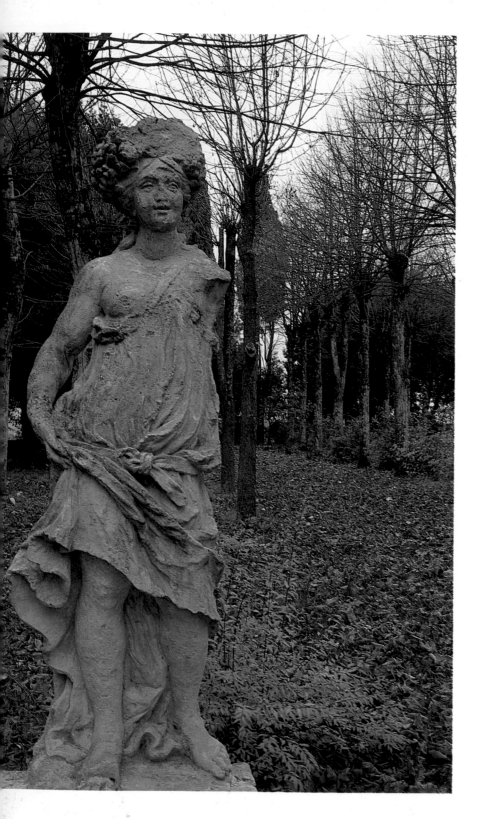

'MOST WORTHY SIR,' begins a letter of 1915, written to the biographer of Baldassare Peruzzi by one of his descendants. It continued: 'Baldassare Peruzzi was born at Ancaiano and there still remains an old tower where tradition says he lived. The local church is not the work of Peruzzi, but of Fontana who designed also, in 1667, the villa of Cetinale, belonging to the Chigi family. The Villa of Vico Bello (near Siena) always of the house of Chigi, was built from the designs of Peruzzi. Greetings from thy friend, Cesare Peruzzi, Tobacconist.'

Peruzzi was a true artist of the Renaissance, at once an architect, painter and theatrical designer, credited with the invention of movable scenery, renowned for his passion for medieval architecture and a master of perspective and *quadratura*. During the Sack of Rome in 1527, he was imprisoned and tortured by the Spaniards and returned to Siena, Vasari recounts, with 'nothing but his shirt'. Made superintendent in charge of the fortifications of the city, he received several commissions from the Chigi family, including Vicobello, which he designed some time between 1528 and 1531 before returning to Rome to make his last great opus, the curving Palace of Massimi alle Collone.

Although on a much smaller scale than his Roman villas, the villa and gardens of Vicobello testify to Peruzzi's reputation for purity and unity of design, so understated sometimes that one could not be sure it was by his hand. Harold Acton dubbed him an 'architect's architect' – and Sir Geoffrey Jellicoe rated Peruzzi second only to Vignola in 'delicacy and refinement'. What remains today of Peruzzi's garden is the layout. Vicobello sits on the ridge of a hill with a view over Siena, but it was conceived to be seen from Siena as an ensemble, the villa and garden representing the distinctive Chigi coat of arms: a pyramid – which could either be of bullions of gold symbolizing their financial power or represent the hills of Siena – topped by a star. A series of terraced walled gardens rise in pyramidal fashion to the top, crowned by, instead of a star, the villa. The arms are repeated throughout the garden, fashioned in box, in stone as punctuation points, or in escutcheons. Peruzzi was also known for his understated use of old materials – brick and uncut stone – and these are evident in the construction of the walls, which 'give opportunity for many charming architectural effects'.

The villa is flanked on one side by the ilex *bosco* Edith Wharton described as 'the indispensable adjunct of the Italian country house',

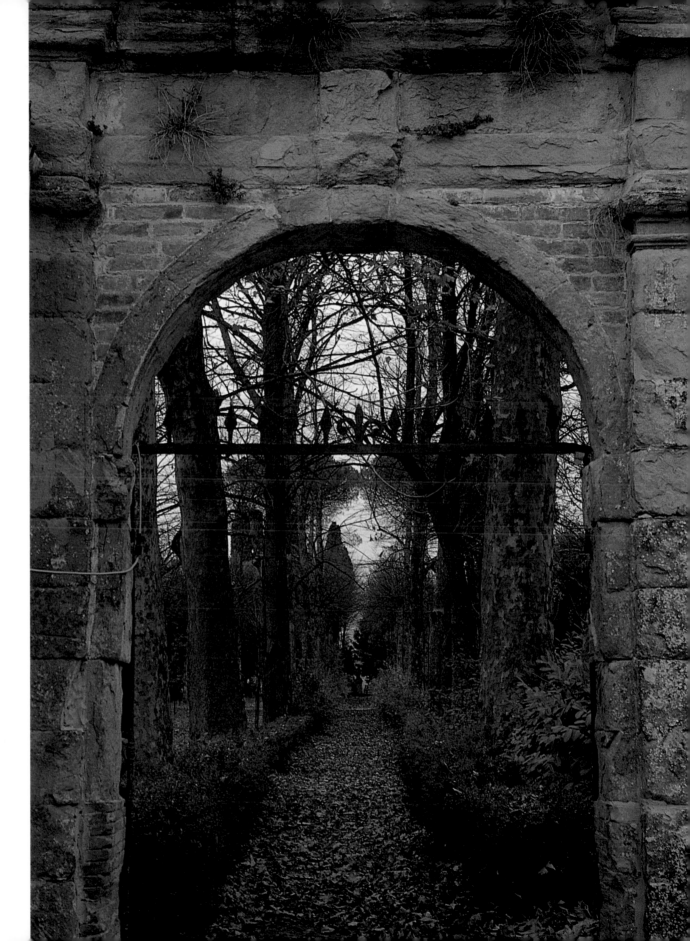

PREVIOUS PAGES *All that is
left of the garden is the simplicity
of its basic plan, the terracing and
perhaps the walls, which are true
to the spirit of Peruzzi if not the
original bricks and stone. The
geometric beds and the pleached
alley have gone.*

*On the lowest terrace (left) the
eccentrically shaped beds, the exotic
bamboo grove and the ginkgo tree,
one of the largest specimens in
Europe, were added during the
romanticizing of the garden in the
nineteenth century. The semi-
circular fishpond near the belvedere
overlooking Siena is said to be one
of Peruzzi's hallmarks.*

*This view of the villa and garden
(right top) shows Peruzzi's severe
Tuscan style and the repetition
throughout the garden – even on
the lemon pots – of the Chigi
impresa. Wharton loved the detail
of architectural features, such as
this small fountain in the middle
terrace (right centre). Another
terrace (right below) was once
planted with clipped ilexes but has
now been replaced by box, and is
dwarfed by an enormous cedar
of Lebanon.*

RIGHT AND OPPOSITE
*The entrance to the ilex bosco
shows Peruzzi's flair for using
and reworking old materials such
as brickwork and stone. Birds
were trapped here as well as in
the ragnaia.*

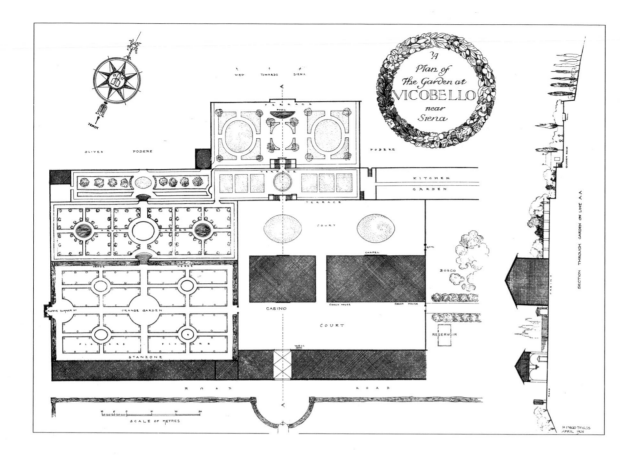

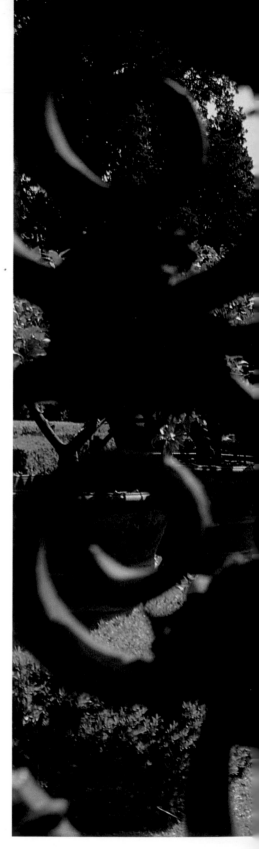

which remains just as she saw it. On the other side of the villa is the upper walled garden where the *limonaia* overwinters the heavy pots of lemons on display in the box parterre from May to November. These are the most glorious feature of the garden of Vicobello today and can best be admired from its well-known summerhouse – which Wharton described as a 'charming garden-house at the end of the path, in the form of an open archway faced with Doric pilasters, before a semicircular recess with a marble seat'. Fruit trees make an orchard in the walled garden directly below it, and a large cedar of Lebanon dominates the terrace below that. All the planting in the garden has been altered several times, the present scheme replacing what Wharton reported nearly a century ago as 'densely shaded' terraces 'planted with straight rows of the square-topped ilexes so characteristic of the Sienese gardens' which descended 'to a level stretch of sward (perhaps an old bowling green)' and ending with the all-too-common *ragnaia* for the trapping of birds.

ABOVE *With his 1905 plan, Inigo Triggs supplied a description of the garden of Vicobello as a 'series of eleven terraces, planted with long rows of square-cut ilexes descending to a meadow or* ragnaia *at the foot of the hill where formerly the young gallants resorted for the snaring of birds'. He went on to list a chapel, a coachhouse and an orange garden, bordered on one side by a long, low* limonaia *and on the other sides by thick-set hedges of cypresses and laurel, and its orange trees set within box-edged flowerbeds. The main walk terminated in the garden house, seen (right) through the star of the Chigi coat of arms.*

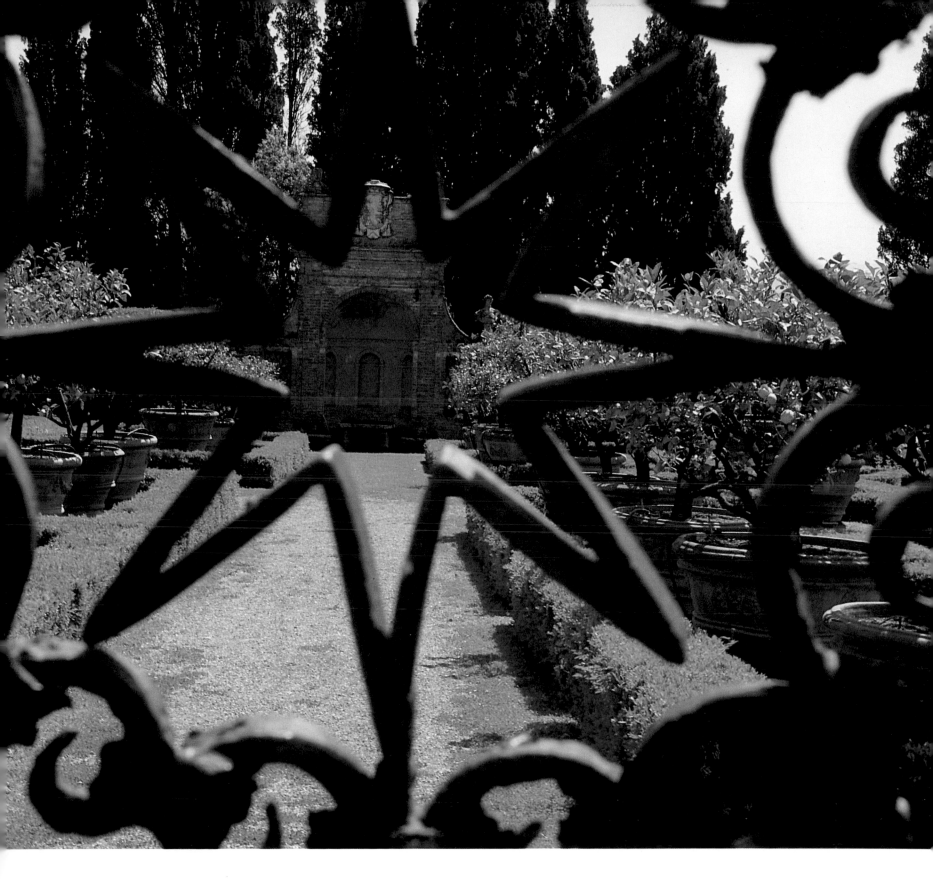

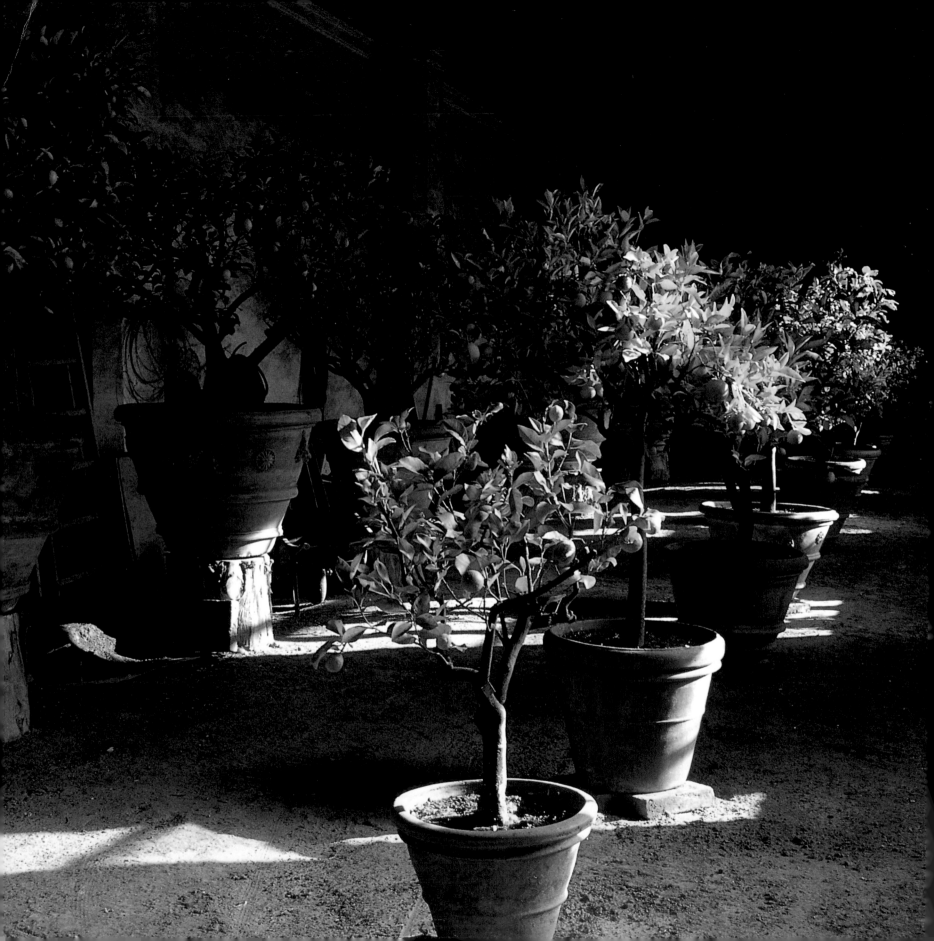

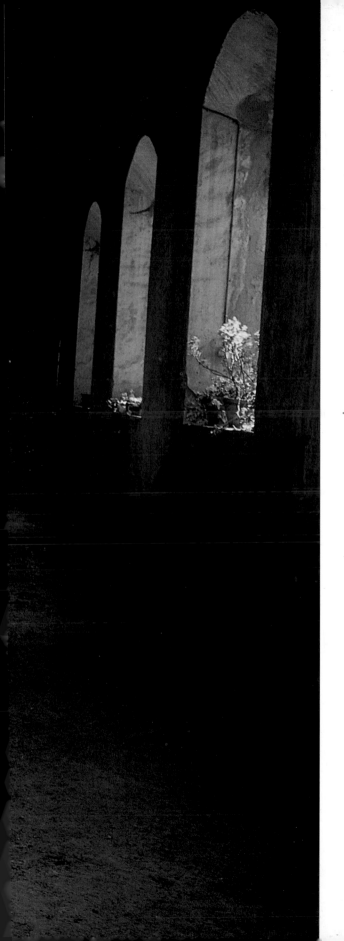

VICOBELLO

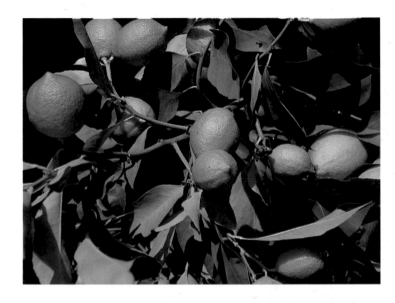

Low-lying winter sun filters through the stone window embrasures of Vicobello's limonaia, *casting shadows onto the earth floor and highlighting the terracotta pots, some of which bear the Chigi* impresa *(right below). If there was one thing you would choose to symbolize the Italian garden it would be not a splashing fountain, a line of box or a piece of a statuary but a single lemon tree planted in an old pot. It is remarkable how the Italians still treasure lemons, long after the days when they were worth a small fortune, and how they remain the pride of these old gardens, evoking the glory of the past. The* limonaia *of Vicobello is looked after by the old gardener Sergio, who, for company, tames and feeds field mice inside it. The lemons have their rituals: it takes eight men to move the 450-pound (204-kilogram) pots in and out of their winter shelter, still employing the old-fashioned system using ropes, pulleys and a wooden cart. The lemons leave the* limonaia *on the first of May and return to their south-facing harbour in early November to sit out the winter on an immaculately swept floor, making the most of the winter sunshine.*

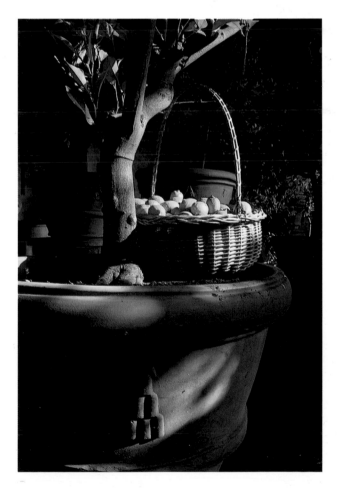

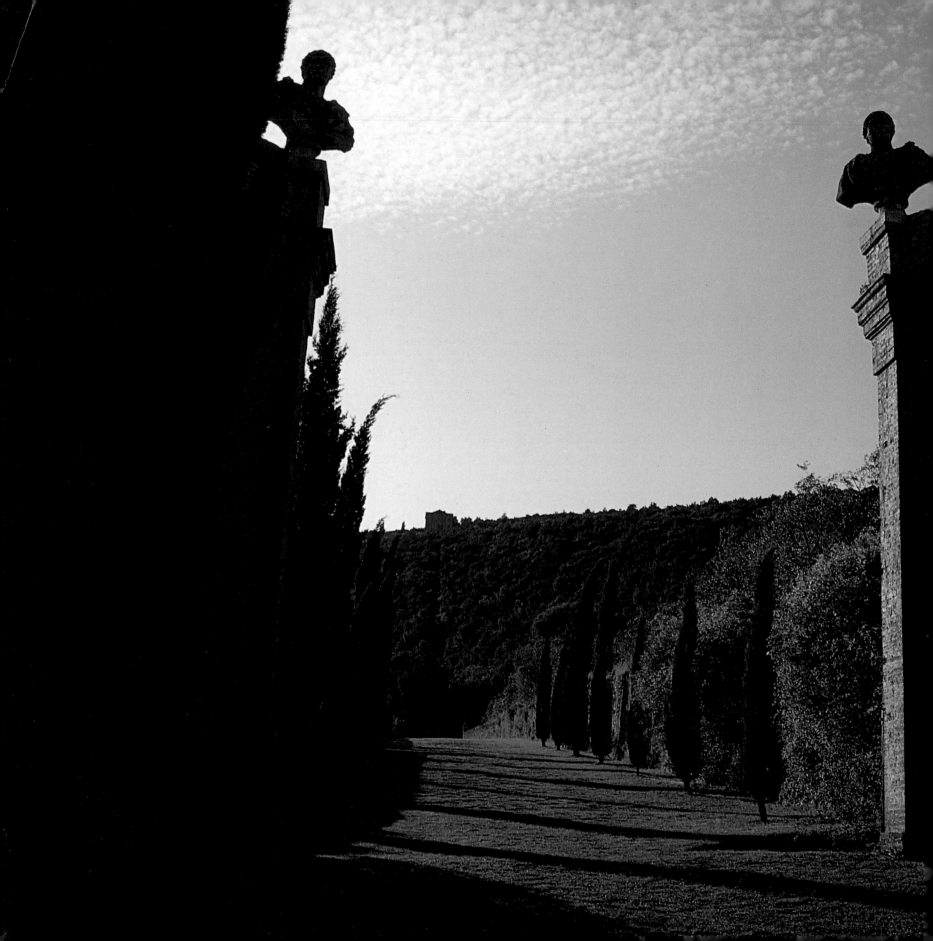

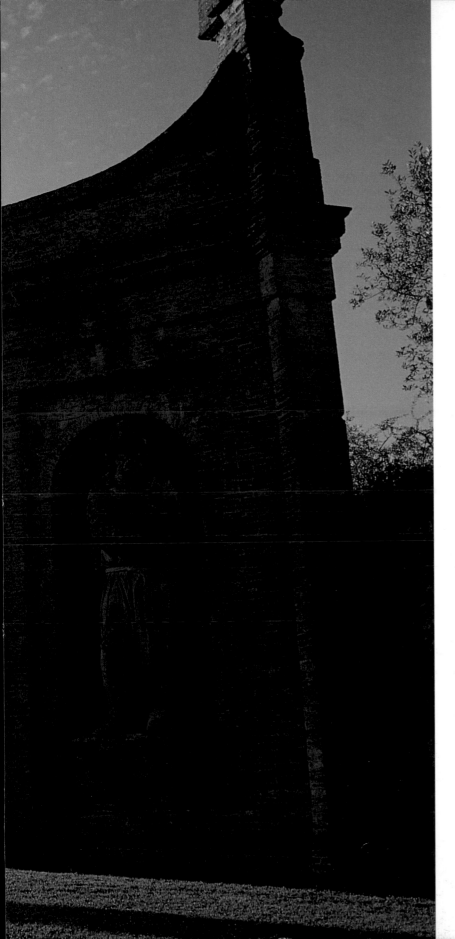

VILLA CETINALE

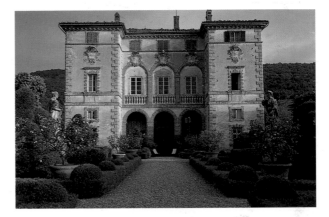

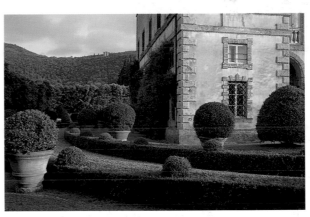

'The house at Cetinale is so charming,' enthused Edith Wharton.
It has now been entirely restored by Lord Lambton and Claire Ward.
Two statues of Spring and Summer, originally from the back gate, preside
over the Lemon Garden. The 'glory of Cetinale', wrote Wharton, 'is its park.
Behind the villa a long grass-walk . . . extends between high walls to a
fantastic gateway' (left), composed of two brick piers whose niches barely
accommodate fifteenth-century statues of the Dacians adapted from the
Emperor Trajan's column in Rome. The tapis vert leads to a crossroads of
the scala santa to the romitorio on the brow of the hill and a path leading
into the Thebaid or Holy Wood, which clothes the hillside with ilex.
Seen from the Lemon Garden, the ascent appears farther and higher
than it really is because of a trick of perspective.

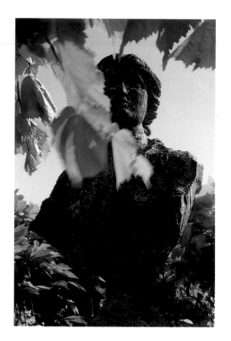

ABOVE *All the statues around the villa were sculpted by Giuseppe Mazzuoli, commissioned by Cardinal Flavio Chigi. Together with wisteria and pleached limes they adorn the balustrade wall.*

OPPOSITE *The old kitchen garden, planted in about 1900 by the English wife of one of the Chigi, has been restored by Claire Ward. The iron hoops, found rusting amongst the weeds, are original and have been revived to carry vines and a large collection of climbing roses. Florentine irises and valerian, common in Italy, spill onto the path in spring, while the quintessentially English sweet william flowers profusely and happily in summer. Swags of pleached lime and lilies in pots (far right) on lovely old stone and brick make a decorative corner.*

LESS THAN A MILE from Baldassare Peruzzi's birthplace at Ancaiano, stands another villa built for one of the Chigi – Villa Cetinale. Designed by Carlo Fontana after he had worked on the Isola Bella, it was completed in 1680, almost 150 years after Peruzzi's death. Perhaps in acknowledgment to Peruzzi's genius and his association with the Chigi, Fontana took Peruzzi's characteristic design of a rectangle with wings, which had served for his grandest Chigi villa – the Villa Farnesina in Rome – and modelled Villa Cetinale on it. Fontana placed the villa in the middle of a 3-mile (4.75-kilometre) axis with a statue of Hercules at one end and a *romitorio* (hermitage) on the other. It paid admirable homage to Peruzzi's reputation for simplicity, accommodating both the surrounding landscape and the agricultural nature of the estate. This is almost unchanged since Edith Wharton's description of it: 'The olive-orchards and corn-fields of the farm come up to the boundary walls of the walk, and the wood is left as nature planted it. Fontana . . . was wise enough to profit by the natural advantage of the great forest of oak and ilex which clothes this part of the country, and to realize that only the broadest and simplest lines would be in harmony with so noble a background.'

The villa was rebuilt from a modest farmhouse for Cardinal Flavio Chigi, the nephew of Pope Alexander VII (Fabio Chigi), the childhood friend of Cardinal Barbarigo, who built Valsanzibio. Pope Alexander had helped Barbarigo become a cardinal, and made Flavio a cardinal at the age of twenty-six – one of the last examples of a practice that had become so common that it gave rise to the word 'nepotism' (from *nipote*, meaning 'nephew'). Pope Alexander VII also gave the newly created Cardinal Flavio Chigi the casino and garden of the Quattro Fontane in Rome, which Barbarigo had built as Secretary to the Pope, and vacated only a few years before, when he was made Bishop of Padua.

Cardinal Flavio Chigi lived in the villa of the Quattro Fontane some ten years before he built Cetinale. To the rear of the property, in a grove of laurel and holm oak he called the Thebaid, he built himself a *romitorio* with frescoes of hermits painted on the walls. Wharton remarked upon these frescoes in her essay on the hermitages, 'What the Hermits Saw', in *Italian Backgrounds*. Cardinal Chigi also commissioned the sculptor Antonio Fontana to make *peperino* (porous rock) statues of animals – dragons, lions, a tortoise. When he converted Cetinale from a farmhouse to a villa and made it his agricultural summer retreat, he brought these

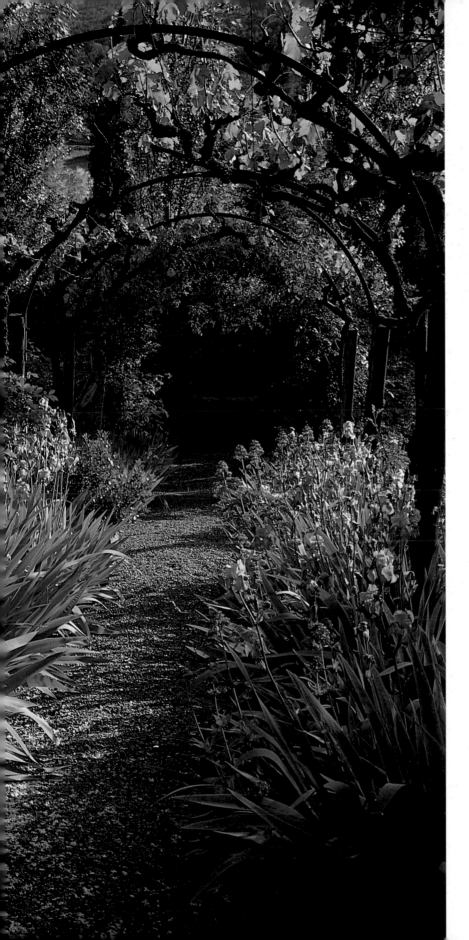

animals with him and placed them in a new Thebaid he made there in the ilex wood. In theory, the idea of the Thebaid came from the Egyptian saints of Thebes who, noted Wharton, 'turned to the desert to escape the desolation of the country and the foulness of the town' and 'took refuge in the burning solitudes of Egypt and Asia Minor'. In practice, it was really Petrarch's concept of *otium* reinterpreted. 'The traditional charm of the life apart was commemorated by the mock "hermitages" to be found in every nobleman's park, or by such frescoes.' The hermit shared his solitude with wild and domesticated animals – hence the statues. Only a few of the animals, the votive chapels, and the statues of the penitent monks and saints are left now, but as you make your way amongst the winding paths, the atmosphere is extremely evocative.

Legend has it that the whole *romitorio*, Thebaid and *scala santa* (holy steps) that led up to it made up a garden of atonement, for it is said that Cardinal Chigi, thwarted in love or ambition, had murdered a rival cardinal in a jealous rage, and built and then ascended the *scala santa* on his knees to beg forgiveness. Lord Lambton scoffs at this and says it was primarily a garden of pleasure with added holy elements. Alternatively, a walk through the garden could be read as a journey by which one leaves the earthly delights of the virile Hercules at the lower end of the garden and makes the steep climb to the *romitorio*, to find oneself already that much closer to God.

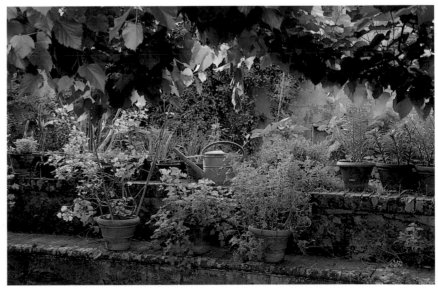

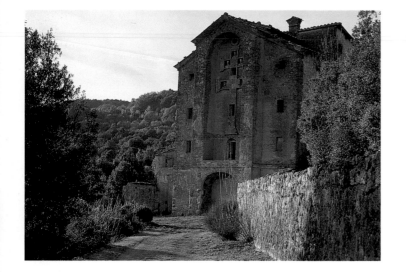

ABOVE *The* romitorio *was designed by Fontana but not built until 1713. There is a Cross of Lorraine on the façade; inside are niches with statues of Jesus and the four Evangelists. Until the end of the nineteenth century it was inhabited by twelve monks.*

BELOW *One of the statues of the Dacians occupying a niche in the gateway at the beginning of the* tapis vert.

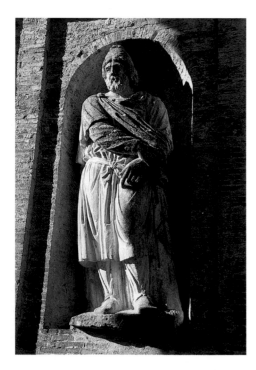

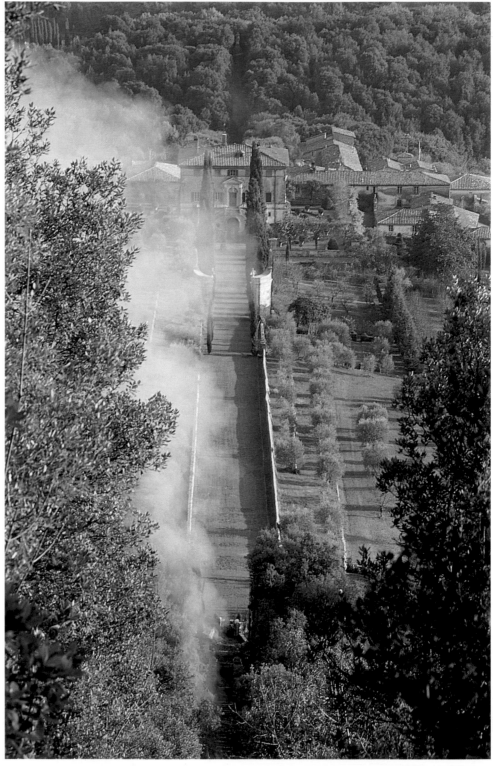

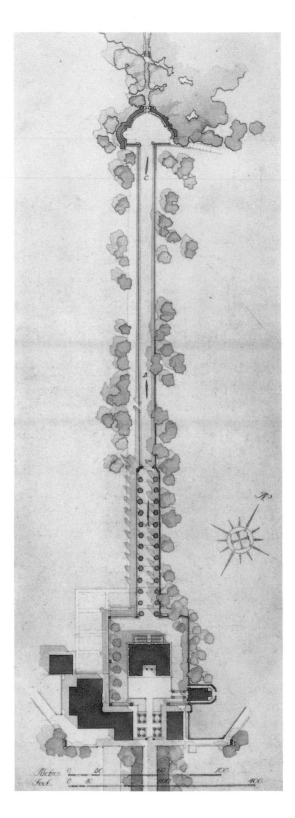

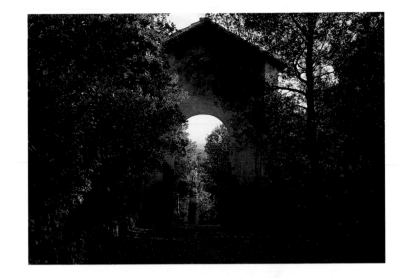

OPPOSITE *The view from the* romitorio *to the villa shows the back of the house much as Wharton described it with '. . . its stately double flight of steps leading up to the first floor, and its monumental doorway opening on a central* salone . . . *The plan of using the low-studded ground floor for offices, wine-cellar and store rooms, while the living rooms are all above stairs, shows the hand of an architect trained in the Roman school.'*

LEFT *The axis from the* romitorio *to the villa, illustrated in Sir Geoffrey Jellicoe's* Italian Gardens of the Renaissance, *recalls Sir Harold Acton's comment on the Villa Cetinale in which he quotes a distinguished mathematician 'who considered there was nothing more beautiful than a straight line'.*

RIGHT *The holy frescoes at the entrance to the Thebaid (top) belie the sybaritic activity conducted there. The famous Sienese horse race, the Palio, was run there sixteen times between 1690 and 1710 because there were riots in the city. It was not only penitent hermits (below) that stood on pedestals: Lord Lambton was told by the Chigi that they were on occasion adorned by painted naked women, and when Cardinal Chigi clapped his hands they all jumped off and joined him for lunch. The* peperino *dragon (centre) was brought from the garden of Cardinal Chigi's villa of the Quattro Fontane in Rome.*

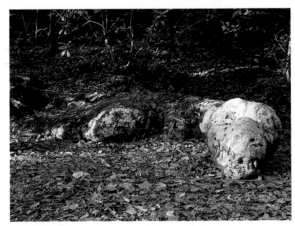

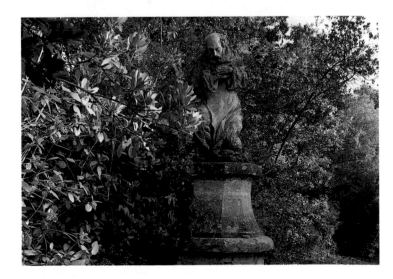

GARDENS
AROUND
ROME

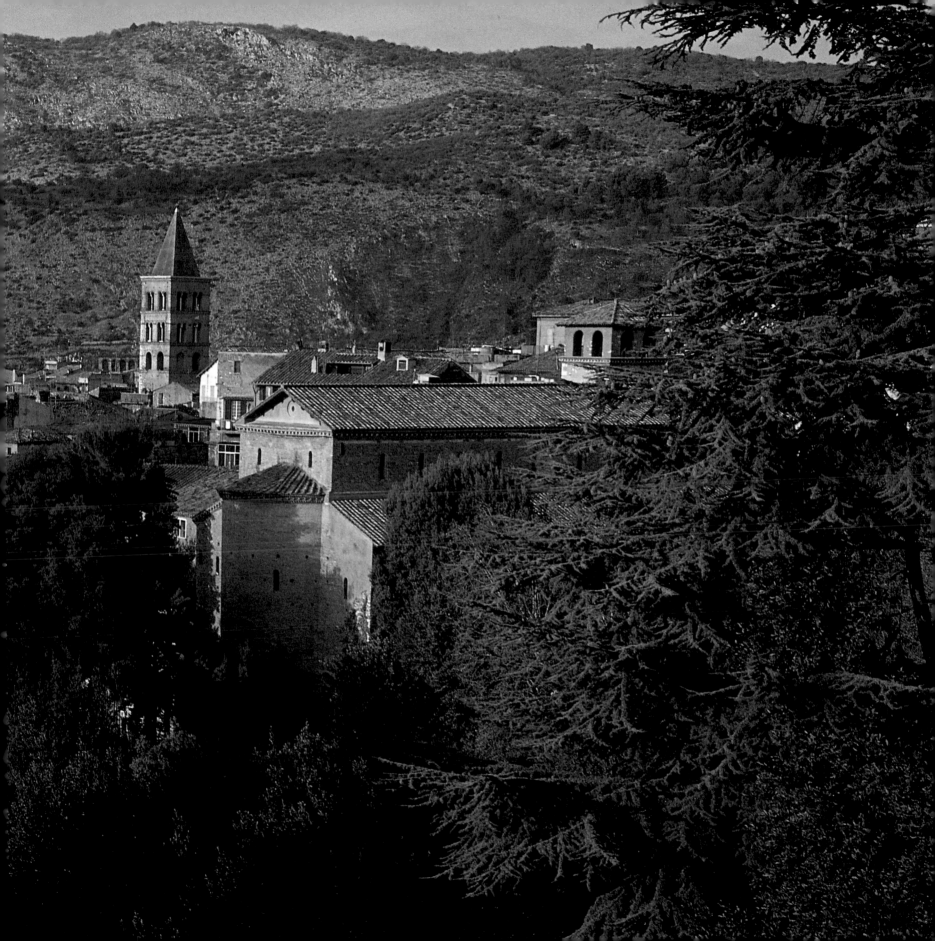

THE STORY of the great Roman gardens of the Renaissance is one of a movement which sought a 'conscious return to the splendour of old patrician life' by reviving the spirit and grandeur of ancient Rome. 'It started', wrote Edith Wharton, as 'the medieval world began to wake from its lethargy and gather up its scattered heritage of artistic traditions', prompting innumerable studies of the ruins of ancient Rome and its classical literature and mythology, and the acquisition of statues and artefacts – as if possessing them would release some of their inherent glory.

The ancient Rome that was so spectacularly reinvented in the gardens of the Renaissance by garden architects was based, for the most part, on concepts elaborated and reinterpreted from ancient Greece and succinctly laid out in the letters of Pliny the Younger, in the writings of Varro and Vitruvius and in the mythological tales recounted by Ovid in his *Metamorphoses*. Petrarch was the first to be so inspired. In 1350 he created in the nutshell of his own modest villa and garden in Provence, France, an allegorical garden and hermitage which became the inspiration behind all the great gardens around Rome.

Unlike Dante and Boccaccio, who thrived on society, Petrarch abandoned 'the haunts of men and crowded cities', which he considered 'enemies', and retreated to Provence to live amongst 'woods which are friends'. He revived Pliny's idea of the life of *otium*, a programme of philosophical contemplation, study and artistic creativity that could be conducted only in the peace of the countryside. 'I cultivate not my land but my mind, and form many

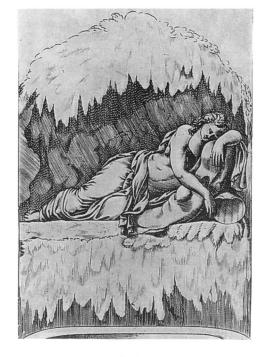

a composition'. Expatiating on the cult of solitary virtue, Petrarch identified his hermitage with the mythological Mount Parnassus of Greece; and he associated the source of the River Sorgue in his nearby grotto with the sacred spring Castalia, which Pegasus had created by a stamp of his hoof. Mount Parnassus was the home of Apollo and his companions, the nine Muses, reigning patrons of the arts and sciences; and Castalia was the source of all artistic creativity and intellectual achievement. The Muses were originally nymphs who lived in caves and grottoes, presiding over springs that represented sources of knowledge and inspiration. This allegory, translated into nymphaeums and rustic grottoes, was to become the most essential and imaginative architectural feature of the Renaissance garden.

Petrarch's hermitage, while identified with Mount Parnassus as a whole, comprised two gardens: one dedicated to Apollo, the god of Reason, who symbolized noble ideals, dignity, restraint and perfection of form, and the other to Bacchus, who represented passion and emotion. This embodied the Renaissance concept of man made complete by thought and action, a duality which in the fifteenth and sixteenth centuries became a symbolic cornerstone in gardens, in which 'thought' was represented by association with Mount Parnassus and 'action' by representations of the labours of the heroic Hercules.

Petrarch had thus taken the garden out of its pragmatic, productive function as a supplier of medicinal herbs and food, and elevated it into ideological and mythological realms. After the popes had returned to Rome from Avignon in 1377, and following the

The Villa Pia, Caprarola and the Villa d'Este were all oriented towards mythological references or ruins of classical Rome. The view from the Cardinal's apartments (previous pages) is directly aligned with the campanile of Tivoli, site of the ancient Roman Temple of Hercules, where it is said Hercules delivered his orations. 'I sleep, while listening to the murmur of the caressing water.' The nymph and her source (above) represented the mysterious spirit of life that the Romans sought to create in a new golden age by reviving the memory of classical Rome. Memory was the mother of the nine Muses, who all lived with Apollo on Mount Parnassus, a favourite theme in Renaissance gardens. At the top of the Villa Medici garden overlooking Rome (right), Mount Parnassus was re-created as an entire hill, encircled by cypresses, with a grotto beneath.

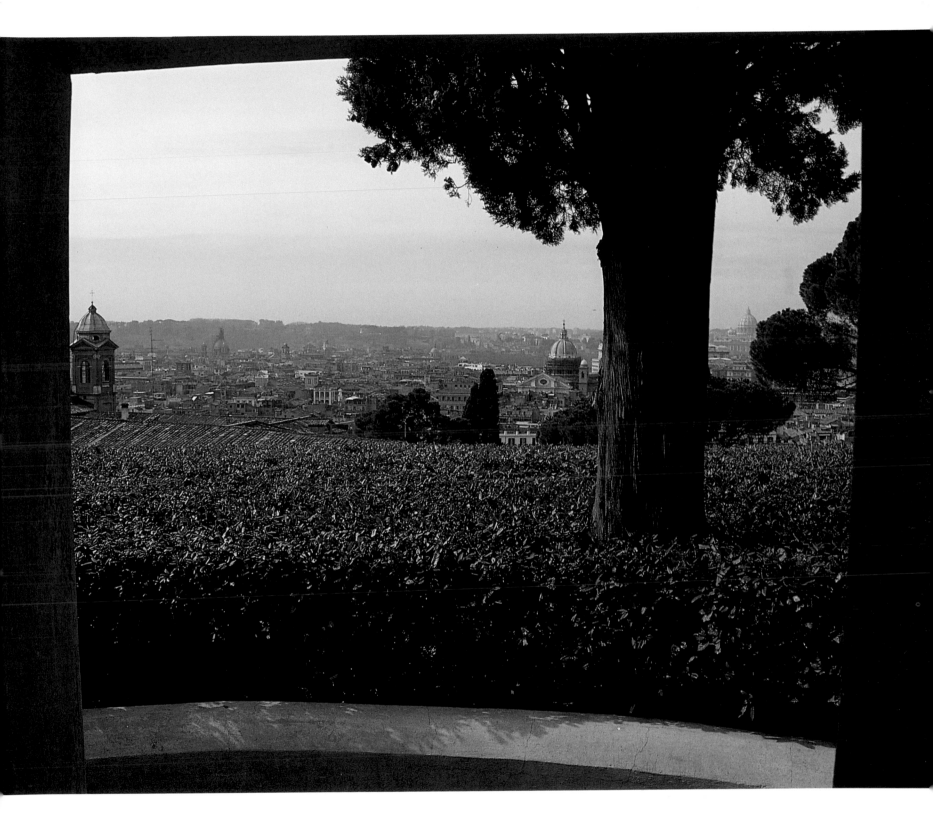

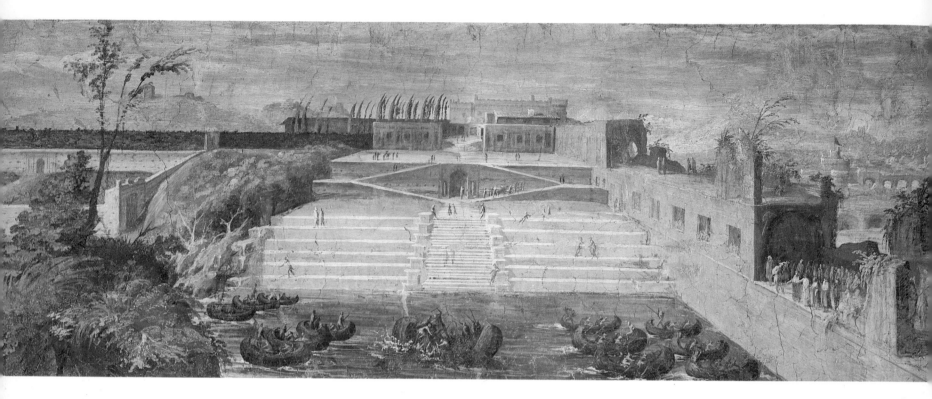

ABOVE *Prospero Fontana's fresco in Castel Sant' Angelo shows the Belvedere Court as it looked in the mid-sixteenth century. 'One of the earliest Roman gardens of which a description has been preserved is that which Bramante laid out within the Vatican in the last years of the fifteenth century,' wrote Edith Wharton. 'This terraced garden, with its monumental double flight of steps leading up by three levels to the Gardino della Pigna, was described in 1523 by the Venetian ambassador to Rome, who speaks of its grass parterres and fountains, its hedges of laurel and cypress, its plantations of mulberries and roses. One half of the garden (the court of the Belvedere) had brick-paved walks between rows of orange-trees; in its centre were statues of the Nile and the Tiber above a fountain; while the Apollo, the Laocoön and the Venus of the Vatican were placed about it in niches.'*

OPPOSITE *'In beauty of site, in grandeur of scale and in the wealth of its Roman sculpture the Villa Pamphili was unmatched,' wrote Wharton. Built in 1648, the Villa Doria-Pamphili retained Renaissance features while also introducing the idea of a villa-garden-park. She added, 'its incomparable ilex avenues and pinewoods, its rolling meadows and wide views over the* campagna *have enchanted many to whom its architectural beauties would not appeal'.*

Papal Schism in 1417, the Church grew powerful once more. This notion of the allegorical garden caught the imagination and found patronage with the wealthy, cultured but fiercely competitive popes and cardinals, who took the concept of Petrarch's intellectual but modestly executed garden hermitage and from it created gardens which became works of art on a monumental scale.

This movement started at the Vatican. The popes, having vaguely identified it with the House of the Lord and its gardens with Paradise, had been developing the papal city in a haphazard way through the years, adding pieces of land and planting trees, but no muse came its way and it remained unprepossessing until 1503, when Cardinal Giuliano della Rovere was elected Pope Julius II. The year following his election he commissioned the architect Donato Bramante to design the magnificent Belvedere Court on the steep slope of the Vatican hill.

Belvedere Court rose in three terraces – linked by flights of stairs and embellished with the colossal statues of two river gods with urns – whose scheme and architectural detail would be widely copied. Bramante incorporated a Statue Court in the top terrace, which became an outdoor museum to display the Pope's statuary, of which there were four principal pieces: Apollo, recalling the Muses of poetry and painters, Venus, Cleopatra and the Laocoön, all set in niches around a fragrant garden of golden citrus fruits. A large statue of Commodus as Hercules identified the garden with the golden apples of the mythological garden of the Hesperides which Hercules, as his twelfth labour, had been sent to steal from the dragon, and introducing the heroic Hercules into garden iconography. Another piece of innovation in this seminal garden, built in 1523 on the very top of its northern bastion, was a small loggia set in a cypress wood, echoing Pliny and Petrarch's *otium* as a restorative place removed from society. It was destroyed by the architect and archaeologist Pirro Ligorio to make way for the Archive Court, but was reinvented by Ligorio in 1558 only 350 feet (106 metres) away from the Belvedere Court as the famous Villa Pia. This became the intimate and secret retreat of popes and cardinals, designed as a kind of open-air salon. It was an enclosed oval court with a fountain in the middle, and a loggia giving on to it, in which cardinals could lunch *al fresco* or retire for quiet contemplation, refreshed by the tinkling fountain and imperceptible breezes. In Edith Wharton's opinion the Villa Pia seemed the 'daydream of an artist who has saturated his mind with the past', and she quoted Burckhardt's description of it as 'the most perfect retreat imaginable for a midsummer afternoon'.

In laying out their gardens in Rome during the last half of the sixteenth century the cardinals borrowed freely from Bramante, Pliny and Petrarch and, advised by their court humanists, archaeologists and architects, played upon their themes in the most vainglorious variations. All vying for the supremacy of the throne in the ruthless game of papal politics, they dressed their gardens in ways that would most impress, and in so doing revealed, like a peacock opening his fan, a magnificent display of the most sophisticated array of iconographical schemes, fountains and architectural recollections of ancient Rome.

The Roman love affair with its illustrious past and quest for personal glorification dominated the sixteenth century; but with the seventeenth century came the Baroque, and as a result of its influence on Roman gardens the emphasis shifted from architecture and sculpture to nature on a large scale. The compact art of the Renaissance garden, so densely packed with detail and layers of meaning, was gradually replaced by the expansive art of landscape design, most beautifully expressed in the Villa Doria-Pamphili.

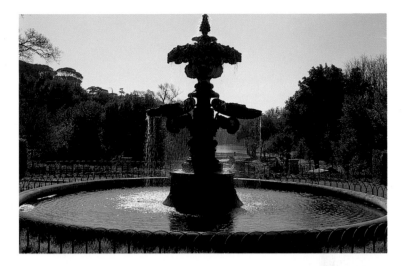

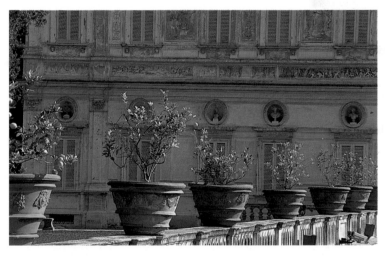

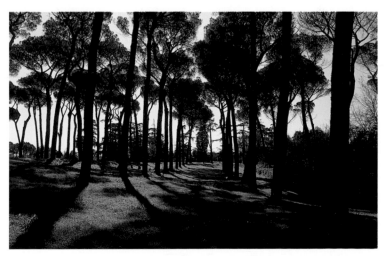

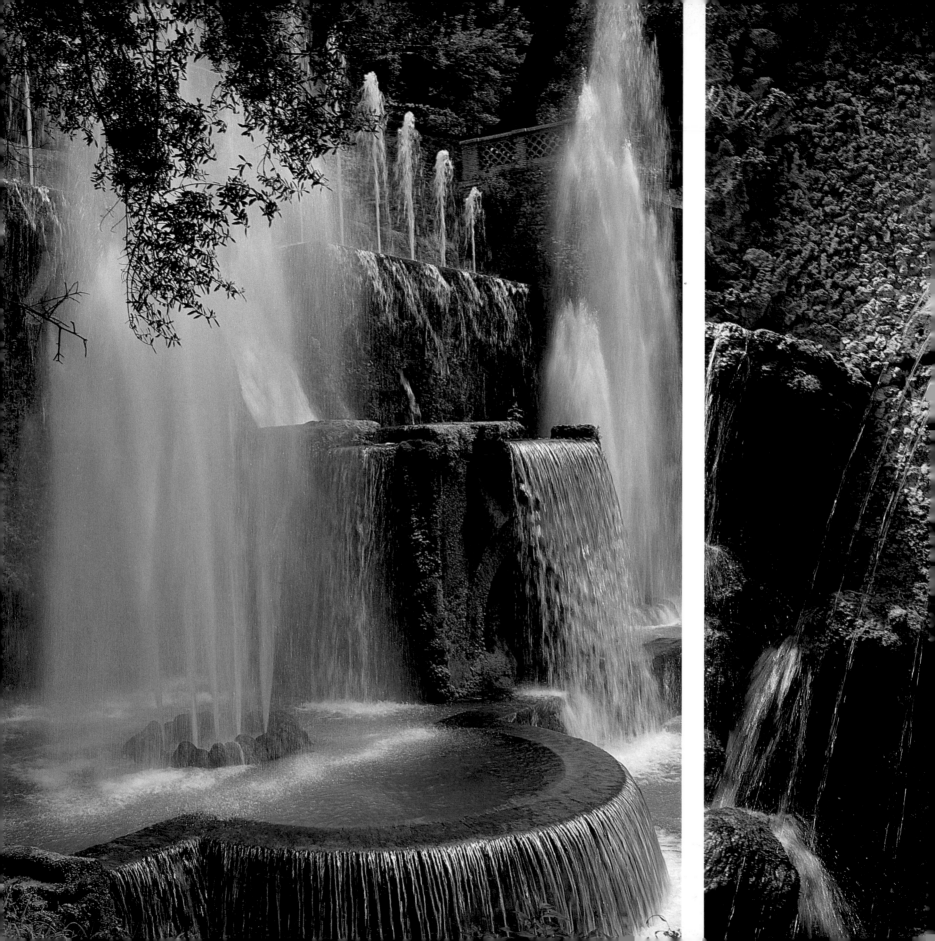

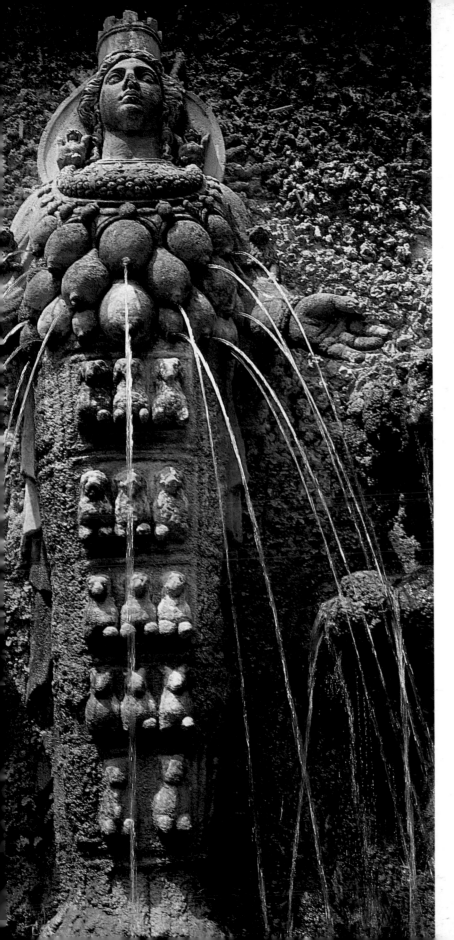

VILLA D'ESTE

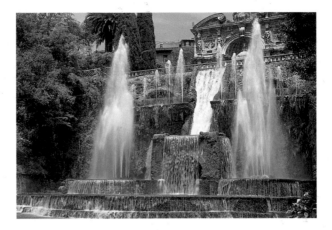

'It is the omnipresent rush of water which gives the gardens of the Villa d'Este
their peculiar character,' noted Edith Wharton. Nowhere was this more
dramatically expressed than in the Fountain of the Organ (far left and above).
It was the wonder of its day, for it played without human intervention.
'To make it more wonderful,' wrote Nicolas Audebert in 1576, 'the view of the
mechanism is denied to visitors.' As the aeolic chamber filled with water, it
created air pressure. The air went into the pipes and water turned the wheel
of a musical score, opening and closing the valves of the pipes. The musical
voice of the Tiburtine Sybil, whose legends and prophecies are the principal
themes of the garden, had a repertoire of five tunes. She foretold the
Apocalyptic flood, which was immediately followed by the roar of the deluge,
created by an enormous volume and force of water. The façade of the upper
portion of the fountain was a wall of marble, glass, gold and mirror
mosaic, dazzling in the sunshine and spray.

The many-breasted Diana of Ephesus (left) originally stood in the centre
of the Fountain of the Organ, the symbol of the all-creating and nurturing
goddesses. She was removed in 1611 by Cardinal Alessandro d'Este, who
erected a tempietto in her place to protect the organ, and the statue is now
elsewhere in the garden. Niccolò Tribolo was the first to use Diana of Ephesus
as an icon, and sent one to King François I of France for Fontainebleau, which is
probably where Cardinal Ippolito II d'Este, who served thirteen years there as
Papal Nuncio, first saw it. Below the statue in the retaining wall, now masked
by modern jets and Pietro Bernini's 1611 cascade, was the grotto of the lesser
sibyls, whose cavernous underground chamber echoed and reverberated her
message, giving the impression that the earth itself was speaking.

THE GARDEN OF THE VILLA D'ESTE was born out of a passion for Classical antiquity and mythology shared by an erudite cardinal and his architect, Pirro Ligorio. The key to understanding its underlying meaning lies in the story, told in frescoes inside the villa, a combination of a tale in Ovid's *Metamorphoses* and local legend.

Ino, who was transformed into the Tiburtine Sibyl, was the sister of Semele, Jupiter's lover. Jupiter's jealous wife Juno persuaded the pregnant Semele to ask Jupiter to reveal himself to her as a god. She, not being a god, could not withstand the bolt of lightning and was instantly killed. Her unborn child, Bacchus, was sewn into Jupiter's thigh, and after his birth was looked after by his aunt Ino. Juno was jealous of Bacchus, and convinced the Furies to render Ino's husband mad. In his madness he smashed their first-born son to death on a rock and Ino fled with her second son Melicertes and flung herself from a cliff into the Ionian sea. Venus saw the innocent Ino and her child drowning and beseeched her uncle Neptune to save them, which he did by turning them into water deities, until they were washed up on the shores of the Tiber. Threatened by Juno once more, Hercules then came to their aid and the prophetess Carmenta made Ino into a prophetess, the Tiburtine Sibyl.

The circular temple at the top of Tivoli's famous cascade was built for the Tiburtine Sibyl. A marble statue of her was later found at the foot of this cliff and taken to the Campidoglio in Rome and the Temple of Jupiter. Here the oracle was consulted by priests who described their vision of the nine suns, which she interpreted as symbolizing the nine stages of man's history. The first sun represented a world without sin; the third war; the fourth the coming of Christ; the fifth his Crucifixion and the ninth the Day of Judgement.

The key characters and events of the legend are mirrored in the garden. Jupiter, Neptune, Hercules and Venus are represented as well as the significance of the fifth and ninth suns in the repeated grouping of fives and nines, and the lower garden's nine paths.

This anonymous seventeenth-century painting based on a sixteenth-century print by Du Perac shows the garden's layout clearly, but not entirely accurately. Ligorio made the temple to the Tiburtine Sibyl at the top of the Tivoli cascades the focal point from which he drew the central axis of the garden, but the artist has straightened out this axis and made it appear to align with the villa. Some of the features shown here, such as the Fountain of Neptune, were never built.

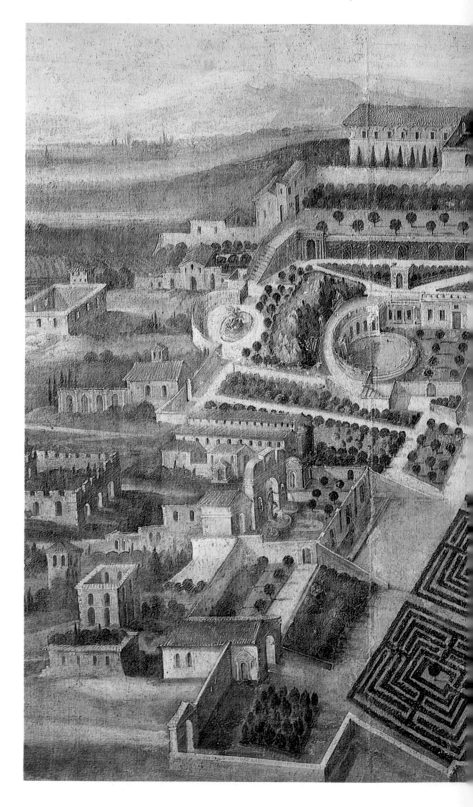

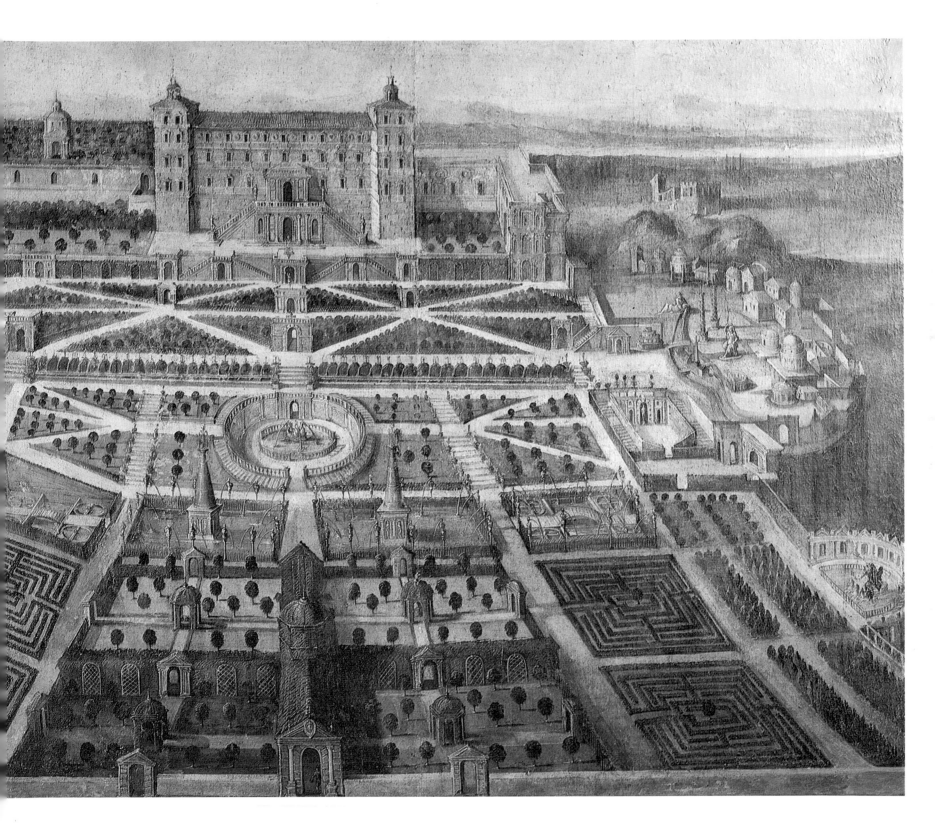

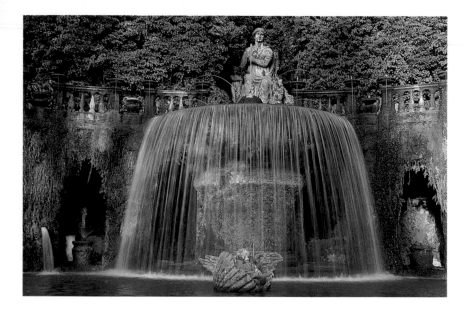

Looking down from a high terrace into the gardens of the Villa d'Este, Edith Wharton appreciated their 'tragic grandeur' and 'depths of mystery'. The concept of 'gardens that were to be, as it were, an organ on which the water is played' was intriguing and for her produced a result that was 'extraordinarily romantic and beautiful' – as long as she did not compare to them the architecture of Raphael, Vignola or even Niccolò Tribolo, whereupon their heavy and fantastic *barochismo* became 'grotesque' and 'disfiguring', their details 'pitiable and tawdry' or 'absolutely puerile'. This is typical of the kind of criticism heaped upon a garden that suffers by comparison to the more restrained Villa Lante or Caprarola, which are generally held up as paragons of architectural genius and innovation.

As a place of metaphor and imagination, the Villa d'Este was the most sophisticated of all the Roman gardens. Created by two of the most erudite minds in Italy, its genius lay in the intricate orchestration of many themes of extraordinary complexity. But the displacing and disappearance of its statues over the years has distorted the music, and in the absence of any original documentation, there is no original score. It remains an enigma. Yet if we judge the evolution of an era by the art that flows from it, then perhaps we should also measure the accomplishments of a garden by its ability to compel painters, composers and writers to want to reinterpret what they see, hear and feel there – and of

scholars to write entire books about it and of garden makers to copy it. The Villa d'Este has been sincerely flattered in this way. Torquato Tasso wrote his *Aminta* here, which received its first reading around the Fountain of Rome, and the court humanist Marc Antoine Muret wrote his tragedies at the villa.

Its ineffable atmosphere inspired arguably the most beautiful paintings ever done of an Italian garden – by Hubert Robert and Jean-Honoré Fragonard, who painted there together during the summer of 1760. 'Monsieur Fragonard is all fire,' wrote their host, the Abbé de Saint-Non, who had use of the villa. 'His drawings are very numerous. They are enchanting. I find in them a kind of sorcery.' Franz Liszt came every year from 1870 to 1884 and paid homage in his exquisite, impressionistic *Fountains of the Villa d'Este* piano piece, which evokes the tinkling fountains, shimmering reflections and water skipping down rills and the play of light on water on a hot, calm summer's day. Six years after Wharton's visit, Henry James, his antennae probing for the intangible, wandered among gardens all mossed over by disuse, their fountains in ruins, and still met the 'haunting genius of style'.

The house of Este, 'that antique brood famed for their passion for war and art', had ruled Ferrara since the thirteenth century, and claimed to be directly descended from Hercules and Galatea. Cardinal Ippolito II d'Este, the son of Duke Alphonso I d'Este and the renowned Lucrezia Borgia, was made Archbishop of Milan at the age of ten, and a cardinal when he was thirty. His maternal grandfather was Pope Alexander VI, whose mistress, the beautiful Giulia Farnese, had persuaded the pope to make her brother Alessandro a cardinal. When Alessandro Farnese was elected Pope Paul III in 1534 instead of an Este it had created bitter rivalry between the two families. Cardinal Ippolito II d'Este considered himself born to the papal throne, but his ambition was so blatant it was looked on with apprehension and he failed, by fair means or foul, to be elected. During the conclave of 1549, he used his power to block the Farnese pope's nephew, Alessandro Farnese II, and the new Pope Julius III rewarded Cardinal d'Este with the governorship of Tivoli, an area rich in Roman ruins, including that of Hadrian's Villa. Este and Ligorio visited all the sites together, and Ligorio immediately began excavating Hadrian's villa, plundering the statues and piecing together its plan.

The cardinal was given a Franciscan monastery on the hilltop of Tivoli, and he and Ligorio began work there in 1550. While the

OPPOSITE *The Oval Fountain was the first to be built in the garden, and one of two made by Ligorio himself. The statue is a copy of an ancient one presented to the Roman people by Pope Pius V after he stripped the Belvedere Court at the Vatican of most of the great collection that Ligorio had gathered together for Pope Pius IV.*

'The poets say that Memory is a divine thing and the mother of the Muses,' wrote Ligorio. Here the Tiburtine Sibyl is transformed into Mnemosyne or Memory. She sits on a chair with her son Melicertes, at the base of a hill representing Tivoli as the new Parnassus. Above her is a statue of Pegasus with his head tilted towards the villa, in recognition of Cardinal Ippolito II d'Este as a long-standing patron of the arts and sciences. The sibyl was beloved of Apollo (the hillside around the fountain was planted with laurel trees in homage to him) who granted her eternal life, but she did not ask for youth, and shrivelled into a cicada-like creature, begging for death. The fountain also represents the first stage in the sibyl's flight after her leap into the sea: the basin of the fountain symbolizes her saviour Neptune, or the sea, and in the centre Venus, who also intervened on her behalf, rises from her shell. The sibyl's journey from Tivoli to Rome continues via the Avenue of the Hundred Fountains to the Fountain of Rome.

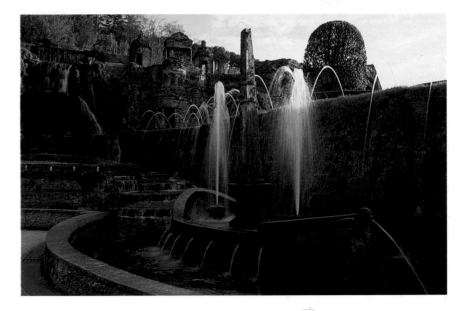

RIGHT ABOVE *The Fountain of Rome, or the Rometta, was the second fountain Ligorio built himself, and one which Cardinal II d'Este loved to contemplate. It celebrated the noble golden age of Rome and served as a spectacular backdrop to the plays that were performed in front of it. The three rivers of Tivoli flow into it from the Avenue of a Hundred Fountains, and are joined by water from the upper part of the fountain, which shows the cascade of Tivoli, the river god Aniene, the Temple of the Sibyl and the Apennines. The stone boat represents the Tiburtine islet of San Bartolomeo on which was the Temple of Jupiter where the sibylline texts were kept. Behind it is the part of the fountain meant to represent the seven hills of Rome with its monuments, including the Pantheon, the Colosseum and the Campidoglio, where the statue of the Tiburtine Sibyl was taken.*

RIGHT BELOW *The Fountain of the Dragon is in the centre of the garden. As his eleventh labour, Hercules had to steal the golden apples from the garden of Hesperides from the dragon and his nymphs. Hercules is represented as a young man and an old man in two statues above the fountain. The fountain also represents the Day of Judgement, as foretold by the sibyl, personified by Jupiter, the father of Hercules. Jupiter formerly sat in a cave, surrounded by the forces of the underworld. On the retaining walls were painted scenes from his life. The figure of Jupiter must have had some personal significance for the cardinal, as he had a statue of the god in the garden in Rome placed beneath his personal coat of arms. The holm oak, sacred to Jupiter, was planted all round the fountain.*

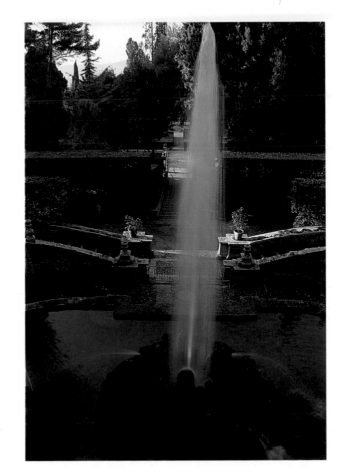

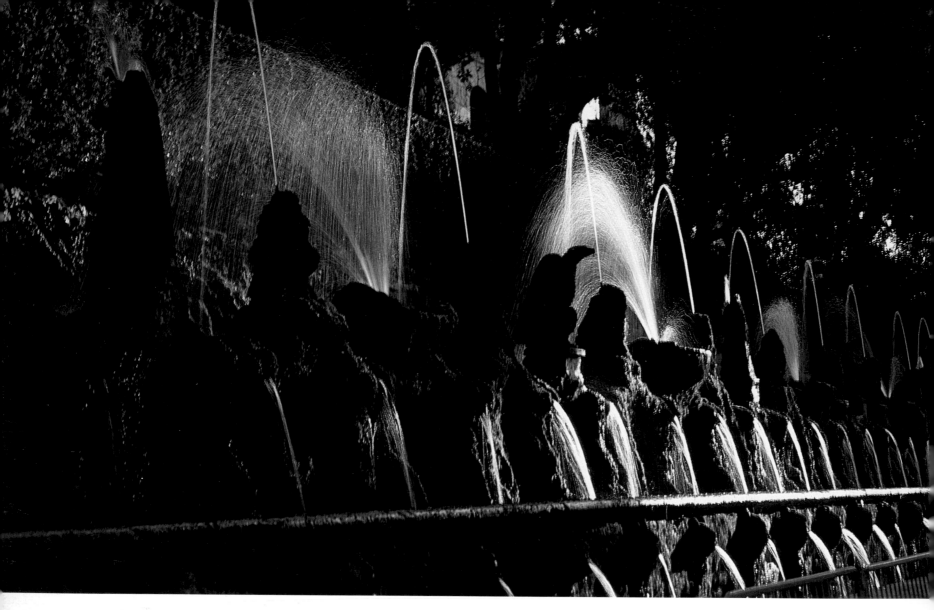

ABOVE *The Avenue of a Hundred Fountains connects the Oval Fountain with the Fountain of Rome. Three terraced channels represent the rivers of Tivoli – the Aniene, the Albuneo and the Erculaneo, which carry water from Tivoli to the Tiber in Rome. The upper channel was originally decorated with twenty-two small boats – separated from each other by three vases. The middle channel was decorated with scenes from Ovid's* Metamorphoses, *and the lower one had heads of small animals spitting water into a channel below. The heads still remain (right). The vases were later replaced by the Este eagles and fleurs-de-lis. Now there are four types of fountain, each sending out a different kind of jet.*

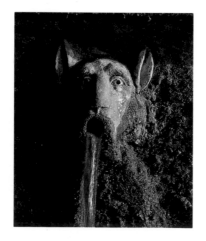

OPPOSITE *The fishpools, or peschiere, contained exotic fish and birds. Swans were to decorate the edges of the pools, along with travertine columns where jets of water shot up and joined each other like rainbows over the pools, recalling the rainbows that appeared to Noah after the Flood. Four fishpools were planned, but only three were built. They were designed to carry water from Diana's breasts to the sea – personified by the Fountain of Neptune with Neptune sitting in a chariot driving sea horses, but this was never built. Nor were the amazing pagoda-like temples in the middle of the fishpools shown in the seventeenth-century painting based on Du Perac's engraving.*

cardinal was simultaneously enlarging and embellishing his garden on Monte Cavallo in Rome with fountains and statues of Jupiter and Apollo and the Muses, the garden at Tivoli was conceived on a far grander scale. A whole part of the old town, including a church, was swallowed up in the landscaping of the garden, causing such resentment among the people of Tivoli that they brought litigation against Este that was still going on at the time of his death in 1572. The landscaping was so monumental that the mis-alignment of the central axis to the villa could only have been deliberate, and was probably the result of Ligorio's wish to link the garden with some important Classical ruins in the Tiburtine landscape. The garden's main axis aligns with the Temple of the Tiburtine Sibyl that sits on top of the hill of the famous Tivoli cascades. Another important axis runs through the centre of the *palazzo* to the Tiburtine amphitheatre outside. Both alignments give a substantial clue that the Sibyl is the central theme of the garden. The cult of Hippolytus, after whom Cardinal Ippolito was named, and that of Hercules, the Este family's mythical ancestor, were also central to the garden's iconography.

Inspired by the use of water he had observed at Hadrian's Villa, Ligorio made it the dominant chord of the Villa d'Este. He brought pure water from a spring in the distant hills to furnish the upper gardens near the villa, and built an aqueduct large enough for a man to walk through from the River Aniene. 'From the Anio', quoted Wharton from Herr Tuckerman, 'throbs the whole organism of the garden like its inmost vital principle.' Water descends through the garden in all its incarnations, permutations and effects. It appears as mist, spray, jets, boiling water and conical spouts. It murmurs, gurgles, roars and spits in witty *scherzi d'acqua*, keeping the garden cool and moist during the baking Roman summers. The greatest attraction of the garden used to be the water-driven automata, the most popular of which was the Fountain of the Owl, which no longer works. Based directly on descriptions given by Hero of Alexandria, its twenty bronze birds sat on branches trilling and chirping in different notes until a big owl appeared and silenced them with his loud and mournful hooting. Water was the mouthpiece though which the message of the prophesying sibyl flowed. It created a harmonious balance between the intellectual, the sensual and the horticultural in a garden where Henry James found 'brave indissoluble unions of the planted and the builded symmetry'.

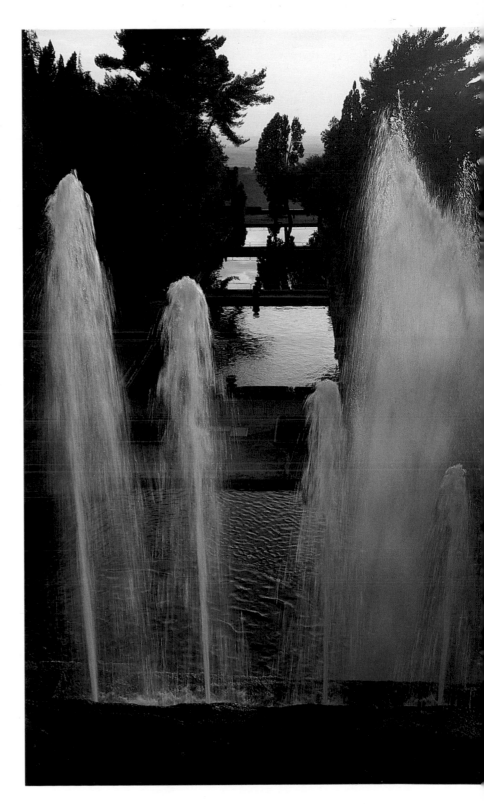

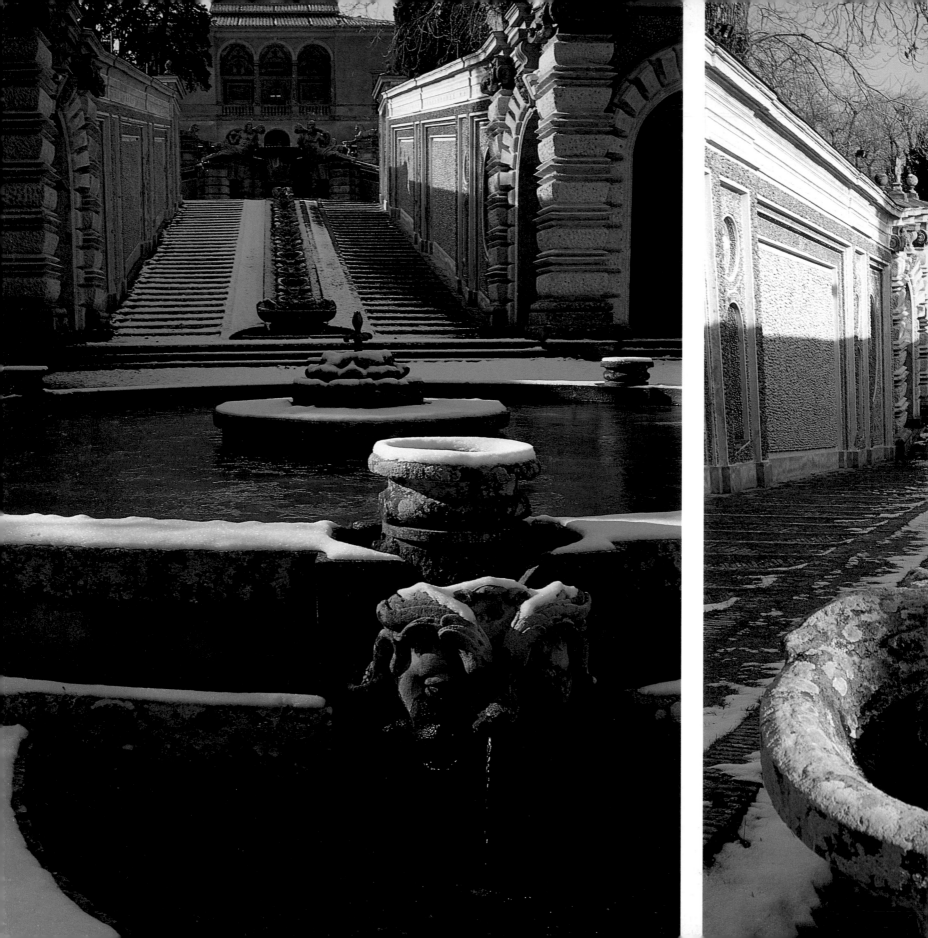

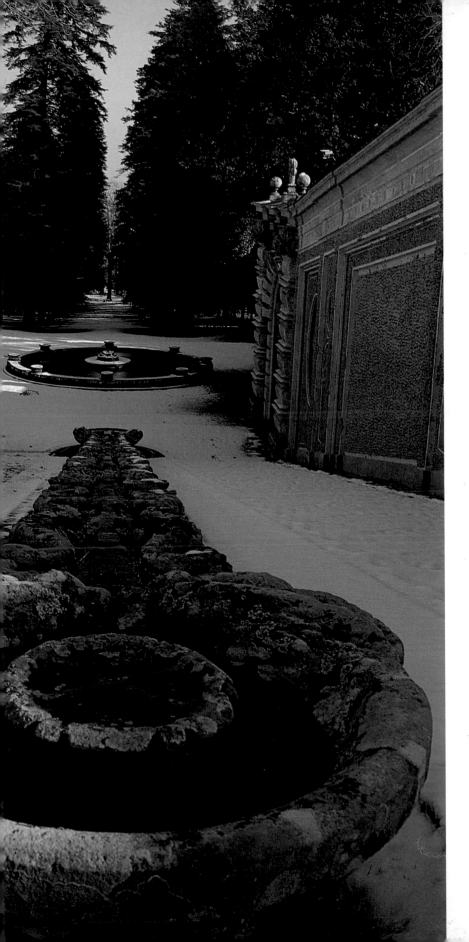

CAPRAROLA

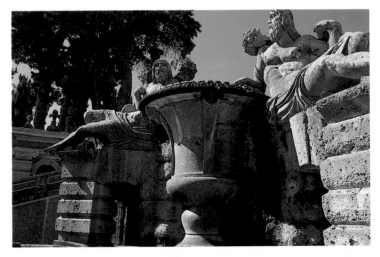

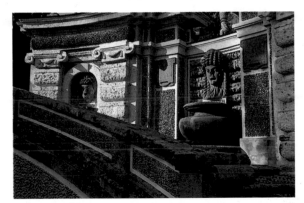

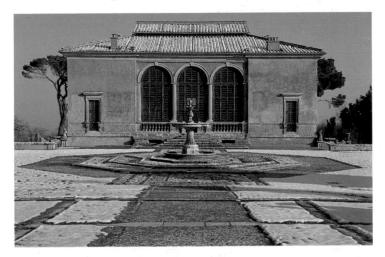

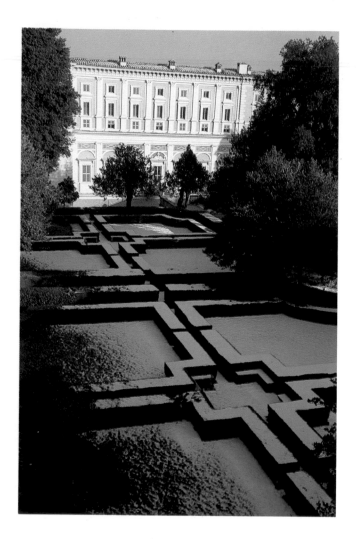

'THERE IS NOTHING IN ALL ITALY LIKE CAPRAROLA,' declared Edith Wharton about the most overwhelming villa ever built there. Cardinal Alessandro I Farnese had purchased the land, situated at the top of the main street overlooking the small town of Caprarola at the foot of the forested Cimini hills, in 1504, to indulge his passion for hunting. The profitable bishoprics that his sister Giulia Farnese was able to secure for him through her liaison with the Pope enabled him to commission Antonio da Sangallo the Younger and the Sienese architect Baldassare Peruzzi, with his love of medieval fortifications and flair for military engineering, to design a pentagonal fortress. Construction had progressed to ground level when Alessandro I was elected Pope Paul III in 1534, and this, together with Peruzzi's death two years later, brought the project to a standstill for the rest of the Pope's lifetime.

On the Pope's death in 1549, Caprarola passed to his nephew, Cardinal Alessandro II Farnese. Caprarola did not interest Cardinal Farnese for many years, as he was intent on acquiring the Villa Madama owned by his sister-in-law Margarita de' Medici. He asked her if he could rent the property, to repair, restore and realize Raphael's plans for Italy's greatest garden of unfulfilled promise, but she refused. In 1556, he commissioned his architect Vignola, who had designed his Roman villa, to draw up new plans to build a splendid palace on the existing foundations at Caprarola. Work resumed in 1559.

Originally conceived as a moated fortress, it was transformed into a splendid palace on top of its old foundations, and Vignola chose to counterpoint the pentagonal exterior with the circular court in its interior. The gardens initially presented Vignola with an awkward design problem, as the somewhat forbidding fortress did not easily lend itself to a pleasure garden. 'The form', said Jellicoe, 'had to be powerful enough to be a significant projection of the odd shape. He chose the firmest shape known to man, the square.' The garden square was the earthy counterpart to the heavenly circle inside the *palazzo*.

The lower gardens, known as the Summer and Winter Gardens, served as *giardini segreti* and were perfectly conventional quartered parterres. The Summer Garden opened out from the summer apartments by means of a bridge over the moat, presided over by two statues of the seasons, known as Horae. It was protected from the scorching summer sun by the wall of the *palazzo*, and contained three fountains to help cool the air, the main one being the Fountain of Venus, the presiding deity of this small garden, which depicted the birth of Venus from the sea. The fountain sent up jets of water in the shape of a Farnese lily making a rainbow in the sunshine. Each quarter of the garden was divided into nine beds planted with roses, in homage to Venus, fruit trees and a variety of flowers.

The Winter Garden was also connected to the winter apartments by a bridge with statues of the seasons holding sundials, and similarly divided into four parterres planted with orange, citron and pomegranate trees, whose fruit would hang decoratively during the winter. The garden was bisected by a long sheltered walk covered in ivy and grape vines, at the end of which was another pergola supported by six rustic satyrs shading the Fountain of Rain with its caverns of pumice stone, moss, dripping water and a naturalistic fishpool.

'To pass from the threatening façade to the widespread beauty of pleached walks, fountains and grottoes', observed Wharton, 'brings vividly before one the curious contrasts of Italian country life in the transition period of the sixteenth century. Outside, one pictures the cardinal's soldiers and *bravi* lounging on the great platform above the village; while within, one has vision of noble ladies and their cavaliers sitting under rose-arbours or strolling between espaliered lemon-trees, discussing a Greek manuscript or a Roman bronze, or listening to the last sonnet of the cardinal's court poet.'

Yet however pleasant the *giardini segreti* may have been, they were always dwarfed by the overwhelming presence of the *palazzo*-fortress looming above them. Something more secluded was needed, something on a more human scale. The Pope, imprisoned in the grandeur of the Vatican, had reached out to the intimacy of a *villa segreto* in the Villa Pia, in order to escape the impersonality of a garden built for public show and pageantry. Duke Cosimo III de' Medici would do the same in building his Garden of the

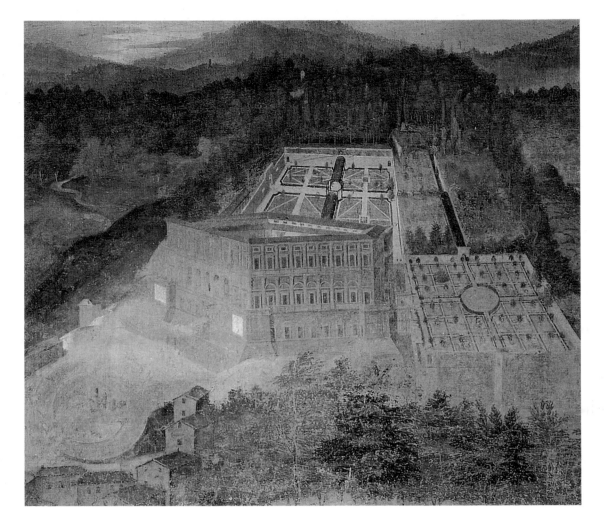

The Villa Farnese at Caprarola as it looked in the 1570s, when this fresco was painted in the Palazzina Gambara at Villa Lante. The Casino Garden had not yet been built into the hillside, but the winter and summer giardini segreti *lead off from the winter and summer apartments.*

The villa sits on an axis between the town of Caprarola and Lake Vico, which lies beyond the hill shown in the background. Hercules is said to have left the lake when he plunged his club into the earth and withdrew it; hence the Farnese impresa of a club surmounted by a lily. A new road was built through the town of Caprarola leading up the hill and through the circular courtyard to make the approach to the rocca more impressive. 'Its five bastions', wrote Wharton, 'are surrounded by a deep moat, across which a light bridge at the back of the palace leads to the lower garden.'

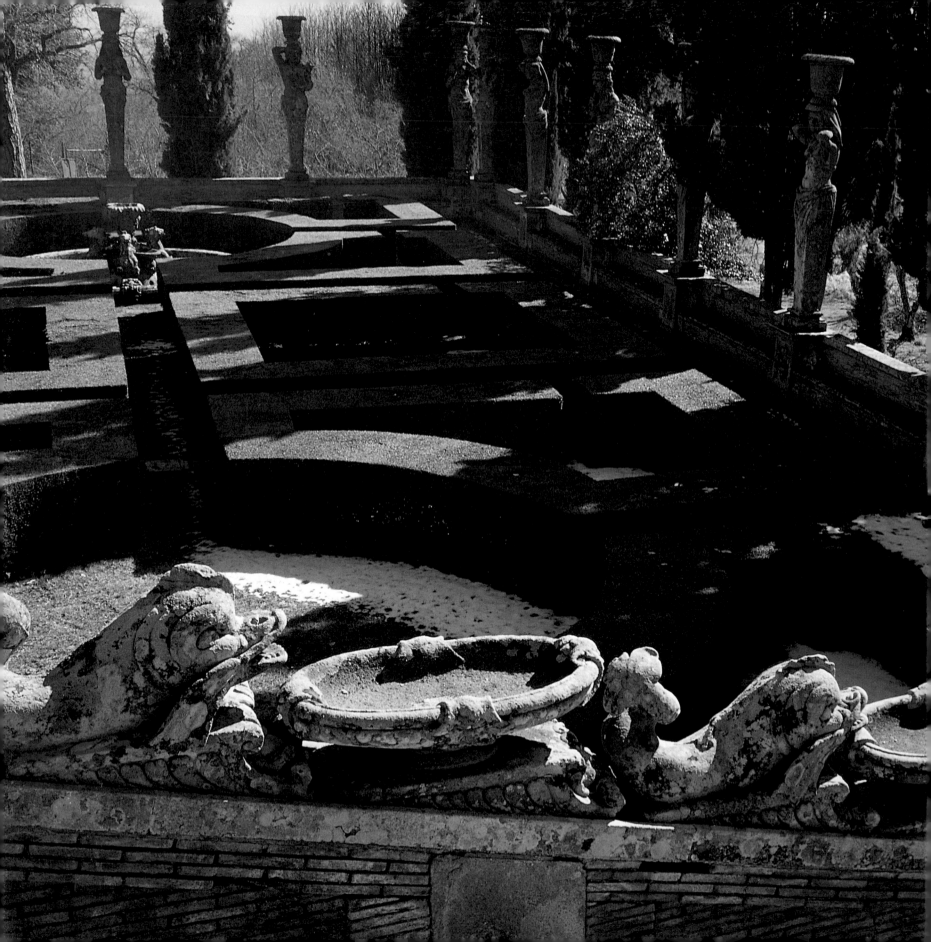

Cavaliere at the very top of the Boboli Gardens. 'The Princes of the Church', wrote Sir Geoffrey Jellicoe, 'sought to surround themselves with lofty grandeur in keeping with their aspirations. Occasionally under the eternal strain of pomp, a great mind exploded, and all the suppressed joy of life flowed forth. What other than human relief-valves are the Casino garden at Caprarola and the Villa Pia in the Vatican gardens?'

This need for a retreat had been partially fulfilled by the hunting lodge that Vignola had already built for Cardinal Alessandro II in 1569, a couple of miles away from the *palazzo*, known as the Barco, where he already entertained fellow cardinals, such as Cardinal Gambara and Cardinal Vicino Orsini from nearby Bomarzo, and, occasionally, the Pope to stag hunts and open-air banquets. He then created an isolated and smaller version of this Barco, in what he called his Barchetto, above the *palazzo*, which he decorated with a miniature version of the recently completed Villa Lante water chain, perhaps in homage to Cardinal Gambara. When Pope Gregory's secretary visited the Barchetto in 1573 he reported seeing a Fountain of the Vase, two river gods, a basin dedicated to the *capra* (goat), as well as the water chain. Another decade would pass before Cardinal Farnese, by this time sixty-four, and suffering severely from gout, decided to turn this little complex into an outdoor dining area. Cardinal Gambara, also grown gouty, chilly and old during his years of *al fresco* dining at his famous table at the Villa Lante, cautioned against such folly, telling him that 'at our age it was more desirable to eat in the shade of a loggia', and recommended building a casino above the fountain, which would offer 'protection for dining in its loggia and a view, in which he might also enjoy the Fountain, towards Caprarola'. Cardinal Farnese took his advice, and built himself a casino, designed by Giacomo del Duca, completed in 1586, but he had only three more years of his life to enjoy it. Giacomo del Duca had succeeded Vignola as Farnese's architect at the Orti Farnesina gardens on the Palatine, and the casino resembles the twin pavilions there designed by Vignola.

The grottoes, with their walls defining the water chain, and the simple parterre garden were added long after Cardinal Farnese's death, by Girolamo Rainaldi in 1620; the famous caryatids were carved by Pietro Bernini and positioned at the same time. For all the rivalry that existed between the Roman cardinals, this garden at least could be seen as a testament to friendship.

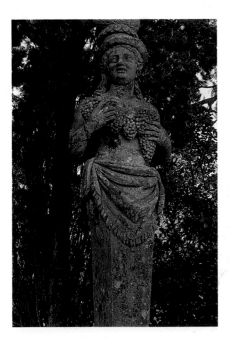

OPPOSITE AND ABOVE The Casino Garden, with its box parterre and caryatids by Pietro Bernini, was much admired by Edith Wharton: 'The composition is simple: around the casino, with its light arcades raised on a broad flight of steps, stretches a level box-garden with fountains, enclosed by the famous Canephorae seen in every picture of Caprarola – huge sylvan figures half emerging from their stone sheaths, some fierce or solemn, some full of rustic laughter. The audacity of placing that row of fantastic terminal divinities against reaches of illimitable air girdled in mountains gives an indescribable touch of poetry to the upper garden of Caprarola. There is a quality of inevitableness about it – one feels of it, as of certain great verse, that it could not have been otherwise, that, in Vasari's happy phrase, it was born, not built.'

VILLA LANTE

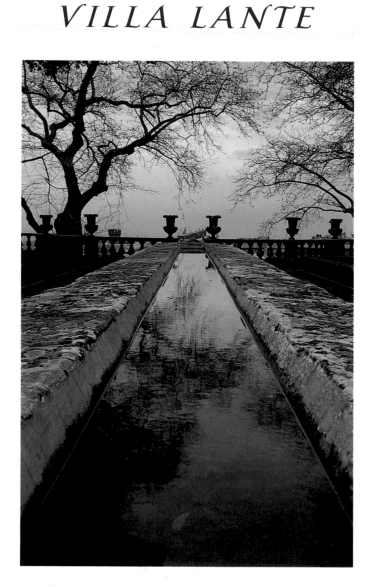

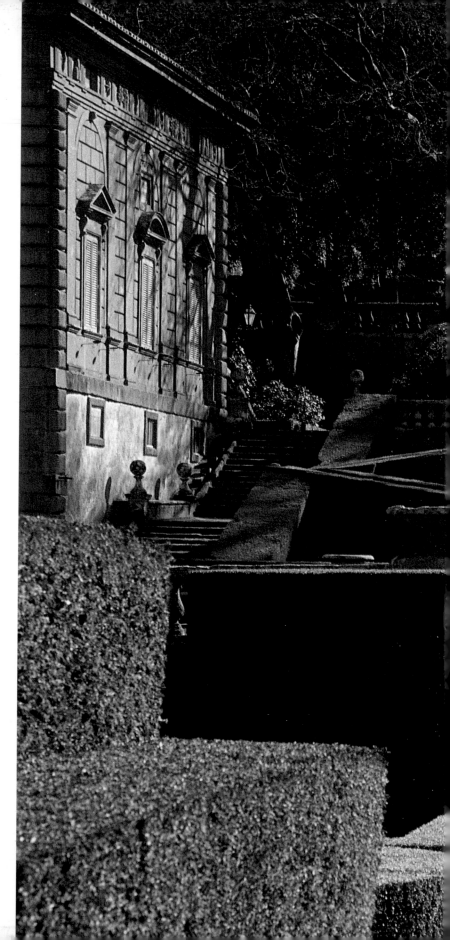

'So perfect is it, so far does it surpass, in beauty, in preservation, and
in the quality of garden-magic, all the other great pleasure-houses of Italy,
that the student of garden-craft may always find fresh inspiration in its study,'
was Edith Wharton's exultant assessment of the Villa Lante. 'If Caprarola is
"a garden to look out from", Lante is one "to look into" . . . the pleasant
landscape surrounding it is merely accessory to the gardens, a last touch of
loveliness where all is lovely. The designer of Lante understood this, and
perceived that, the surroundings being unobtrusive, he might elaborate the
foreground.' The Cardinal's Table (above) and the Fountain of the Moors
(right) are part of its elegant and intelligent iconographical scheme.

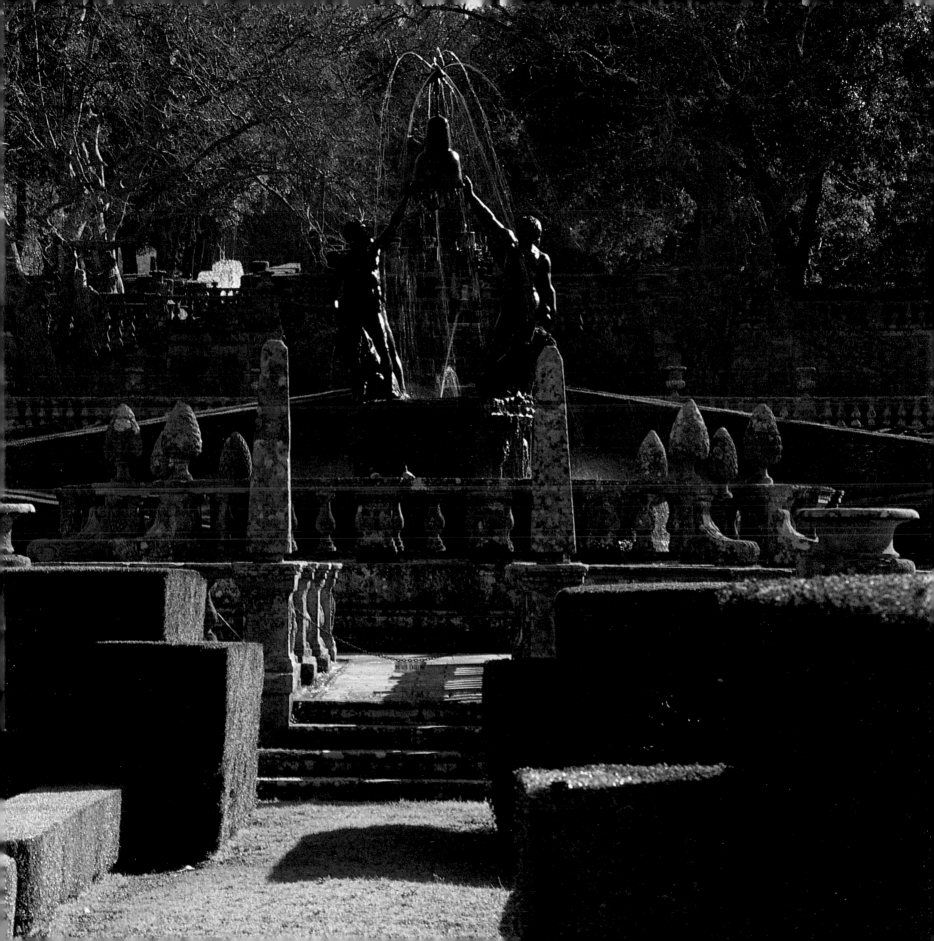

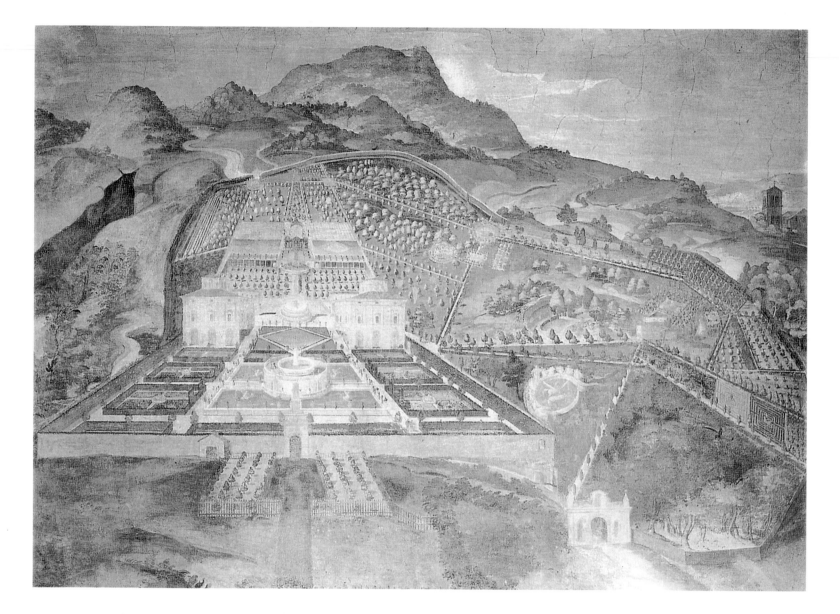

This fresco inside the Palazzina Gambara shows the grid-like plan of the garden, revealing its duality as a formal garden and as a boschetto. Within the formal garden there is a further duality with one side the mirror image of the other, making it a hymn to symmetry, the laws of proportion, and the counterpointing of circles and squares that Vignola had begun to explore at Caprarola. The garden is similar to Bramante's Belvedere Court at the Vatican, in that it is arranged on three levels and the twin palazzini echo his twin towers. The two palazzini, more like garden ornaments than a cardinal's residence, replace the usual single palazzo, and are, observed Wharton, 'part of a garden scheme, and not dominating it', allowing the garden to take centre stage. The boschetto, planted with fruit trees and untended vines, depicts the Golden Age of Man's innocence and Nature's fruitfulness. The allegory, taken from Ovid's Metamorphoses, in which he described a time 'when men of their own accord did what was right . . . The earth itself, untouched by the hoe, produced all things spontaneously', is also represented in fountains dedicated to acorns and ducks, which symbolize natural abundance, and to the unicorn and dragon, which represent purity.

The most important fountain, that of Pegasus (opposite), surrounded by herms of the nine Muses, further identifies the boschetto as Parnassus, home of the Muses, recalling the Oval Fountain with Pegasus at Villa d'Este.

IN SEPTEMBER 1568 Cardinal Alessandro II Farnese wrote to his protégé Cardinal Gianfrancesco Gambara to tell him that his architect Vignola was on his way to Bagnaia and ready to receive his instructions. He also wished him 'every contentment', as well he might, for the quintessential Renaissance garden Vignola and Cardinal Gambara devised together became the best loved of all Italian gardens.

Cardinal Gambara was a model of piety and probity. He was appointed cardinal by Pope Pius IV to serve on the Inquisition in charge of heretical literature, and was subsequently made Bishop of Viterbo by the austere Pope Pius V. Initially he resided in the small castle of Bagnaia, a medieval town at the foot of the Cimini hills renowned for its mineral waters. A hunting park had been created on the hill above the town by previous cardinals, who had built a hunting lodge and an aqueduct that would provide the freshest, clearest and most admired water of any of the villas. While Cardinal Gambara was contemplating the villa and garden he wanted to lay out inside this walled park, the two great rivals, Cardinal Farnese and Cardinal d'Este, were completing theirs. The Farnese garden was monumental in its physical scale; the Este garden was stupendous in its intellectual and iconographic complexity. Cardinal Gambara, who was not a rival but a friend of both cardinals – related to Cardinal Farnese by marriage and the executor of Cardinal d'Este's will – made a garden of extraordinary sophistication on a very small scale based on the archetypal themes of man's fall from grace and his redemption. The garden at Villa Lante is the story of paradise – paradise lost and paradise regained – told in a wood and three terraces.

The mythological concept of the twin peaks of Mount Parnassus and its sacred spring, home of the Muses, dominates the hillside. Two *palazzini*, echoing the peaks, prominently frame a long water chain inside the formal garden, and outside, in the *boschetto*, is a large pool with Pegasus surrounded by the nine Muses. These two halves make up the whole, and this duality is repeated throughout the garden. The *boschetto* represents the Golden Age of innocence and Nature's abundance. The garden charts the story of the consequences of original sin. Man has lost his innocence. Nature no longer produces freely, and man must live by the cultivation of his garden and his intellect, guided and inspired by the Muses, as patrons of the arts and sciences. Thus the garden honours man's endeavours to feed his body and nourish his soul.

This story is told in a sequence of three terraces, beginning at the top. The highest describes the retributive Flood as related by Ovid. 'The sky god Jupiter in his anger resolved to send rain pouring down from every corner of the sky, and so destroy mankind beneath the waters . . . the greater part of the human race were swallowed up by the waters and dolphins took possession of the woods . . . a high mountain, called Parnassus, raises twin summits to the stars . . . and the little boat which carried Deuclaion and his wife ran aground here.' However, humanity is eventually saved from the waters: 'Jupiter knew they were both guiltless, true worshippers of God . . . and he bid Neptune to recall the waves and rivers . . . and the sea had shores once more. The swollen rivers were contained within their own channels.' The second terrace celebrates the harvest and the third is a hymn to civilization, where man finds salvation through his intelligence and his creativity.

The genius of the Villa Lante garden is not merely in the far-reaching complexity of its concept but also in the way in which it makes use of the very achievements it celebrates. The triumphs of ancient Roman architecture, the laws of mathematics and proportional relationships, and the literature of Petrarch and Ovid are all there. What Jellicoe called 'the highest beauty man can obtain – the calm formality of architecture' is perhaps what elicits admiration for the garden as an unconscious response to the achievements of civilization.

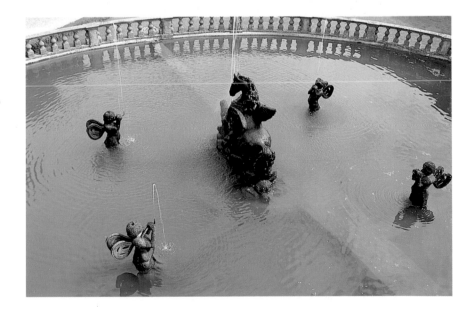

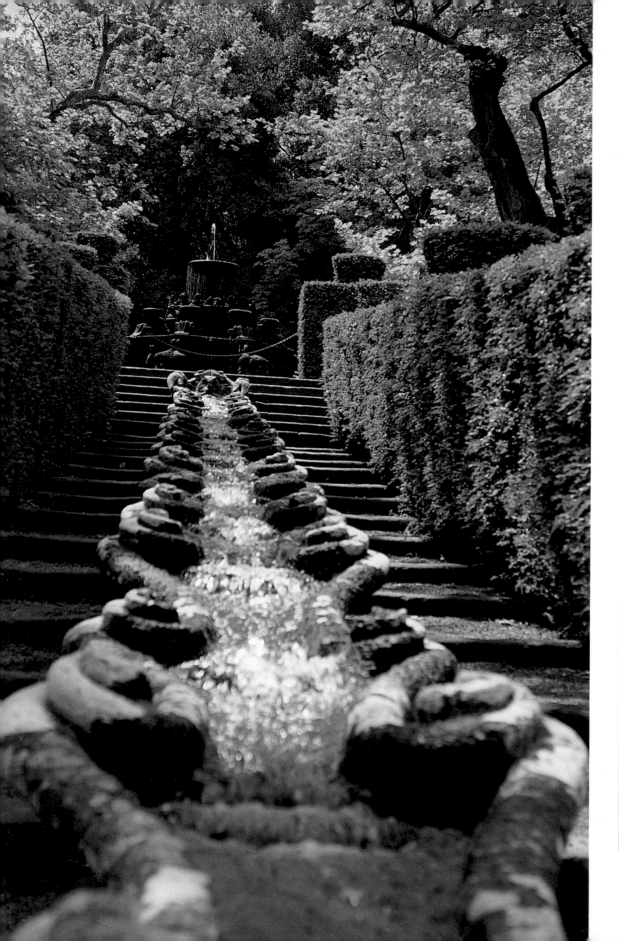
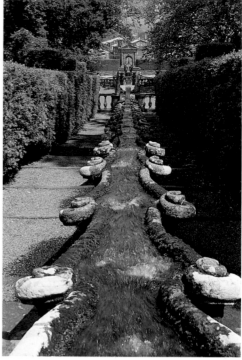
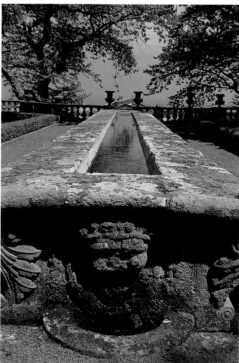

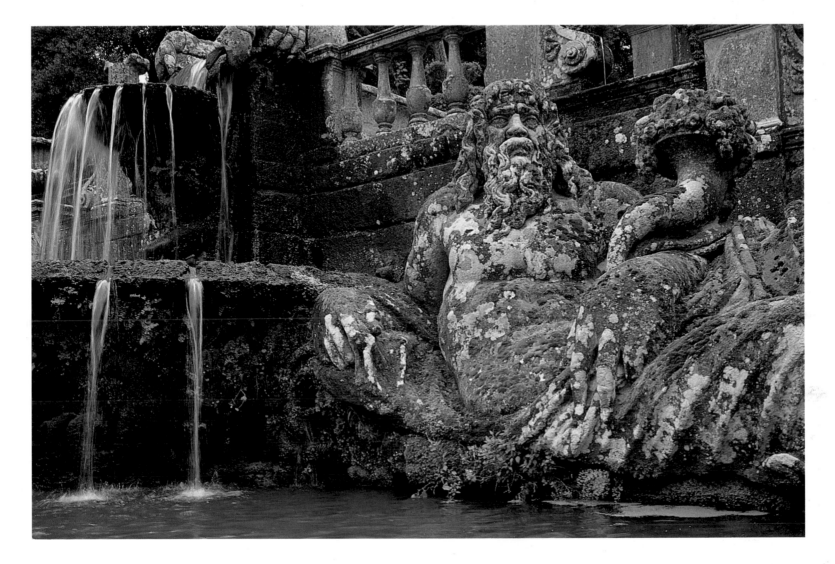

Water pours into the garden through the Fountain of the Deluge and in a
huge waterfall from the cornices of the two loggias to the Muses and gathers
in the Fountain of the Dolphins (far left) on the upper terrace, named after the
dolphins which encircle it. The flood waters are then recalled and 'channelled'
into a catena d'acqua: a water chain. This was designed as an elongated
crayfish (a pun on Cardinal Gambara's name, which resembles the Italian
word for 'crayfish'), with a little crustaceous head at the top and pincers at the
bottom. From the Fountain of the Dolphins there is an uninterrupted view to
the lowest terrace of the garden and the Fountain of the Moors (left above) past
the Cardinal's Table on the middle terrace (left below). Four little water jets
punctuate the long canal in the centre of the table.

On the middle terrace is the Fountain of the River Gods, the Tiber and the
Arno, who irrigate the fields (above). Originally there was a siren representing
fertility straddling the pincers, but she has now gone. The water would have
flowed under her into the basin. On either side of the gods are niches
containing statues of Flora, the goddess of flowers, and Pomona, the goddess
of fruit and the harvest, whose garden, Ovid tells us, 'was her passion and
her love. No other nymph could tend a garden more skilfully . . .' The harvest
was produced for the Cardinal's Table where, inspired by Pliny, Cardinal
Gambara dined al fresco.

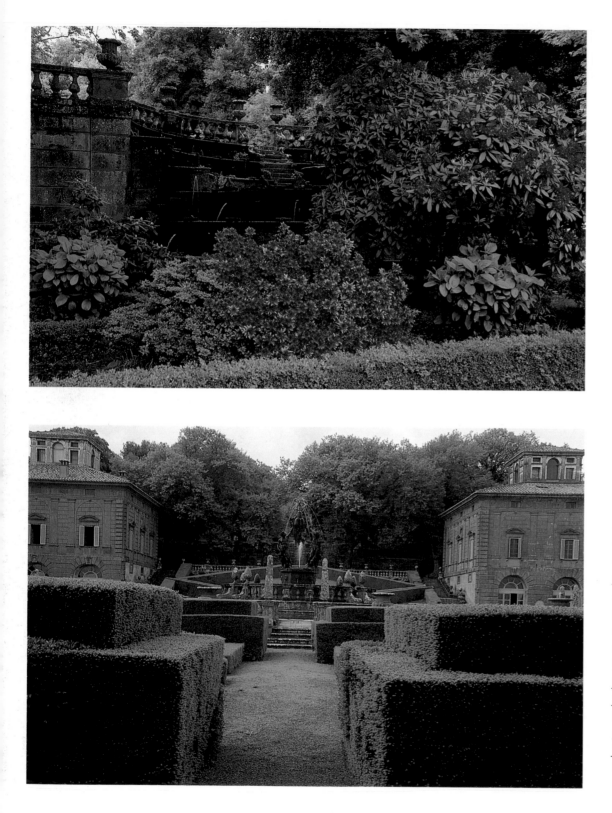

LEFT ABOVE *The Fountain of the Lights was modelled on Bramante's staircase in the exedra of Belvedere Court, but consists of channels of water instead of steps. On one side there was a grotto to Venus as a sleeping nymph watched by satyrs, and on the other a grotto to Neptune. Azaleas, rhododendrons and hydrangeas did not exist in sixteenth-century Italy, and their introduction obscured the view, intended to run from the bottom terrace right to the top. The box hedges on the slope between the two palazzini were also kept low to keep clear the perspective view of the Cardinal's Table and the water chain. Plane trees were planted, in the tradition of Pliny, but were not allowed to fudge the design, as the vegetation does now.*

LEFT BELOW *The design of the palazzini closely resembles the hunting lodge Vignola designed for Cardinal Farnese at Caprarola. Cardinal Gambara built only one palazzino of the planned two during his lifetime because Cardinal Carlo Borromeo, who arrived for a visit, told him that the money would be better spent on the poor. Cardinal Gambara, being obedient, obliged and built a convent in the town. The second palazzino was built in 1598 by Cardinal Montalto, who had no such scruples.*

RIGHT *The parterre was divided into twelve compartments originally containing herbs, each one surrounded by evergreen hedges, with low fences and fruit trees. In the centre of the Fountain of the Moors was a meta sudans ('sweating spire') fountain from ancient Rome: a foaming, bubbling, almost shapeless pyramid of continuously pulsing water. It was later replaced by Giambologna's statue of four Moors. The idea for the little boats in the fishpools was borrowed from the Rometta at the Villa d'Este by Cuzzio Maccarone, fontaniere (fountain maker) for both gardens, but instead of obelisks and a temple to Jupiter they contain men with arquebuses and trumpets.*

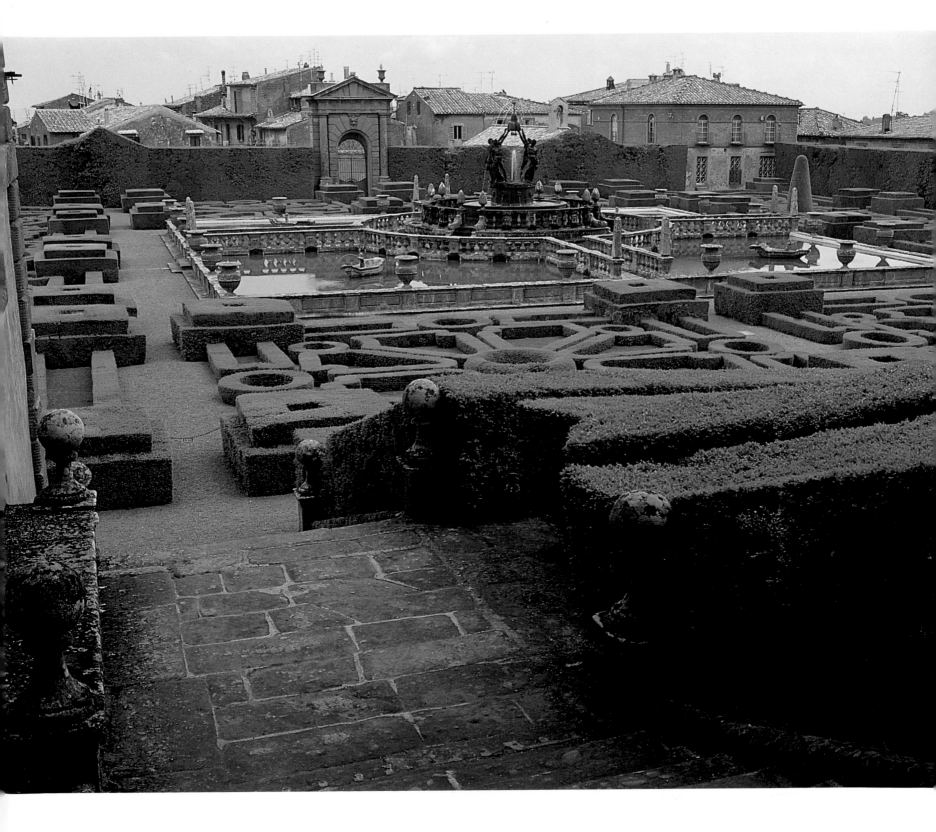

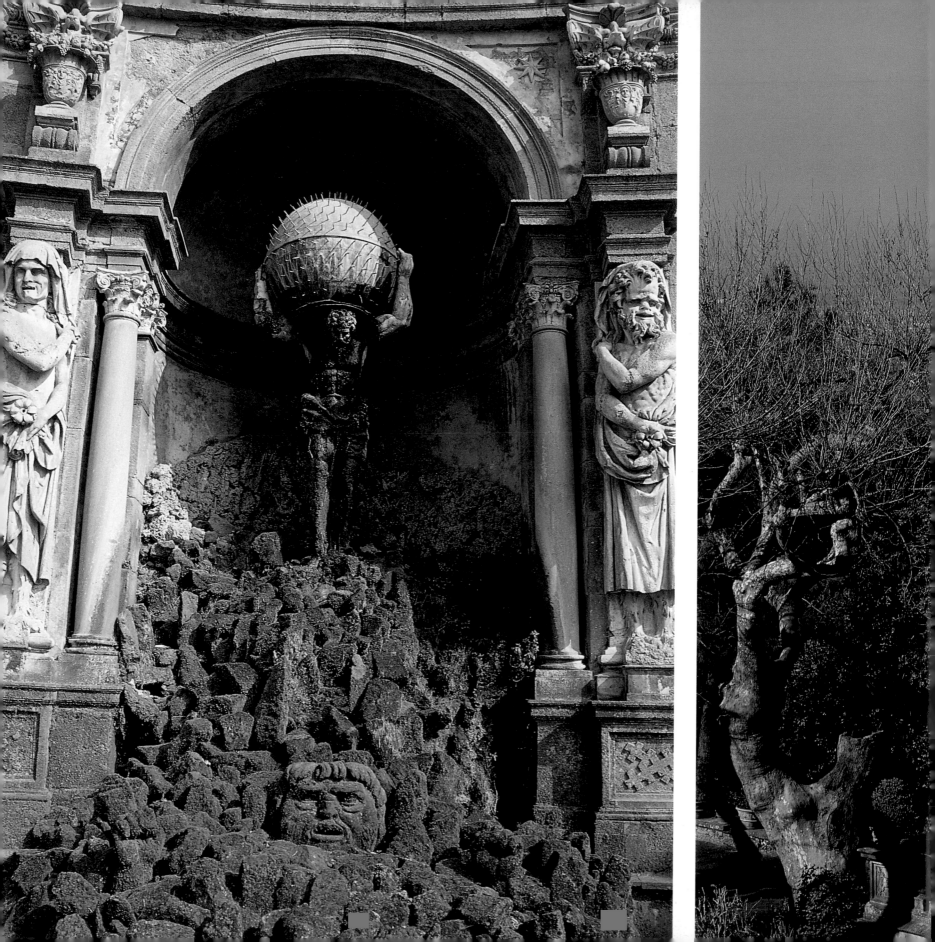

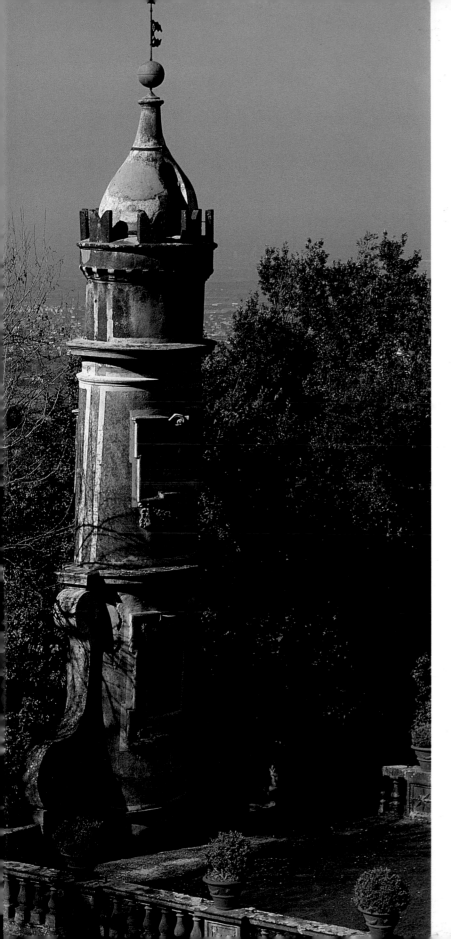

VILLA ALDOBRANDINI

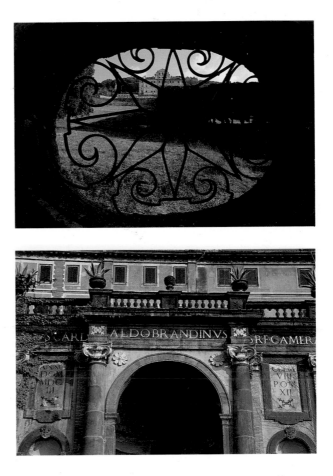

The view from the main piazza of Frascati through the Aldobrandini star to the villa (top). Rough grass has replaced the parterres, but the ilex avenue leading up to the retaining wall of the villa's front terrace remains, decorated with Pope Clement VIII's impresa (above). On the terraces flanking the villa, the 'swallow-tailed crenellations' on the twin turrets reminded Edith Wharton of 'a fantastic reversion to medievalism, more suggestive of "Strawberry Hill Gothic" than of the Italian seventeenth century' (left). The niche was once alive with a fountain. Pope Clement (far left) is represented in the central niche of the famous water theatre behind the villa as Atlas, bearer of the globe of divine wisdom, while below him the trapped head of Tantalus emerges from the rocks, punished for revealing the secrets of the gods to mankind by being unable to quench his thirst.

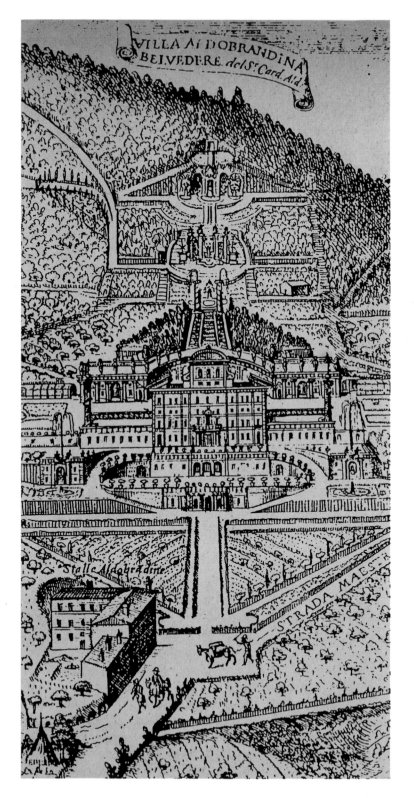

THE GARDENS OF THE VILLA ALDOBRANDINI were designed to present a striking view encompassing the whole hillside, beginning at the very top and descending by means of cascades and waterfalls to the villa and continuing along the ilex avenue down to the main piazza of the town of Frascati. Yet the grandiose water effects had dried up by the time Edith Wharton saw it, and she found as many faults with the Villa Aldobrandini as she had found reasons to praise Villa Lante. She dismissed the villa as belonging to 'the first stage of the Baroque before that school had found its formula'. Its famous water theatre, designed by Giacomo della Porta, she judged 'a heavy and uninspired production'; it was too close to the villa, it was out of scale with it and there was a 'distinct lack of harmony between the two façades'. The only feature that did meet with her approval was 'the upper garden' in the *bosco*.

'It was in the guidance of rushing water', wrote Wharton, 'that the Roman-garden architects of the seventeenth century showed their poetic feeling and endless versatility; and the architecture of the upper garden at the Aldobrandini merits all the admiration which has been wasted on its pompous theatre . . . John Evelyn', she continued, 'could not say too much in praise of the glorious descent of the cascade from the hilltop.' Best admired from the top floors of the villa, this descent, already dry and probably – she

LEFT *Greuter's view of the Villa Aldobrandini in 1620 shows its dramatic position on a wooded hillside at the edge of the town of Frascati, and the stages of the water's descent, beginning in the woods at the Fountain of the Shepherds and ending in the water theatre.*

OPPOSITE *Looking down the cascade towards the villa (top). The continuous cooling presence of the water and the spectacular sight of the cascades rushing down through the woods throughout the baking summer months must have been one of the most exciting garden 'sensations' in Italy. The twin pillars of Hercules at the top of the water staircase (detail centre) are decorated with the Cardinal's impresas. Jets of water shot out through the tops of the pillars and swirled down in rivulets. Giacomo della Porta took the idea of the nymphaeum and transformed it into a grand water theatre (below). Wharton felt that it had been built too close to the villa, but this was dictated by the steep gradient of the hill. To have placed it further back would have meant building a higher retaining wall, already high enough, and obscuring the view of the cascade. The semicircular exedra shape was the most efficient way of retaining the earth against the slope of the hillside.*

provides no details – also derelict when Wharton saw it, began at the top of the mountain with a reservoir. This dropped down as a waterfall into the Fountain of the Shepherds, and was channelled into the next terrace, which was laid out with parterres, before falling into the next stage through the Rustic Fountain. It was then carried through to the Pillars of Hercules and cascaded down the eight stairs of the water staircase, where it came to the edge of the water theatre, sent up a spray in the shape of the Aldobrandini star and disappeared above the globe carried by Atlas, where it fell as a veil of water on to the rocks and the basin and into the earth.

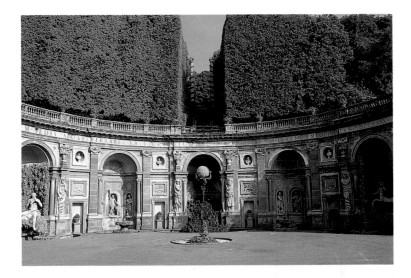

The creation of these grandiose water effects was only possible at Frascati after the end of the sixteenth century. Although the town had been colonized by prominent humanist cardinals, who were drawn to the ruins of the ancient town of Tusculum, where Cicero and Lucullus had lived, and by the splendid views over the Campagna to Rome, water was scarce. The Roman aqueducts had fallen into disuse and disrepair. Competition for prestige and water was fierce, and anyone who was suspected of diverting water had their garden vandalized. This was the situation until the close of the sixteenth century, when dried-out Frascati found itself with a benefactor who controlled the strings to the Papal purse. In 1598, Pope Clement VIII Aldobrandini gave his nephew, the Secretary of State, Cardinal Pietro Aldobrandini a modest villa he had inherited just above the town, in recognition of Cardinal Aldobrandini's skilful negotiation of peace with France in 1595. This had led two years later to the successful annexation of the Duchy of Ferrara, following the death of Cardinal Ippolito II d'Este's brother, Duke Alfonso II d'Este, that brought the Este fortune into the coffers of the Church. These diplomatic coups brought great kudos to the Aldobrandini name, which the family lost no time enshrining. The inscription emblazoned in gold across the top of the water theatre commemorates these deeds.

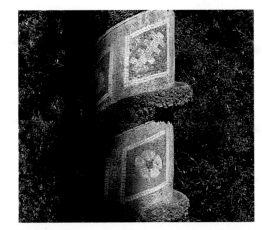

Pope Clement VIII visited all the most famous gardens in 1598, announcing that he wanted his Frascati garden to rival all other gardens, but most of all Villa Lante. The villa was enlarged according to plans by Giacomo della Porta, one of many followers of Michelángelo, and the water theatre and upper garden were added. The lengthy process of collecting water from the spring of Molara on the Monte Algido was instigated at the same time, and construction proceeded speedily and without interruption in the hope that the elderly Pope would live to enjoy it. It took five years,

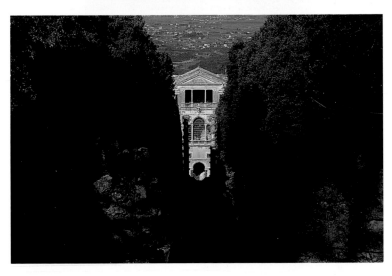

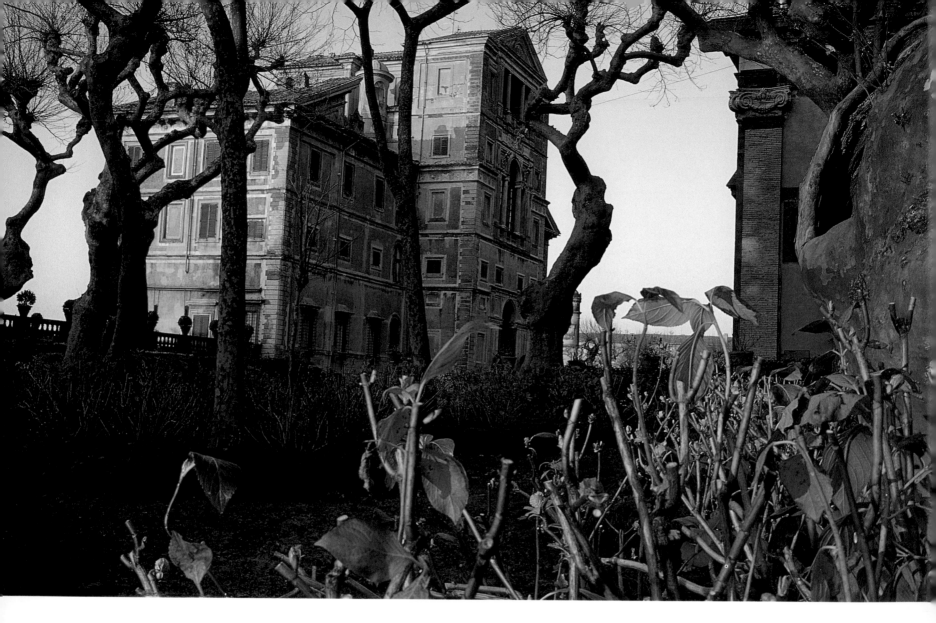

but it was the architect, not the Pope, who died, in 1602, a year before the villa was finished. Carlo Maderno executed della Porta's designs, Giovanni Fontana was put in charge of the water displays, and the hydraulic effects were the work of Maccarone, the famous *fontaniere* of the next generation, who was still at work on the Villa d'Este.

The desire to outdo all other rivals did not end with the Pope's death. In the early years of the seventeenth century Cardinal Pietro Aldobrandini despatched Giovanni Guerra to his favourite gardens, to sketch their principal features. He took the idea of turning a whole hill into a water course from Villa Lante; the veil of water descending from the globe was inspired by the Fountain of Tivoli

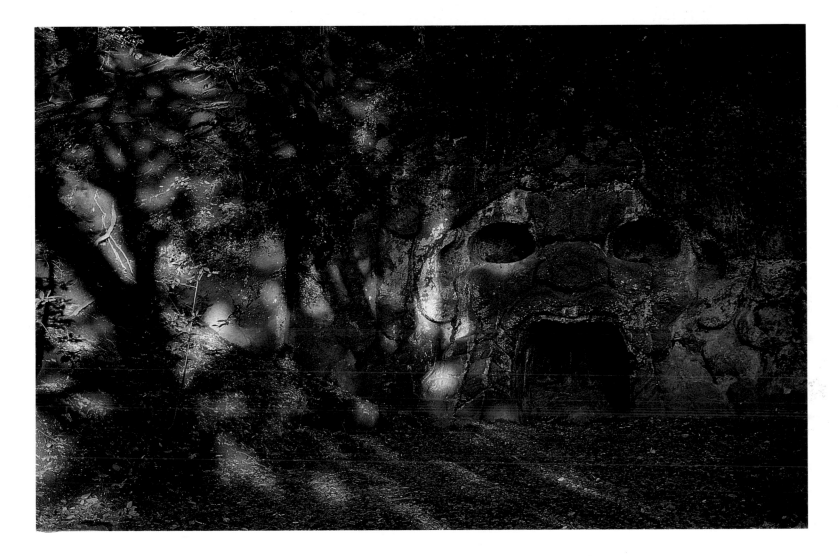

at Villa d'Este, and the Mouth of Hell from Bomarzo. 'The Villa Aldobrandini,' said Jellicoe, 'splendid in itself, welds all other villas into practically one scheme.'

The statue of Hercules reaching to Atlas was copied from a book widely used at the time – *Imagines* by Philostratus – and may signify the Cardinal as Hercules reaching out to receive wisdom from the Pope. It is linked with the Pillars of Hercules above the *scaletta d'acqua,* which represented the promontories at the straits of Gibraltar, marking the limits of the known world of antiquity. The exedra had two rooms built at either end. On one side was a chapel dedicated to St Sebastian, the patron saint of the Aldobrandini, representing the temple of religion, and on the other was a room with a scaled-down fountain showing Mount Parnassus as the hills of Frascati. The exedra was enlivened with acoustic devices activated by water, which produced birdsong, the horn of a centaur, a faun sounding its syrinx and the hissing of a tigress accosted by a lion. Added to that were weather effects of thunder, hail and mist. Underneath Mount Parnassus was an organ that emitted gentle aeolian music, echoing the music of the wind on the mountain. Apollo and his Muses played instruments whose cacophony made Charles de Brosses cringe. Although the Cardinal's inscription across the exedra states he had 'erected this villa as a place of repose after his work in the city', one wonders if he would not have found more peace if he had pitched a tent in the noisiest piazza in Rome.

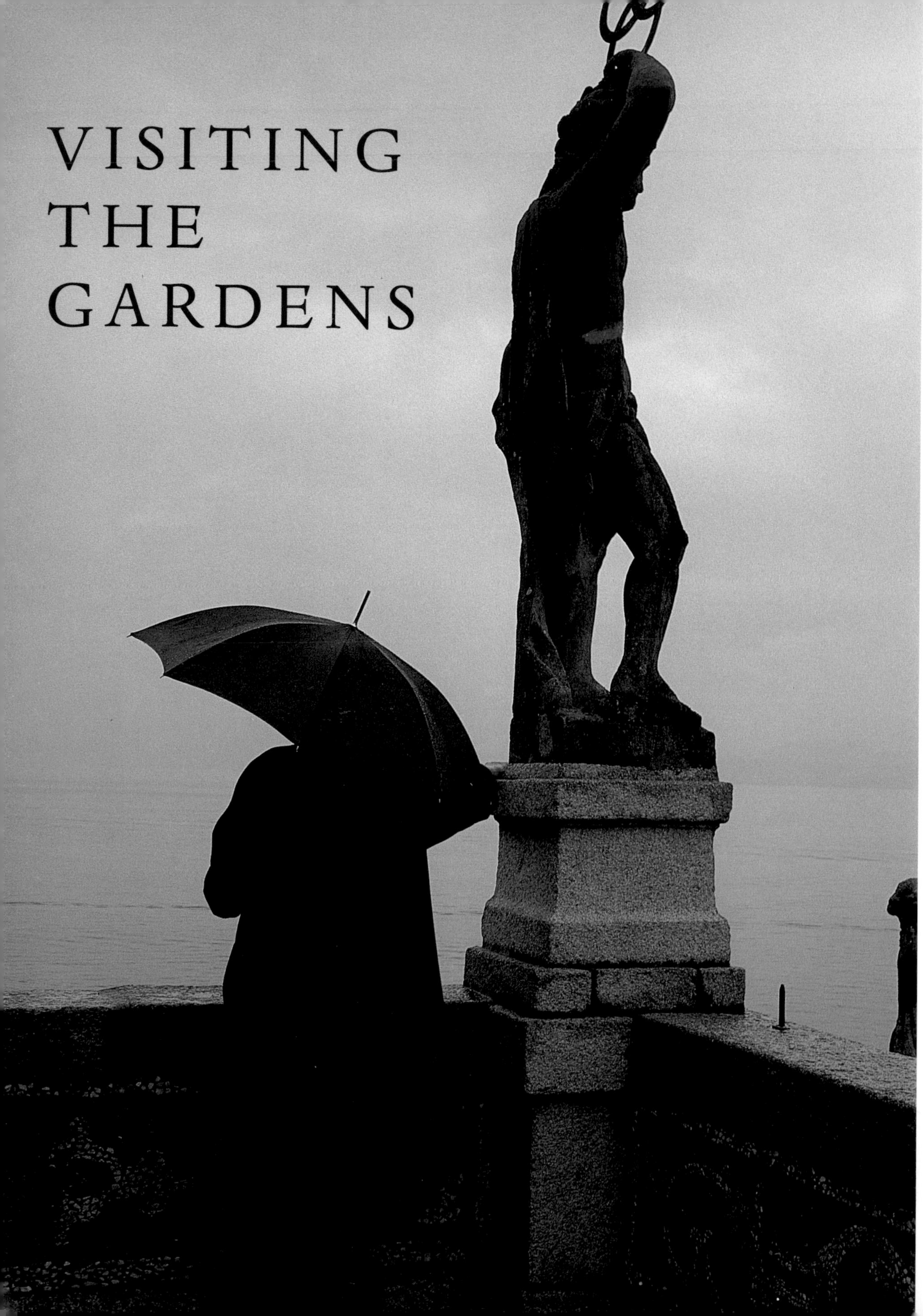

VISITING THE GARDENS

In cases where different guidebooks give different names for the same villa, alternatives have been given, after the name used in this book. Relevant phone numbers have been supplied where available. It is worth telephoning first, as some villas may be open only by appointment.

LOMBARDY

ISOLA MADRE
28050 Isole Madre (VB)
Tel: 323 31261
One of the Borromean Islands, on Lake Maggiore; reached by boat from Stresa, Baveno or Pallanza

ISOLA BELLA
28050 Isola Bella (VB)
Tel: 323 30556
One of the Borromean Islands, on Lake Maggiore; reached by boat from Stresa, Baveno or Pallanza

VILLA D'ESTE
Via Regina 40
22012 Cernobbio (CO)
Tel: 031 511471/512471
On the west shore of Lake Como, 33 miles/53 km N of Milan and 3 miles/5 km N of Como

VILLA CARLOTTA
Via Regina 2
22019 Tremezzo (CO)
Tel: 344 40405/41011
On the west shore of Lake Como, 18½ miles/30 km north of Como, on the S340 between Tremezzo and Cadenabbia; or by boat from Bellagio or Como

VILLA CICOGNA
Villa Cicogna Mozzoni
Piazza Cicogna 8
21050 Bisuschio (VA)
Tel: 332 471134
5 miles/8 km north of Varese
on the S344

VENETO

VILLA PISANI
Via A. Pisani 6
30039 Stra (VE)
Tel: 49 9800590
On the Brenta canal, 5 miles/8 km
east of Padua on the S11

CASTELLO DEL CATAIO
35041 Battaglia Terme (PD)
Tel: 49 526541
About 10½ miles/17 km south-west of
Padua on the SS16 towards Monselice

GIUSTI GARDENS
Giardino Giusti/Palazzo Giusti
Via Giusti 2
37129 Verona
Tel: 45 8034029
City centre, on the east bank of the
River Adige

PADUA BOTANIC GARDEN
Via Orto Botanico 15
35123 Padua (PD)
Tel: 49 656614
City centre

VALSANZIBIO
Villa Barbarigo/Villa Pizzoni
Ardemani
35030 Valsanzibio di Galzignano (PD)
Tel: 49 9130042
11 miles/18 km south of Padua,
3½ miles/6 km west of Battaglia Terme
on the A13 or the S16

VILLA CUZZANO
Villa Arvedi-Cuzzano
Cuzzano
37023 Grezzana (VR)
Tel: 45 907045/907135
5½ miles/9 km north of Verona
towards Negrar

FLORENCE

VILLA PRATOLINO
Parco di Villa Pratolino
Demidoff
loc. Pratolino
Via Fiorentina 6
50030 Vaglia (FI)
Tel: 55 2760529–538
7½ miles/12 km north of Florence

VILLA CASTELLO
Villa Medici Castello
loc. Castello
Via di Castello
50141 Firenze
Tel: 55 454791 (porter's lodge)
South of Sesto Fiorentino, 3½
miles/6 km north-west of Florence

BOBOLI GARDENS
Piazza Pitti 1
50125 Firenze
Tel: 55 218741 (tours)
City centre, behind the Pitti Palace

VILLA PETRAIA
Villa Medicea della Petraia
loc. Castello
Via della Petraia 40
50141 Firenze
Tel: 55 452691
South of Sesto Fiorentino, 3½
miles/6 km north-west of Florence

VILLA GAMBERAIA
Via del Rossellino 72
50135 Firenze-Settignano
Tel: 55 697205
1¼ miles/2 km on the far side of
Settignano, 5 miles/8 km north-
east of Florence

SIENA

VILLA GORI
Via di Ventena 8
53100 Siena
Tel: 39 577 2209 (tourist office)
North of Siena on the road to
Vicobello near the Monastera
Osservanza

VICOBELLO
Villa Vicobello
Via Vicobello 12
Vico Alto
53100 Siena
Tel: 39 577 2209 (tourist office)
Just outside the city walls of Siena

CETINALE
Villa Cetinale
Cetinale
Sovicille
53018 Siena
Tel: 39 577 2209 (tourist office)
8 miles/13 km south-west of
Siena, between Ancaiano and
Celsa, via the S73

ROME

VILLA MEDICI
Via Trinità dei Monti
00187 Rome
On the Pincian Hill at the top of
the Spanish Steps

VILLA DORIA-PAMPHILI
Villa Doria-Pamphili Belrespiro
Via Aurelia Antica,
Via di S. Pancrazio
or Via Vitellia
00165 Rome
Tel: 6 5899359/5813717 (tours)
South-west of the city centre,
entrance beyond the Porta San
Pancrazio

CAPRAROLA
Villa Farnese
Piazza Farnese
01032 Caprarola (VT)
Tel: 761 646052
11 miles/18 km south-east of
Viterbo off the Via Cimina

VILLA D'ESTE
Piazza Trento 1
00019 Tivoli (Roma)
Tel: 774 312070
Town centre, 18½ miles/30 km
east of Rome on the S5

VILLA LANTE
Via J. Barozzi 71
01031 Bagnaia (VT)
Tel: 761 288008
1¾ miles/3 km east of Viterbo

VILLA ALDOBRANDINI
Via G. Massaia 18
00044 Frascati (Roma)
Tel: 6 9426887
13½ miles/22 km south-east of
Rome on the S215

OPPOSITE *A rainy day at the*
Jardin d'Amour at Isola Bella.

GLOSSARY

Terms and Italian words as they are used in this book

agrume	citrus fruit
barco	wild ground used for hunting; later a park
broderie	arabesque design made of box, turf or gravel
boschetto	little wood
bosco	wood
campagna	countryside
casino	ornamental lodge, pavilion or small house in the grounds of a large house
catena d'acqua	water cascade (literally 'chain')
exedra	semicircular or rectangular recess sometimes with raised seats or any apse or niche opening into a larger space
fontaniere	fountain maker or operator
giardino segreto	secluded or enclosed (literally 'secret') garden
herm	sculpted head or armless bust on a pedestal base
limonaia	lemon house
leporarium	place where rabbits or hares are kept
loggia	gallery or room open on one or more of its sides, either part of a large building or a separate structure
mascherone	carved mask of a face, often grotesque
mosaico	mosaic
nymphaeum	shrine or grotto dedicated to the nymphs
otium	leisured repose
parterre	low, level, formally patterned flower garden, usually close to a house
peperino	light porous volcanic rock used for sculpture
peschiera	fishpond
piano nobile	main floor of a large house
prato	open lawn or meadow
prospettiva d'acqua	water vista (literally 'perspective')
ragnaia	thicket designed for netting small song birds such as thrushes for the table
romitorio	hermitage
scalinata	stairs, staircase
scherzi d'acqua	water tricks, surprise showers
tapis vert	literally 'green carpet': stretch of grass cut in a regular (usually rectangular) shape
tramontana	cold dry wind north wind blowing down from the Italian mountains
vasca	basin or tank
villeggiatura	summer holiday season, withdrawal to a summer residence

BIBLIOGRAPHY

Harold Acton, *Tuscan Villas*, Thames and Hudson, London, 1973.

Marella Agnelli, *Gardens of the Italian Villas*, Weidenfeld & Nicolson, London, 1987.

Sophie Bajard and Raffaelo Bencini, *Villas and Gardens of Tuscany*, Pierre Terrail, Paris, 1993.

Julia Cartwright, *Italian Gardens of the Renaissance*, Smith Elder & Co., London, 1914.

Judith Chatfield, *A Tour of Italian Gardens*, Ward Lock, London, 1988.

—, *The Classic Italian Garden*, Rizzoli, New York, 1991.

David R. Coffin, *Gardens and Gardening in Papal Rome*, Princeton University Press, Oxford and Princeton, New Jersey, 1991.

—, *The Villa in the Life of Renaissance Rome*, Princeton University Press, New Jersey, 1979.

Eleanor Dwight, *Edith Wharton: An Extraordinary Life*, Harry N. Abrams, New York, 1994.

Christopher Hibbert, *The Rise and Fall of the House of Medici*, Penguin Books, Harmondsworth, 1979.

Sir Geoffrey Jellicoe, *The Studies of a Landscape Designer Over Eighty Years*, vol. 1, Garden Art Press, London, 1993.

William Winthrop Kent, *The Life and Works of Baldassare Peruzzi of Siena*, Architectural Book Publishing Co., New York, 1925.

Francis King, *Florence: A Literary Companion*, John Murray, London, 1991.

Claudia Lazzaro, *The Italian Renaissance Garden*, Yale University Press, New Haven and London, 1990.

R. W. B. Lewis, *Edith Wharton – A Biography*, Harper & Row, New York, 1975.

Ian Littlewood, *A Literary Companion to Venice*, St Martin's Griffin, New York, 1991.

Percy Lubbock, *Portrait of Edith Wharton*, Jonathan Cape, London, and Appleton Century Crofts, New York, 1947.

Georgina Masson, *Italian Gardens*, Thames and Hudson, London, and Harry N. Abrams, New York, 1961.

Janet Ross, *Florentine Villas*, J. M. Dent & Co., London, and Dutton & Co., New York, 1901.

J. C. Shepherd and G. A. Jellicoe, *The Italian Gardens of the Renaissance*, Academy Editions, London, 1994.

H. Inigo Triggs, *The Art of Garden Design in Italy*, Longman & Co., London, 1906.

Edith Wharton, *A Backward Glance*, Scribner, New York, 1962.

—, *Valley of Decision*, John Murray, London, and Scribner, New York, 1902.

—, *Italian Villas and Their Gardens*, John Lane: The Bodley Head, London, and Century, New York, 1904.

—, *The Letters of Edith Wharton*, R. W. B. Lewis and Nancy Lewis (eds), Macmillan Publishing USA, New York, 1988.

AUTHOR'S ACKNOWLEDGMENTS

Had Edith Wharton picked her publishing team herself, she could not have been better served by the clarity and intelligence of both my editor, Caroline Bugler, and Anne Wilson, the designer. In fact, Mrs Wharton owes the revival of her book to Caroline Bugler, who returned from one of her Italian art pilgrimages with the idea and has guided me over the past two years with the wisdom of Solomon, the patience of a saint and the cool of the proverbial cucumber. The other genius-in-residence and leading light on this project is the queen of visual flair, Anne Wilson, who also designed my Monet book. The initial selection I ask her to make of the strongest, most evocative pictures always inspires and sets the 'tone' for the text which she subsequently illustrates and makes work in her inimitable, wonderful and, to me, utterly mysterious way.

I am very fortunate to have had the unflappable and extraordinarily articulate editor Anne Askwith, who has been a tremendous help on the book, and my thanks go to Hilary Mandleberg for skilfully streamlining that first unwieldy Lombardy chapter. And thanks once again to 'mon capitaine' and muse, Erica Hunningher, for her many suggestions and unfailing support throughout; to Elena Pizzi, my lifeline to the gardens themsleves, for her translation, her moral support; and to her husband Ezio, thankfully always on the end of my mobile phone as I travelled often circuitously from garden to garden.

I am most grateful to all the garden owners, but especially Count Fabio Pizzoni Ardemani, Count Niccolò Giusti, Lord Lambton and Claire Ward. The Beinecke Library provided unpublished writings and letters by Wharton. The London Library, as always, was a writer's best friend, and those books in print they could not provide Primrose Hill Books quickly obtained for me. And finally to my friend and *brujo*, Sally Monaghan Stubbs, on whose birthday I finally finished the book.

All the photographs in this book were taken with a Leica R5 camera and lenses and with Fuji Velvia 50 ASA film.

PUBLISHERS' ACKNOWLEDGMENTS

The Publishers would like to thank Scott Marshall of the Edith Wharton Restoration at the Mount, the Italian Tourist Board, Ian Chilvers, Fred Gill, Hilary Mandleberg and Sarah Labovitch for their assistance, and Kathie Gill for the index.

Project Editor Caroline Bugler	Editor Anne Askwith
Picture Researcher Sue Gladstone	Picture Editor Anne Fraser
Editorial Director Erica Hunningher	Art Director Caroline Hillier
Production Vivien Antwi	

PHOTOGRAPHIC ACKNOWLEDGMENTS

The Publishers have made every effort to contact holders of copyright works. All copyright holders we have been unable to reach are invited to contact the Publishers so that a full acknowledgment may be given in subsequent editions. For permission to reproduce the paintings and archive material, and for supplying photographs, the Publishers thank those listed below.

(L=left, R=right, A=above, B=below)

Alinari 10
Courtesy the Archives of the American Illustrators Gallery, New York City © Copyright 1996, by ASaP of Holderness, NH, 03245 USA. Authorized by the Maxfield Parrish Family Trust 136
Nobile Fabio Pizzoni Ardemani 91
Signor Ottavio Arvedi, Villa Arvedi, Grezzana, Verona 100
Ashmolean Museum, Oxford 13
Edith Wharton Restoration at the Mount, Lenox, Massachusetts 17,18
Courtesy of the Lenox Library Association, Lenox, Massachusetts 15
Lilly Library, Indiana University, Bloomington, Indiana 16,19
National Portrait Gallery, Smithsonian Institution/Art Resource, New York 8
Private Collection 24–25, 47, 51R, 61, 66, 68, 80, 84, 129, 142, 151L
Scala, Florence 106A, 110, 117, 124, 156
© Tate Gallery, London 22

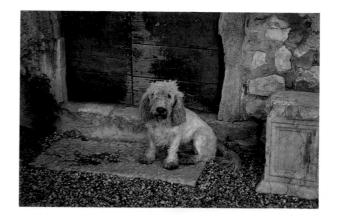

The ferocious guard dog at the Villa Cuzzano waiting to take his place in stone on a pedestal for posterity.